Promoting the Socio-Economic Wellbeing of Marginalized Individuals Through Adult Education

Sampson Tawiah
Durban University of Technology, South Africa

Itumeleng Innocentia Setlhodi
University of South Africa, South Africa

A volume in the Advances in Higher Education and Professional Development (AHEPD) Book Series

IGI Global
PUBLISHER of TIMELY KNOWLEDGE

Published in the United States of America by
IGI Global
Information Science Reference (an imprint of IGI Global)
701 E. Chocolate Avenue
Hershey PA, USA 17033
Tel: 717-533-8845
Fax: 717-533-8661
E-mail: cust@igi-global.com
Web site: http://www.igi-global.com

Library of Congress Cataloging-in-Publication Data

Names: Tawiah, Sampson, 1976- editor. | Setlhodi, Itumeleng, 1975- editor.
Title: Promoting the socio-economic wellbeing of marginalized individuals through adult education / Sampson Tawiah, Itumeleng Setlhodi.
Description: Hershey : Information Science Reference, [2023] | Includes bibliographical references and index. | Summary: "The book covers a wide range of topics, including sustainable economic change, leadership and management within adult education, and quality assurance in adult education, among others. By promoting the socioeconomic wellbeing of marginalized individuals through adult education, this book is a must-read for anyone interested in creating a fair and just society. The integration of ICT into adult education practices is a major focus of the book, offering a practical approach to bridging the digital divide and improving access to education for marginalized individuals"-- Provided by publisher.
Identifiers: LCCN 2023024057 (print) | LCCN 2023024058 (ebook) | ISBN 9781668466254 (hardcover) | ISBN 9781668466292 (paperback) | ISBN 9781668466261 (ebook)
Subjects: LCSH: Adult education--Economic aspects. | Adult education--Social aspects. | Marginality, Social. | Web-based instruction--Social aspects. | Educational equalization.
Classification: LCC LC5215 .P78 2023 (print) | LCC LC5215 (ebook) | DDC 374--dc23/eng/20230607
LC record available at https://lccn.loc.gov/2023024057
LC ebook record available at https://lccn.loc.gov/2023024058

This book is published in the IGI Global book series Advances in Higher Education and Professional Development (AHEPD) (ISSN: 2327-6983; eISSN: 2327-6991)

British Cataloguing in Publication Data
A Cataloguing in Publication record for this book is available from the British Library.

For electronic access to this publication, please contact: eresources@igi-global.com.

Advances in Higher Education and Professional Development (AHEPD) Book Series

ISSN:2327-6983
EISSN:2327-6991

MISSION

As world economies continue to shift and change in response to global financial situations, job markets have begun to demand a more highly-skilled workforce. In many industries a college degree is the minimum requirement and further educational development is expected to advance. With these current trends in mind, the **Advances in Higher Education & Professional Development (AHEPD) Book Series** provides an outlet for researchers and academics to publish their research in these areas and to distribute these works to practitioners and other researchers.

AHEPD encompasses all research dealing with higher education pedagogy, development, and curriculum design, as well as all areas of professional development, regardless of focus.

COVERAGE

- Adult Education
- Assessment in Higher Education
- Career Training
- Coaching and Mentoring
- Continuing Professional Development
- Governance in Higher Education
- Higher Education Policy
- Pedagogy of Teaching Higher Education
- Vocational Education

IGI Global is currently accepting manuscripts for publication within this series. To submit a proposal for a volume in this series, please contact our Acquisition Editors at Acquisitions@igi-global.com or visit: http://www.igi-global.com/publish/.

The Advances in Higher Education and Professional Development (AHEPD) Book Series (ISSN 2327-6983) is published by IGI Global, 701 E. Chocolate Avenue, Hershey, PA 17033-1240, USA, www.igi-global.com. This series is composed of titles available for purchase individually; each title is edited to be contextually exclusive from any other title within the series. For pricing and ordering information please visit http://www.igi-global.com/book-series/advances-higher-education-professional-development/73681. Postmaster: Send all address changes to above address.

Titles in this Series

For a list of additional titles in this series, please visit:
http://www.igi-global.com/book-series/advances-higher-education-professional-development/73681

Innovations in Teacher Development, Personalized Learning, and Upskilling the Workforce
Sriya Chakravarti (Higher Colleges of Technology, UAE)
Information Science Reference • © 2023 • 242pp • H/C (ISBN: 9781668455180) • US $215.00

Improving Higher Education Models Through International Comparative Analysis
Valerie A. Storey (Franklin University, USA) and Thomas E. Beeman (St. Joseph's University, USA)
Information Science Reference • © 2023 • 360pp • H/C (ISBN: 9781668473276) • US $215.00

Essential Practices for Building STEM Enrichment and College Bridge Programs
Calvin Briggs (Southern Center for Broadening Participation in STEM, USA) and Christopher K. Bass (Clark Atlanta University, USA)
Information Science Reference • © 2023 • 300pp • H/C (ISBN: 9781799871224) • US $215.00

Innovations at the Brazilian Federal Network of Vocational Education
Fábio Diniz Rossi (Federal Institute of Education, Science, and Technology of Farroupilha, Brazil) Anderson Yanzer Cabral (Federal Institute Rio Grande do Sul, Brazil) and Juliano Cantarelli Toniolo (Federal Institute Rio Grande do Sul, Brazil)
Information Science Reference • © 2023 • 300pp • H/C (ISBN: 9781799883593) • US $215.00

Addressing the Queen Bee Syndrome in Academia
Karis L. Clarke (Clark Atlanta University, USA) and Noran L. Moffett (Independent Researcher, USA)
Information Science Reference • © 2023 • 300pp • H/C (ISBN: 9781668477175) • US $215.00

For an entire list of titles in this series, please visit:
http://www.igi-global.com/book-series/advances-higher-education-professional-development/73681

IGI Global
PUBLISHER of TIMELY KNOWLEDGE

701 East Chocolate Avenue, Hershey, PA 17033, USA
Tel: 717-533-8845 x100 • Fax: 717-533-8661
E-Mail: cust@igi-global.com • www.igi-global.com

Editorial Advisory Board

Table of Contents

Detailed Table of Contents

This chapter presents a case study of how an air service provider (Evergreen, pseudonym) in Singapore builds an adult education ecosystem with strong partnerships to promote the wellbeing of its badly hit aviation workforce during the Covid-19 pandemic. It illustrates how Evergreen envisions changes and pushes the boundaries by actively establishing partnerships with the institutes of high learning, the government agencies, industry associations, and training partners, and at the same time building a learning culture for a resilient workforce. Everygreen turns Covid-19 from a risk into opportunities to strengthen partnerships with high levels of trust, commitment, and open participation. This is accomplished in part by co-creation of learning materials, experiences, and environments with partners with a focus on resilience and sustainability. The findings identify important qualities that can be established as best practices for organisations and policy makers to further improve their adult education provision and promote the wellbeing of their workforce.

This chapter raises an argument as to whether provision of adult basic education in the Eastern Cape Province of the Republic of South Africa can lead to bigger issues in the form of developing human capital which, in turn, will lead to inclusion of those once marginalised and excluded in the economic activities of South Africa. The main research question—To what extent does adult basic education and training (ABET) provision contribute to human capital development?—was pursued to probe the perceptions of educators in ABET centres and those in the education districts. A survey design, underpinned by the interpretivist paradigm, was used in this investigation, employing qualitative research method. One hundred and five (105) educators in the ABET centres and six (6) in the district offices participated in the study. The educators in ABET centres and those in district offices were purposefully selected. Data collection took place through questionnaires and interviews. The qualitative data were transcribed word for word for purposes of tracing any observable themes.

This chapter explores the link between Paulo Freire's ontological and epistemological philosophies and the community literacy and numeracy group (CLING) project in South Africa. The CLING project is based on the belief that literacy is about mastering reading, writing, and arithmetic skills. It also empowers individuals to reach their full potential and achieve success and fulfilment. The authors discuss how apartheid obstructed the education of black individuals, but Freire's ideologies and educational philosophies aimed to raise awareness and liberate individuals from illiteracy, economic struggles, and inequality. The authors emphasise the importance of critical literacy in promoting social justice. Using a qualitative approach, the authors gathered data from both primary and secondary sources and selected twelve individuals who provided information-rich insights. It was discovered that literacy education, including reading and writing, has helped marginalised individuals and empowered men and women.

There is need to build teaching capacity in pursuance of strengthening instruction and support for improving learning, particularly for adult learners. To expound the enhancement of increasing teaching capacity for effective student support through letsema in an ODeL Institution, presenting transactional distance theory and narrating experiences, with emphasis on collective effort through letsema practice. The

An individualistic education can hardly minimize community-based problems; hence, community education could play a magnificent role towards reducing community-based problems. Although the literature about community education appears to be in abundance, the literature about community education and community-based problems seems to be few. For this study, the researcher's aim is to strengthen and sustain a responsibly coherent community to minimize ritual murder through community education. The researcher adopted a participatory action research approach to involve community members in the fight against ritual murder in their community. The researcher employed qualitative techniques to collect data. Twenty-two (22) participants were selected purposively. The participants formed a focus group that had discussions and interviews. The study concluded that ritual murder is a serious community-based problem threatening communities. Community education is recommended to modernize culture and tradition for reducing ritual murder.

The purpose of this chapter is to explore the effects of technology integration in mathematics teaching to promote wellbeing of learners during Covid-19. An interpretive approach together with face-to- face interviews were utilized to gather information from nine participants who teach grade ten mathematics from each of the three senior secondary schools in the OR Tambo Coastal District. The findings revealed that several teachers lacked the formal technology expertise required to embrace online learning successfully and found a dearth of learner connections while teaching online. It was also found out that there was a lack of access to technology. It is recommended that the department of basic education should ensure that all learners have the data card loaded with uncapped data for learning to run smoothly. It was advised that professional development programs be established to train teachers in the design, use, and application of ICT technologies for online teaching.

Preface

Welcome to this highly anticipated edited reference book on *Promoting the Socio-Economic Wellbeing of Marginalized Individuals Through Adult Education*. We, Sampson Tawiah and Itumeleng Innocentia Setlhodi, as the editors of this groundbreaking publication, are thrilled to present a compelling collection of research and knowledge aimed at driving real change in the field of Adult Education.

Adult Education has emerged as a powerful academic discipline that transcends traditional boundaries in an ever-evolving world. It encompasses many specialized areas, including Educational Foundations, General Education, Sociology, Distance Education, Educational Leadership and Management, and Information and Communication Technology. At its core, Adult Education seeks to empower the educationally disadvantaged, both young and old, and elevate them into the very heart of our socio-economic fabric, enabling them to live fulfilling lives. This Edited Book will serve as a catalyst, bringing together a wealth of best practices and cutting-edge research to accelerate the socio-economic advancement of individuals in the Digital Age.

This book is not merely a compilation of theoretical musings but a clarion call to action. It is aimed at students, scholars, and education providers driven by a profound desire to improve the socio-economic wellbeing of those marginalized by society. If you believe, as we do, that education is key to unlocking a brighter future for all individuals, particularly those who have been systematically excluded, then this book is your essential companion.

In today's interconnected world, where access to information and opportunities is increasingly mediated by technology, integrating Information and Communication Technology (ICT) into education becomes paramount. The digital divide poses a formidable challenge, and our book delves into the critical importance of leveraging ICT in adult teaching and learning. By harnessing the power of technology, we can empower adult learners with the necessary skills and competencies to thrive in an ever-changing landscape.

We invite you, as postgraduate students, scholars, researchers, policymakers, education providers, government officials, managers of Higher Education Institutions, curriculum developers, advocates of blended teaching and learning, and scholars of STEM education, to embark on this transformative journey with us. Together, let us explore the nuanced dimensions of promoting the socio-economic wellbeing of marginalized individuals through Adult Education.

The chapters within this book delve deep into various key themes, shedding light on sustainable economic change, Adult Education in the Digital Age, best practices that have yielded tangible results in Adult Education, effective leadership and management within the realm of Adult Education, decolonization and social justice in the era of digital migration, the transformative potential of ICT for Sustainable Socioeconomic Development, strategies for integrating ICT into Adult Education practices, the evolution of Adult Education in the 21st Century, quality assurance measures in Adult Education, the rich history of Adult Education in South[ern] Africa, and the theoretical foundations that underpin Adult Education.

Moreover, we have curated chapters that explore vital aspects such as inclusion in Adult Education, the transformative power of adult learning during the transformation age, the potential of Adult Education to effect positive change in correctional centers and prisons, the acquisition of technical and vocational skills by adult learners, the intersection between Adult Education and social change, the recognition of Adult Education as a public responsibility, the profound relationship between development and Adult Education, the boundless potential of Adult Education beyond borders and limitations, and the limitless possibilities of Adult Education beyond the traditional classroom setting.

We extend our heartfelt gratitude to all the esteemed authors who have poured their expertise and insights into this book. Their unwavering dedication to research and scholarship has been instrumental in shaping this compelling resource. We would also like to express our deep appreciation to the diligent reviewers whose invaluable feedback and guidance have ensured the highest quality of content.

We implore you to seize the opportunity presented by this edited reference book. Let it inspire you to take bold action, revolutionize Adult Education, and create a truly inclusive and equitable society. Together, let us forge a future where every individual can unlock their full potential through lifelong learning regardless of their background or circumstances.

Chapter Overview

Chapter 1: Building Strong Adult Education Partnerships for the Wellbeing of the Aviation Workforce During the Covid-19 Pandemic

In this thought-provoking chapter, Zan Chen from the Institute for Adult Learning at Singapore University of Social Sciences presents a compelling case study on how an air service provider, referred to as Evergreen (pseudonym), in Singapore, effectively established an adult education ecosystem with robust partnerships to promote the wellbeing of its aviation workforce during the challenging times of the Covid-19 pandemic.

The chapter delves into the visionary approach adopted by Evergreen, showcasing how the organization proactively sought to embrace change and push boundaries by forging strong partnerships with institutes of higher learning, government agencies, industry associations, and training partners. By cultivating a learning culture focused on resilience and adaptability, Evergreen transformed the risks posed by the pandemic into opportunities for growth.

One key aspect highlighted in the study is the importance of building partnerships based on trust, commitment, and open participation. Through co-creating learning materials, experiences, and environments in collaboration with their partners, Evergreen successfully nurtured an ecosystem that fostered the resilience and sustainability of its workforce. The chapter outlines Evergreen's specific strategies and practices, providing valuable insights for organizations and policymakers seeking to enhance their adult education provision and promote the wellbeing of their workforce.

By drawing upon this case study, readers will gain a deeper understanding of the qualities and approaches that contribute to successful adult education partnerships, particularly in times of crisis. The findings presented in this chapter offer practical recommendations and best practices that can be leveraged by organizations and policymakers to create a supportive and thriving learning environment for adult learners, ultimately benefiting both individuals and the overall workforce wellbeing.

Chapter 2: Adult Basic Education Provision and Human Capital Development: Exploring the Perceptions of Adult Educators

In this thought-provoking chapter, Mziwoxolo Richmond Krexe from Walter Sisulu University in South Africa delves into the critical question of whether the provision of Adult Basic Education in the Eastern Cape Province of the Republic of South Africa can lead to significant human capital development, ultimately resulting in the inclusion of marginalized individuals in the country's economic activities.

The main research question of this study is addressed: To what extent does Adult Basic Education and Training (ABET) provision contribute to human capital development? To shed light on this question, the author explores the perceptions of educators working in ABET centers and those in education districts. The research employs a survey design grounded in the interpretivist paradigm and utilizes qualitative research methods.

The study includes the participation of 105 educators from ABET centers and 6 educators from district offices, who were purposefully selected for their valuable insights. The data collection process involved questionnaires and interviews, ensuring a comprehensive understanding of the educators' perspectives. The qualitative data from these sources were meticulously transcribed to identify and trace emerging themes.

By examining the perceptions of adult educators within the ABET system, this chapter provides valuable insights into the role of Adult Basic Education in fostering human capital development. Through a thorough analysis of the data collected, readers will gain a deeper understanding of the potential impacts and effects of ABET provision on the economic inclusion of marginalized individuals.

This chapter contributes to the broader discourse on human capital development and its relation to Adult Basic Education. It sheds light on the experiences and perspectives of educators, providing a nuanced understanding of the challenges and opportunities inherent in ABET provision. The findings presented in this chapter serve as a valuable resource for policymakers, educators, and stakeholders involved in adult education, offering insights into enhancing the effectiveness and impact of Adult Basic Education programs for the betterment of individuals and society.

Chapter 3: The Ontological and Epistemological Connection between Paulo Freire's Literacy Education and the CLING Project in South Africa

In this enlightening chapter, Zamalotshwa Florence Thusi and Sampson Tawiah from the School of Education at Durban University of Technology in South Africa explore the profound connection between Paulo Freire's ontological and epistemological philosophies and the Community Literacy and Numeracy Group (CLING) project in South Africa.

The CLING Project operates on the belief that literacy encompasses more than just acquiring basic reading, writing, and arithmetic skills. It recognizes literacy as a transformative force that empowers individuals to reach their full potential, overcome economic struggles, break free from the shackles of illiteracy, and combat inequality. The authors delve into the historical context of apartheid, which hindered the educational opportunities of black individuals in South Africa. However, they highlight how Paulo Freire's ideologies and educational philosophies emerged as a powerful tool for raising awareness and liberating individuals from the chains of illiteracy, fostering empowerment, and advocating for social justice.

To comprehensively understand the subject matter, the authors employ a qualitative approach, gathering data from various primary and secondary sources. Additionally, they select twelve individuals who have participated in the CLING Project, ensuring a rich and diverse set of insights. Through this meticulous research process, the authors uncover the transformative impact of literacy education, encompassing both reading and writing, on marginalized individuals and the empowerment experienced by men and women who have engaged with the CLING Project.

This chapter serves as a compelling exploration of the profound connection between Paulo Freire's educational philosophies and the CLING Project in South Africa. By shedding light on the transformative potential of literacy education, the authors underline the importance of critical literacy in promoting social justice and addressing the historical inequalities ingrained in the fabric of society.

Through their research findings, the authors offer valuable insights for educators, policymakers, and stakeholders involved in literacy education and community development. By embracing the principles of Freirean pedagogy and recognizing the power of literacy as a tool for liberation and empowerment, societies can foster a more just and equitable future for all individuals.

The exploration of the ontological and epistemological connection between Paulo Freire's literacy education and the CLING Project in South Africa presented in this chapter provides a thought-provoking contribution to the field of education, emphasizing the transformative potential of literacy in the pursuit of social change and empowerment.

Chapter 4: Increasing Teaching Capacity for Supporting Students in an ODeL Institution: Employing Letsema

In this insightful chapter, Itumeleng I. Setlhodi from the University of South Africa explores strategies to enhance teaching capacity in supporting adult learners in an Open Distance e-Learning (ODeL) institution, with a specific focus on the General Education and Training Certificate: Adult Basic Education and Training (GETC: ABET) program.

The GETC: ABET program plays a vital role in providing learners with foundational knowledge and skills necessary for social and economic development and promoting justice and equality. However, national statistics reveal a significant gap between the number of learners enrolling in the program and those who successfully complete it. To address this issue, the author conducted a qualitative study exploring strategies to motivate adult learners to achieve the GETC: ABET program.

Through interactive individual and focus interviews involving 35 participants, the study identified interventions employed by teachers to encourage learners and provide support, aiming to minimize or eliminate barriers that hinder program completion. The findings underscore the critical role of teacher interventions in ensuring learners complete the program. Consequently, the Department of Higher Education and Training has an opportunity to strengthen these strategies to facilitate higher completion rates among learners.

Based on the study's findings, this chapter proposes essential strategies for consideration by community colleges and the broader education community. These strategies aim to enhance teaching capacity and support systems, enabling educators to effectively motivate and guide adult learners in completing the GETC: ABET program.

By delving into the nuances of teaching in an ODeL environment and offering practical strategies, this chapter contributes to the ongoing discourse on improving student retention and success rates in adult education. The proposed strategies provide educators, policymakers, and institutions with valuable insights on how to address the challenges faced by adult learners and promote a supportive learning environment conducive to program completion.

As we explore the potential of Letsema - a term used in Setswana meaning "working together" - this chapter emphasizes the collective responsibility of community colleges and educational stakeholders to increase teaching capacity and provide the necessary support for adult learners. By employing these strategies, we can create an educational landscape that empowers adult learners to overcome barriers, fosters their success, and ultimately promotes lifelong learning for all.

Chapter 5: Unpacking the Interdependence of CET College Leadership: A Systems Thinking Perspective on Organizational Change and Governance in South Africa

In this chapter, Lynette Lulama Mbatha from the University of KwaZulu Natal in South Africa delves into the intricate dynamics of leadership within the Community Education and Training (CET) colleges in the context of adult education. With a focus on organizational change and governance, the chapter takes systems thinking perspective to examine how various stakeholders perceive the interdependence of different aspects of CET college leadership, how change processes are managed, and the effectiveness of organizational change initiatives.

Adult education plays a pivotal role in South Africa's national skills development agenda, aiming to enhance the skills and employability of the adult population. The landscape of adult education in South Africa encompasses diverse forms, including adult basic education and training (ABET), technical and vocational education and training (TVET), community education and training (CET), and higher education. Recognizing the significance of adult education, the South African government has made substantial investments in this sector to combat unemployment, alleviate poverty, and stimulate economic growth.

Leadership and management within adult education face distinct challenges within the South African context. These challenges encompass a large and diverse learner population, limited resources, and the necessity to balance the expectations of various stakeholders. Against this backdrop, the chapter critically examines the understanding of stakeholders regarding the interconnectedness of different facets of CET college leadership in driving organizational change. Additionally, it explores how change processes are effectively managed within these institutions.

Employing a systems thinking perspective, the author provides insights into the complex dynamics of leadership within CET colleges. By adopting this holistic approach, the chapter sheds light on the interrelationships and interdependencies among various components of leadership, including governance structures, decision-making processes, stakeholder engagement, and the implementation of organizational change initiatives.

The findings presented in this chapter contribute to a deeper understanding of how CET college leadership operates within the realm of adult education in South Africa. They offer valuable insights into the challenges faced by leaders in managing organizational change in the context of adult education. Furthermore, the chapter highlights the importance of systems thinking in comprehending the complexities of leadership and governance, providing a framework for enhancing effectiveness and driving positive change.

Educators, policymakers, administrators, and stakeholders involved in adult education and leadership will find this chapter to be a valuable resource. The insights presented here can inform strategic decision-making, foster effective governance structures, and ultimately contribute to the improvement of adult education institutions in South Africa.

Chapter 6: Assessment of Indigenous Languages Archives Preservation in South Africa

Authored by Nkholedzeni Sidney Netshakhuma from the University of Mpumalanga, this chapter focuses on assessing the role of indigenous language archives preservation by the Mpumalanga provincial archives in South Africa. The central objective of this study is to explore how the preservation of indigenous language archives can contribute to the promotion of socio-economic wellbeing among marginalized societies.

Indigenous language archives hold immense value in understanding and documenting the cultural heritage and history of communities and individuals. These archives play a crucial role in affirming the socio-economic wellbeing of marginalized societies by providing access to information and resources that empower and uplift communities. However, during the era of apartheid in South Africa, the use of indigenous language archives for educational purposes was denied, denying communities their rights to access and utilize these valuable materials.

This chapter critically examines the efforts made by the Mpumalanga provincial archives to preserve indigenous language archives and their impact on the socio-economic wellbeing of marginalized societies. By recognizing and preserving these archives, communities and individuals gain a sense of recognition and validation, reinforcing their cultural identity and heritage.

The study explores the significance of indigenous language archives in educational curricula, highlighting the importance of incorporating these materials to promote inclusive and diverse learning experiences. It underscores the need for recognition and utilization of indigenous language archives to enhance educational practices, foster cultural understanding, and promote socio-economic development among marginalized communities.

Through an assessment of the Mpumalanga provincial archives' efforts, this chapter provides valuable insights into the current state of indigenous language archives preservation in South Africa. It sheds light on the challenges and opportunities in preserving these archives, while emphasizing the potential socio-economic benefits that can be derived from their accessibility and utilization.

Researchers, educators, archivists, policymakers, and stakeholders in the field of indigenous language preservation and socio-economic development will find this chapter thought-provoking and informative. It serves as a call to action for recognizing the value of indigenous language archives and their potential to empower marginalized communities and individuals in South Africa. By prioritizing the preservation and accessibility of these archives, we can promote cultural preservation, social inclusion, and sustainable development in the diverse landscape of South Africa.

Chapter 7: The Contribution of Community Education towards Minimizing Ritual Murder in the Community for Good Social Order

Authored by Avhurengwi Samson Mabade from Walter Sisulu University, South Africa, this chapter focuses on the role of community education in addressing the issue of ritual murder within a community. While individual education alone may not effectively address community-based problems, community education can play a significant role in reducing such issues. Despite the abundant literature on community education, there is a noticeable lack of literature specifically addressing community education in relation to community-based problems.

The primary objective of this study is to explore how community education can contribute to the responsible and coherent functioning of a community, ultimately working towards minimizing ritual murder. Adopting a participatory action research approach, the researcher actively involved community members in the fight against ritual murder within their community. By engaging community members in the research process, a collaborative and inclusive approach was fostered, empowering the community to actively address this issue.

Qualitative research techniques were employed to collect data for this study. Through purposive sampling, twenty-two participants were selected to form a focus group for discussions and interviews. The findings of the study highlight the severity of ritual murder as a community-based problem that threatens the overall well-being of the community. Furthermore, the study underscores the potential of community education as a means to modernize cultural practices and traditions, thereby reducing instances of ritual murder.

In conclusion, this chapter sheds light on the crucial role of community education in addressing community-based problems, specifically focusing on the issue of ritual murder. By actively involving community members and promoting a responsible and coherent community, community education can contribute to creating a safer and more harmonious social order. The chapter emphasizes the need for modernizing cultural practices and traditions through community education to combat ritual murder effectively.

This chapter serves as a valuable resource for researchers, educators, policymakers, and community leaders interested in community education and its potential impact on social issues. By recognizing the significance of community education in tackling community-based problems, we can foster a sense of collective responsibility, strengthen social cohesion, and strive for a more peaceful and just society.

Chapter 8: Technology Integration in Mathematics to Promote Wellbeing of Learners During Coronavirus Pandemic: A Case Study in the OR Tambo Inland District

Authored by Thabisa T Maqoqa from Walter Sisulu University, South Africa, this chapter focuses on the effects of technology integration in mathematics teaching during the Covid-19 pandemic and its impact on the wellbeing of learners. The primary objective is to explore how technology integration can support learners' wellbeing and educational experiences during these challenging times.

Using an interpretive approach and face-to-face interviews, the researcher engaged nine participants who teach grade 10 mathematics from three senior secondary schools in the OR Tambo Coastal District. By purposefully sampling these participants, valuable insights were gathered regarding their experiences and perspectives on technology integration in mathematics education during the pandemic.

The findings of the study reveal several key points. Firstly, it was observed that many teachers lacked the necessary formal technology expertise to fully embrace online learning and encountered difficulties in establishing meaningful connections with learners in the online environment. Additionally, a lack of access to technology was identified as a significant barrier to effective technology integration in mathematics education.

Based on these findings, recommendations are made to address the challenges faced by educators and learners. The chapter suggests that the Department of Basic Education should prioritize ensuring that all learners have access to data cards loaded with uncapped data to facilitate smooth online learning experiences. Furthermore, the establishment of professional development programs for teachers is recommended, focusing on enhancing their skills in designing, using, and applying ICT technologies for online teaching.

This chapter provides valuable insights into the practical implications of technology integration in mathematics education during the Covid-19 pandemic. It highlights the challenges faced by educators and learners and offers recommendations to improve the overall learning experience and promote learner wellbeing.

Researchers, educators, policymakers, and stakeholders in the field of mathematics education and technology integration will find this chapter particularly relevant. By recognizing the importance of technology integration and addressing the associated challenges, we can create a supportive and engaging learning environment that promotes the wellbeing of learners, even in times of crisis.

Chapter 9: Strategies for Motivating Learners to Complete the General Education and Training Certificate Level 1 in South Africa

Co-authored by Itumeleng I. Setlhodi and Motlagoiloe S. Moroe from the University of South Africa, this chapter addresses the issue of low completion rates among learners in the General Education and Training Certificate: Adult Basic Education and Training (GETC: ABET) program in South Africa. While the program aims to provide learners with foundational learning and empower them for social and economic development, national statistics reveal a significant gap between enrollment and completion numbers.

To explore potential strategies for motivating adult learners to complete the GETC: ABET program, the authors conducted a qualitative study. Interactive individual and focus interviews were conducted with a total of 35 participants. Through these interviews, the study sought to identify the interventions used by teachers to encourage learners to complete their studies and the support provided to minimize or eliminate barriers that hinder program completion.

The findings of the study shed light on effective strategies employed by teachers to motivate learners. These strategies address various factors that contribute to learner disengagement or dropout, such as personal challenges, lack of support, and limited resources. By implementing targeted interventions, teachers can play a vital role in supporting learners and fostering a conducive learning environment that encourages completion.

Based on the study's findings, this chapter proposes essential strategies for consideration by community colleges and the Department of Higher Education and Training. These strategies aim to strengthen the teachers' approaches and enhance learner motivation to complete the GETC: ABET program. By implementing these strategies, institutions can improve completion rates and ensure that more learners benefit from the educational opportunities provided.

This chapter is a valuable resource for educators, policymakers, and stakeholders involved in adult education in South Africa. It highlights the importance of addressing the challenges faced by learners and offers practical strategies to promote learner motivation, engagement, and program completion. By adopting these strategies, institutions can create a supportive learning environment that empowers learners to overcome barriers and successfully complete their education, contributing to their personal growth and societal development.

Chapter 10: Marginalization of Older Adults in the Digitalization Drive in Ghana: Exploring the Potentials of Adult Learning and Education

Authored by Ellen Abakah and Kofi Konadu Berko from the Department of Adult Education and Human Resource Studies at the University of Ghana, this chapter delves into the digital divide experienced by older adults in Ghana within the context of the country's digitalization efforts. In recent years, the rapid advancement of the internet and information communication technologies (ICT) has brought about significant changes in various aspects of life. Governments around the world have embraced digitalization as a means to provide services online. However, despite the increasing number of internet and ICT users globally, there remains a persistent divide in access and utilization of these technologies, particularly among different age groups.

Focusing specifically on the Ghanaian context, this chapter critically examines the digital divide that exists between younger and older adults. It explores the implications of Ghana's digitalization initiatives and the role of adult learning and education in addressing the digital inequalities faced by older adults in the country. The chapter argues that the continued marginalization of older adults in the digital space could contribute to a new form of social exclusion. To counter this, the authors propose leveraging adult learning and education as a means to bridge the generational gap and promote digital inclusion.

By analyzing Ghana's digitalization policies and frameworks, the chapter highlights the need to prioritize adult learning and education within the broader digitalization agenda. It emphasizes the potential of adult learning and education to empower older adults with digital skills and knowledge, enabling them to actively participate in the digital society. By addressing the specific needs and challenges faced by older adults, Ghana can work towards bridging the digital divide and ensuring that digitalization benefits all segments of the population.

This chapter serves as a valuable resource for policymakers, educators, and stakeholders involved in digitalization and adult education in Ghana. It highlights the importance of recognizing and addressing the marginalization of older adults in the digital era. By integrating adult learning and education into digitalization strategies, Ghana can foster digital inclusion, promote social equity, and harness the full potential of its population in the digital age.

In conclusion, this edited reference book presents a comprehensive and insightful exploration of various aspects of adult education in the South African context. Through the collective contributions of esteemed scholars and experts in the field, this book provides a rich tapestry of knowledge and research findings that shed light on critical issues and challenges faced in adult education and its impact on individuals, communities, and society as a whole.

The chapters in this book delve into a wide range of topics, spanning from building strong adult education partnerships in the aviation industry during the Covid-19 pandemic to the preservation of indigenous language archives, and from the interdependence of CET college leadership to the role of technology integration in promoting learner well-being. Each chapter offers unique perspectives, empirical evidence, and valuable insights that contribute to our understanding of adult education in South Africa.

Throughout this book, a common thread emerges - the recognition of adult education as a powerful tool for social and economic development, promoting justice, equality, and well-being. The authors consistently emphasize the need for inclusive and learner-centered approaches, as well as the importance of addressing barriers and inequalities in access to education.

Moreover, this book underscores the critical role of partnerships, collaboration, and stakeholder engagement in strengthening adult education provision. The case studies, research findings, and proposed strategies provide valuable guidance for policymakers, educators, and practitioners in designing effective adult education programs and initiatives.

As editors, we are grateful to the esteemed contributors who have shared their expertise, knowledge, and research findings in this volume. Their dedication and commitment to advancing adult education in South Africa is commendable, and we believe that their contributions will inspire further research, innovation, and action in the field.

We also extend our gratitude to the readers and scholars who will engage with this book. It is our hope that this edited reference will serve as a valuable resource, stimulating critical thinking, dialogue, and transformative practices in the realm of adult education.

Finally, we express our gratitude to the publishing team for their support and guidance throughout the editing process. Their expertise and commitment have been instrumental in bringing this book to fruition.

In conclusion, this edited reference book serves as a testament to the vibrancy and significance of adult education in South Africa. It illuminates the challenges, opportunities, and transformative potential of adult education and underscores the importance of continuous efforts to enhance access, quality, and inclusivity in adult learning and development.

We hope this book will inspire researchers, educators, policymakers, and all those invested in adult education to explore further, innovate, and collaborate towards building a stronger, more equitable, and empowered society through lifelong learning.

Sampson Tawiah
Durban University of Technology, South Africa
Itumeleng Innocentia Setlhodi
University of South Africa, South Africa

Acknowledgement

The editors express their heartfelt gratitude to the scholars who contributed to making this book production a success. Their resilience and hard work have not gone unnoticed. We are grateful for this contribution towards the body of knowledge in academia to encourage and conscientize education providers, governmental officials, students and academics to use this work as an enabler towards addressing the needs of the marginalized in society and the world. We thank IGI Global Publishers for their relentless efforts and assistance towards our academic journey.

Chapter 1
Building Strong Adult Education Partnerships for the Wellbeing of the Aviation Workforce During the COVID-19 Pandemic

Zan Chen
https://orcid.org/0000-0002-5633-8743
Institute for Adult Learning, Singapore University of Social Sciences, Singapore

ABSTRACT

This chapter presents a case study of how an air service provider (Evergreen, pseudonym) in Singapore builds an adult education ecosystem with strong partnerships to promote the wellbeing of its badly hit aviation workforce during the Covid-19 pandemic. It illustrates how Evergreen envisions changes and pushes the boundaries by actively establishing partnerships with the institutes of high learning, the government agencies, industry associations, and training partners, and at the same time building a learning culture for a resilient workforce. Everygreen turns Covid-19 from a risk into opportunities to strengthen partnerships with high levels of trust, commitment, and open participation. This is accomplished in part by co-creation of learning materials, experiences, and environments with partners with a focus on resilience and sustainability. The findings identify important qualities that can be established as best practices for organisations and policy makers to further improve their adult education provision and promote the wellbeing of their workforce.

DOI: 10.4018/978-1-6684-6625-4.ch001

INTRODUCTION AND THEORETICAL APPROACH

During the Covid-19 pandemic, millions of individuals in direct aviation jobs (at airlines, airports, aircraft manufacturing, and air traffic management) and aviation-supported jobs (e.g., tourism jobs impacted by the lack of air travel, catering supplies, professional services required to run a global transport system) stood at risk of losing their livelihoods (IATA, 2021). The impact of the COVID-19 pandemic and rapid technological developments have seen air service providers rethink their business operations and training models. They have been pushed to innovate faster, invest in the skills of their workforce, products, and services and to work with greater speed and flexibility. Combined with policy, social and economic changes, for some providers the opportunity to diversity has been revolutionary, sparking new collaborative partnerships and smart ways of working that are likely to continue into the long-term horizon.

In the context of Singapore, government plays a critical role in pushing adult education and lifelong learning, as best exemplified by the national SkillsFuture movement since 2015. The SkillsFuture movement, which aims to foster a skilled, diverse and future-ready workforce through training and adult education, has been lauded as potential solutions to global economic pressures and inequality (Ong, 2018; Watermeyer et al., 2022). SkillsFuture has introduced a comprehensive range of programs and initiatives targeted at different stakeholders, including initiatives for individuals, such as education and career guidance, a one-stop online portal that informs Singaporeans of their learning and career choices, enhanced internships for youth; and SkillsFuture Credit to all Singaporeans aged 25 years old and above and mid-career subsidies to all Singapore Citizens aged 40 and above. Enterprises were provided with resources such as the new Skills Frameworks for 34 industry sectors, and SkillsFuture Enterprise Credits to build deep skills for a lean workforce and enhance business competitiveness. During the pandemic, the Singapore government allocated generous funding for adult education and spent about $2 billion in supporting skills development and keeping jobs of its people in 2021 (Singapore Budget n d). In addition to relevant government agencies that fund adult education, there are a diverse range of other stakeholders integrated at different layers and levels (Chen et al., 2021). These include private adult education providers, in-house training providers within enterprises, EdTech companies that offer training and technology solutions, the institutes for higher learning (universities and polytechnics) that offer professional learning and lifelong learning to their alumni and workforce, licencing boards, unions and professional bodies and of course the adult educators and learners themselves. Together, they create a complex environment in which the adult education providers operate. The ecosystems that adult education providers engage in and with are embedded in specific economic and social arrangements (Desjardins &

Loannidou, 2020). They "lie at the intersection of a variety of other systems including a nation's education and training system, labour market and employment system and other welfare state and social policy measures" (Desjardins, 2017, p.232). Yet, there is little elaboration about specific qualities of the adult education ecosystem and how it is developed. Understanding the specificities of the adult education sector, its learning communities and stakeholders helps to identify and examine what types of partnerships, relationships and interactions that exist (Chang & Gütl, 2007) and how an ecosystem approach could support workforce development and skills formation for other sectors, like in this case the aviation sector.

Set in the broader context of an ecosystem, the landscape is dynamic and constantly evolving. As the ecosystem continues to shift - priorities, circumstances and boundaries continue to change. The COVID-19 pandemic, by forcing businesses and education and alike to reduce human interactions and physical contact, has further accelerated the changes towards digitization, online learning, and automation. A key question is how organisations manage the dynamics and uncertainties that are inherently part of the evolving and moving ecosystem?

Using an ecosystem approach, the case reported in this chapter illustrates how an adult education and training team within an air service provider (Evergreen, pseudonym) envisions changes and pushes the boundaries by actively establishing partnerships with the institutes of high learning, the government agencies, industry associations, and training partners, and at the same time building a learning culture for a resilient workforce.

Ecosystem

To unpack the idea of ecosystem perspective I begin with why this perspective is important, drawing on the literature of business ecosystems.

Structural changes in economies across the globe mean it is increasingly less likely that single firms "can offer all the elements a customer needs – let alone to experiment with them" (Jacobines, 2019). These structural changes include rolling back of regulations that protect firms that had exclusive rights to particular customers. Digitization is increasingly seeing a blurring between products and services, enabling previously unconsidered combinations and linking previously unrelated goods and services, provided through networks of suppliers (ibid). As a result, ecosystems "are on the rise" (ibid). Businesses are no longer viewed as singular units but as part of a business ecosystem (Boustras, 2014). In such a system, there is both competition and cooperation present simultaneously. Gueguen, Pellegrin-Boucher and Torres refer to this as "coopetition" (2006, p.6). It is a way of identifying new market opportunities and implementing development strategies. There are calls in literature for organisations to "shift and expand their mindset … [from] an outside-in perspective" (Panetta, 2017). That is, shift from mechanistic views to what is called an open systems' view (McKinsey, 2019), to what we refer to as being part of multiple ecosystems.

Being part of an ecosystem is important in order to deliver value creation and perceive and act on new opportunities (Boustras, 2014; Jacobines, 2019; McKinsey, 2019; Panetta, 2017). It requires flexible organisational boundaries that make the most of opportunities afforded though being part of multiple business ecosystems (McKinsey, 2019). One important aspect is getting stakeholder interests aligned (Stanczky, 2017) to develop and maintain collaborative partnerships.

Partnerships

Partnerships in general are understood as being a means to work together to design context specific strategies, adapt policies to specific conditions and take initiatives on shared priorities (OECD, 2001). Partnerships are necessary to achieve desired outcomes (Kilpatrick & Guenther, 2003), often motivated by some combination of risk sharing, obtaining access to new markets and pooling complementary skills (Powell et al., 1996). More specifically, the purposes of multiple partnerships include the ability to stretch limited resources, undertake market scanning, reduce costs, offer distinctive products and services, co-brand with respected partners, develop staff capabilities, and share risks (Ferrier et al., 2008).

Within the context of adult education and training, providers also seek partnerships to fill a learning or training gap, improve career opportunities for their staff, meet policy initiatives, and sometimes to take up grants (Kilpatrick & Guenther, 2003; Owen & Bound, 2001). Partnerships contribute to building knowledge and community capacity (Chaskin et al., 2008) and towards the development of a learning ecosystem. Opportunities for partnerships are not afforded the ecosystem within which they work, not just from the initiative of the provider. According to Walcutt and Schatz (2019), as a learning ecosystem continues to evolve with less defined boundaries, it relies upon a greater diversity of expertise and actors and agile partnerships. For training providers, these may include – employers, other providers, unions, associations, chambers, unions, government agencies, particularly funding bodies, licensing bodies, communities of interest and more.

In Australia where public providers, in amongst the growing percentage of private providers, social partnerships play a significant role (Kilpatrick & Guenther, 2003; NCVER, 2007). These partnerships make a difference by identifying, acknowledging and addressing local needs and developing local capacity for roles to support learning (Billett et al., 2007). In the same vein, Allison, Gorringe and Lacey (2006) describe partnerships in the vocational education and training sector as creative association between providers with the community and/or business and/or other institutions and organisations to build capacity, make the most of available resources. The focus and outcomes of social partnerships places at its centre the social good of the client group(s) being served. This differs from market driven partnerships where social good may be an outcome, but it is not a focus. Historically the Australian government funding of partnerships/collaborative efforts brought a focus to community and business partnerships designed to promote a culture of corporate and individual social responsibility in Australia. Such government support contrasts with the emphasis on competition in the training sector.

The process of developing partnerships develops social capital – a network of relations built on trust, reciprocity and loyalty (Casey & Delaney, 2022; Kilpatrick et al., 2010). To develop collaborative partnerships requires dedicated resources, existing networks of relationships that can be grown and nurtured, leadership, and inhouse support for staff participation, problem solving and action (Chaskin, 2001). The process involves determining goals, and developing ways of working (Bound, 2007), and often involves phases of development of connecting, interacting, participating and committing (ibid). Governance of partnerships starts within the organisation; the degree of autonomy staff have, the design and flow of their work, the extent – or lack of – knowledge building within the provider. Establishing, developing, and maintaining partnerships also require (Kilpatrick & Guenther, 2003, p.28):

- Opportunities and structures for interaction which facilitate two-way information flows, networking and collaboration. Formal structures of boards and committees tend to enhance the effectiveness of partnerships that are beyond the early, initiation stage.
- Brokers or intermediaries play a key role in forging a learning culture (Kearns & Papadopoulos 2000); industry or government bodies can facilitate interaction.
- Human infrastructure that includes enabling leadership (leaders being not only people in positions of authority and power, collaborations work more effectively when others take responsibility for getting things done), and training brokers and/or local coordinators who facilitate the operation of ongoing relationships. Interpersonal, conflict resolution and teamwork skills are important.
- Some shared visions, values and trust among the partners in the collaboration; partnerships with a vision that allows a mix of meeting the needs of individuals, the community and the region/industry are the most successful.

All these suggested a relational approach in developing partnership. However, current knowledge of the efforts required to foster a sustained relational partnership for adult education remains sketchy. The case reported here tries to uncover the efforts for and features of a sustained relational partnership to help the aviation service provider navigate the challenges in times of constant changes.

Data Collection and Analysis

This chapter sets out to uncover how Evergreen (the in-house adult education team within an air service provider) responds and overcomes challenges presented by changing circumstances. The data reported in this chapter is drawn from a larger study on the training and adult education landscape in Singapore. A total of 18 case studies of adult education providers (including private training providers, the institutes of higher learning, in-house training units and Edin Singapore were conducted in 2022. Our overall aim is to identify important qualities that can be established as best practices for organisations to further improve their adult education provision and promote the wellbeing of its workforce.

The sampling of interviewees of this case included individuals undertaking different roles or function, for example, senior management representatives from the organisation, learning and development head, adult educators and their learners. They were invited to offer views on a range of topics, including business models, purpose and practices of partnerships, deployment of resources, use of technology, learning cultures within the organisation, design of work, and practice of training and learning. Given COVID-19 restrictions, all interviews were done online via zoom. The interviews were recorded with the consent of participants. They were later transcribed, and the transcriptions were then analysed using Braun and Clarke's (2006) multi-stage thematic analysis. Thematic analysis was selected as it provides a method by which to determine themes within each participant's experiences and perspectives (ibid). We note that respondents reported challenges and tensions brought by the changing landscape. We focus particularly on the efforts to forge an effective partnership to navigate those changes. The following section is a descriptive depiction of their challenges and efforts. This description provides contexts for the in-depth discussion of the characteristics of adult education partnerships that follows.

The Case of Evergreen

Evergreen is an in-house training centre of a leading global air and travel services provider. Established in 1959 in Dubai with only five employees, the company now employs over 41,000 staff offering quality and safe ground handling, cargo, travel, catering and retail services in 36 countries across six continents. In Singapore, the company has four decades of experience and is staffed with 1800 people locally. The company management team strongly advocates investments in their people and recognizes the importance of continuous professional development, which leads to the setup of Evergreen – the in-house training centre focusing on improving current skills and continuous growth for a resilient and sustainable workforce.

The aviation industry is one of the most heavily hit industries by Covid-19. As the international boarders closed, the number of airlines handled by this air and travel services provider shrunk drastically from 1,500 to 100 flights a day. The passengers per flight also decreased from a full capacity of around 320 to as few as five passengers. Consequently, the changes created excess manpower and machinery downtime for this airline service provider. One of the biggest challenges was then to keep the staff on the pay roll and minimize the impact on their well-being. Evergreen proactively strengthens partnerships and turns this crisis into opportunities for sustainable developments by harnessing the capability and managing the well-being of their workforce.

On the economic well-being end, Evergreen leverages on the full suite of support package from government agencies to help those affected by Covid-19 situations and keep them on the job. They do this by working closely with community centres, unions, business federations and other industry bodies to deploy its temporarily redundant workforce to other industries or community groups that need more manpower, for example, to distribute tokens and provide signpost and vaccination support. The external deployment provides short-term job opportunities for their excessive workforce during the pandemic and allows them to return back to this air service provider when Covid-19 eases and airline operations resume. A senior executive explained the external deployment as follows:

So, we actually deployed quite a bit of our staff externally. So, to agencies like People's Association. Even SingPost, they needed people, we have excess staff. So basically, we deployed our staff to them, they paid our staff through us. So we kept them on our payroll but they are kind of like – like we became like a manpower provider, in a way. But that is to keep them on the job. And some of them are already back with us. In fact, slowly, slowly over time, we took back all our staff who were external.

Evergreen well recognises the pain and reluctance of those deployed staff. They put in great efforts to ensure the staff are prepared for the external deployment. A support framework is developed for employees, which provides counselling services to guide them through periods of change. Employees are also assisted in training and workplace learning to obtain skills that allow them to adapt to new work and industry environments, and gaining exposure to and work experiences in new sectors or industries.

In addition to external deployment, Evergreen also taps on generous training funds from the government to develop those in the pay roll with new skills and capabilities. Previously, due to time and budgetary constraints, training opportunities were mainly provided to supervisory positions or limited to technical skills. Evergreen makes good use of operation downtime during Covid-19 and government training subsidies to expand training coverage to include generic skills and advocate equal training opportunities for all staff. As one senior executive shared:

"They [government bodies] gave us this ETSP, Enhanced Training Support Package. We had like 90% subsidy for training, even like what we called human skills. Basically, things like maybe communication skills, how to manage conflicts, how to lead by mentoring and coaching. You know all the supervisory level kind of skills or even leadership skills, right, we took this opportunity to send our staff. ... We make sure, we try to put almost every one of our local staff through it."

The investment and support in upskilling and reskilling have lifted the spirits of its workforce. Evergreen collaborates closely with industry partners and institutes of higher learning to develop modular and personalized training programs and placement opportunities. Staff are motivated in acquiring new, industry-attuned knowledge and skills that not only benefit their current work but also position themselves for continued professional success. The senior executive shared that:

"…..when I started sending these guys, a lot of them, the feedback was very good and a lot of them were really driven in the course. We started during the lockdown phase. So, we were doing virtual but the people were really very happy. Every single trainer wrote to me and said, eh, your guys, really driven to learn."

The above examples show how Evergreen develops and leverages on external partnerships to maintain the jobs and economic wellbeing of its staff. Another significant effort is to harness internal resources with job redesign and creating new roles. During the lockdown, the company uses the operation downtime to upgrade its systems and employ technological infrastructure. One big challenge was staff's potential fears or psychological resistance to new technologies, worrying that technologies will replace manual work and consequently lead to job losses. Evergreen facilitates dialogues and interactions to first address those concerns in advance before implementing the changes and redesign job based on the strengths and needs of the staff. In the following example, a senior executive described how an admin staff landed in a new role in e-learning courseware design when he recognized her talent and interest in digital technology and encouraged her to upskill for the new role.

"Like this girl that I – so the admin staff that was doing this, of course she panicked. She said, eh, am I going to lose my job? I said, no. Look, today you spent an hour a week, just to do this. I said, I could have made use of you in this hour, for better

things. And at the end of the day, like for her, I actually offered her – I said, look, do you like, you know, learning new stuff? I even asked her say – because she described herself as an arty person. So I said, wow, you like all these digital technologies. I said, would you like to learn how to create e-learning courseware?... So in fact, I actually relook at her job role, her job scope. Her JD [job description]. So, her JD now becomes bigger, more high value work rather admin, issue receipts. So now, she helps me with other stuff. She could take on projects that could help us, you know, improve other areas of work."

This role change alleviated the panic the staff felt when administrative procedures were automated with technologies. This exemplified how Evergreen is empathetic and highly attuned to the psychological wellbeing of its staff in the face of technological advancements and changes. Open dialogues and counselling as shown in this example are critical to support its staff to navigate through the changes and even change or expand roles for more meaningful work.

As the training centre in the air service provider, Evergreen is undergoing changes not only from the aviation sector, but also from the adult education sector. As we know it, Covid-19 has accelerated the use of learning technologies and adult education and training has become more virtual (e.g., Chen& binte Hardy, 2023; Chen et al, 2021). To Evergreen, this move to online learning is a challenge but more an opportunity for pedagogical experimentations. They do this by proactively partnering with the Institutes for Higher Learning. They sign memorandums and collaborate on technology-enabled training projects which allow Evergreen to access the learning technologies in the universities and polytechnics. For example, Evergreen has converted its ramp training to Virtual Reality and through that, it not only sustains training during the lockdown but also enhances the learning experience and outcomes. Evergreen also converts classroom training contents to online learning by working along with final-year students from the polytechnics to co-create e-learning contents. In addition, partnership with the Institutes of Higher Learning also helps to improve the pedagogical competencies of Evergreen's training staff. Through co-designing continuing professional development programmes with the Institutes for Higher Learning, Evergreen upskills the pedagogic practices of its inhouse trainers and workplace mentors to embrace more interactive and learner-centered pedagogies and builds up their online training capabilities which cascades down to better learning experience and outcomes for its workforce, in both classroom and blended learning environments. Trainers also use strategies like peer mentoring to bridge the inter-generational learning challenges in the classrooms and engage in regular dialogic feedback from learners. The shift from lectures to case studies makes learning more authentic, it also flattens the power relationship between the learner and allows for open dialogue and coaching for deeper learning. As the senior executive shared:

"In the past, it's just downloading – this is the rules, this is what you supposed to, not supposed to do. You don't really go into the why and the impacts, the consequences if you drive haphazardly, if you use a handphone. So what we have done is, - the students have done with our help is to convert some of these past incidents to case studies, where the people come in, they discuss then they do presentation. They say, how can this be avoided. So basically, more interactions as well as more engagement and hopefully more insights into the safety into the airside."

In addition to leveraging on formal partnerships to build up trainer capabilities, Evergreen also encourages its trainers to improve skills and capabilities through informal channels. For example, trainers are encouraged to attend Toastmasters sessions to improve public speaking and communication skills. They are also supported to take learning leave to join professional networks for trainers to share and learn from other training professionals. There are company learning hours preserved for peer sharing, learning and reflection. The company also provides staff with LinkedIn Learning account for their self-learning. All these broadens the ecosystem of learning for their trainers, and ultimately for their learners.

While Evergreen forges a wide range of internal and external partnerships, it is notably difficult to establish partnership with competitors. A set of historical and habituated tensions within and between major competitors whose interests are divergent have marked the air services industry in Singapore. To Evergreen, staff poaching is a recognized threat that have hampered sharing of training resources and collaborative efforts. The current leadership in Evergreen determines to break the traditional adversary relationship by having informal "coffee sessions" with its major competitors. Over time, they build trust and open to discuss the challenges and exchange ideas to solve those common issues of interest together. These coffee sessions break the ice and have led to recognition of shared interests across the parties, who gradually co-develop new programmes together. At the same time, Evergreen strategically involves the government body and airport management to drive some of the initiative to minimise the poaching threat. The steps from reaching out to the traditional adversarial party, establishing mutual recognition of interests to enacting mutual, collaborative engagement require tremendous effort. This in turn paves way for a more collaborative adult training ecosystem for the aviation sector as a whole. I will return to this point in the next section.

DISCUSSION

Evergreen puts in great effort to forge strategic partnerships for the wellbeing of its staff. It proactively leverages on government support, partners with union, social agencies and community groups to keep key staff on the payroll and deploy excess staff, so that their economic wellbeing can be preserved during the pandemic. It also turns Covid-19 from a risk to opportunities in upskilling and reskilling its workforce by strengthening partnerships with the institutes of high learning, industry associations, and its competitors. The upskilling and reskilling are well received by its staff. The training and placement do not only provide new skills and knowledge for continued career progression and success, but also opportunities for staff and managers to reflect on and actively engage with how quickly industries and technologies are changing. These training and placement experiences then become interesting and enriching on their own. In a sense, Evergreen aims to foster its learning culture and build a learning ecosystem for a resilient workforce.

The data reveals important qualities of a sustainable relational partnership. The term "relational" is to feature the long-term relationships on the basis of mutual benefits, trust, commitment and open participation; as opposed to a "transactional" approach, which is usually short term, with low levels of trust, unequal power distribution and closed participation. If we return to the Evergreen case, we could consider what a sustained relational partnership might look like.

Firstly, a sustained relational partnership seeks to build a long-term relationship with high levels of trust and mutual benefits. Partnership essentially recognizes shared interests (Casey & Delaney, 2022) towards a common goal or purpose to add value to the participating partners. In the example of external deployment, Evergreen provides counselling services and training to prepare their to-be-deployed staff for the change. This entails more than effort to support their own staff deployment, but taking the steps to train them for the new work and industry environments that would in turn benefit their industry partners and community groups who receive those deployed staff. Here mutual benefits include successful excess staff deployment for Evergreen, improved productivity and performance of its deployed staff and partners, and improved trust between Evergreen and staff (for care and continuous support in times of difficulties), between Evergreen and its partners (efforts to minimize risks for disappointing results of deployment).

Literature has established the vital role trust plays in all long-term partnerships (e.g., Das, 2018; Giddens, 1991; Sztompka, 1999). Further theoretical and sociological discussion of trust is beyond my purpose here. But importantly, I stress, trust is being built through continuous effort and patience. In the coffee session example with its competitors, Evergreen demonstrates deliberate effort and unprecedented openness to identify mutual goals, develop ways of working, adjust and negotiate practicalities of the partnership, which gradually foster a "shift from mistrust to trust, from withholding to sharing" (Casey & Delaney, 2022, p. 62), from competition to collaboration.

Secondly, it continuously seeks and establishes diverse partnerships for multiple purposes. Research has elaborated on many benefits of partnership to management, employees, companies, and unions (Ferrier et al., 2008; Geary & Trif, 2011; Kilpatrick & Guenther, 2003; Kochan & Riordan, 2016). The case of Evergreen in this study suggests that partnership in adult education with diverse organisations and agencies creates the opportunities to capitalize, exchange and remobilize a range of tangible and intangible resources such as technologies, learning materials, knowledge, networks, services and manpower. Strategic use of internal and external resources allows its company to digitalise operation systems, deploy temporarily excessive staff, expand job roles, improve training offerings and pedagogies, reskilling and upskilling workforce to stay relevant with industry changes. Efforts in forging and strengthening partnerships lead to improved productivity, greater job security, and a learning ecosystem for a sustainable workforce. Importantly, this learning ecosystem can support development of other important qualities in organizational and employment life (Casey & Delaney, 2022) and facilitated participatory power (Casey et al., 2016) from a motivated workforce that generate a mutual social-economic benefit in the long run.

Thirdly, a sustained relational partnership builds strong emotional attachment and commitment. Evergreen is empathetic to the potential fear and anxiety of its employees in face of changes accelerated by the pandemic. It puts in tremendous efforts to partner with the government, union industry associations and social groups to first attend to the economic and psychological wellbeing of its staff. Dialogue sessions between management and staff are organised to create partnership among themselves. "Employee as partners" practice may represent a significant change in the ways of working. The collective capacity and moral capital of mutual respect (Casey & Delaney,2022) are being built through jointly addressing the challenges and negotiating solutions. While providing staff with expanded access to training and professional development opportunities, Evergreen also built strong commitment through their encouragement, support, modelling and inclusiveness. With secured jobs and aspirations into newly deployed jobs or expanded roles, staff feel stronger sense of belongs to the organisation, and in return they tend to show greater work effort and commitment (Chen & Ramos, 2022; De Cooman, et al 2013).

Fourthly, a sustained relational partnership encourages co-creation, open communication and participation. Evergreen strategically reaches out to its competitors and built alliance with them to jointly solve problems that cannot be solved by any single organization. The risk-taking in sharing (Casey & Delaney, 2022) has subsequently opened paths for co-creation of new programmes and further development. Its "Employee as partners" practice allows staff and management to express and embrace multiple perspectives that foster open communication and greater participation.

Whilst the findings point out strongly key features of a sustained relational partnership, these are by no means exclusive or prescriptive. Partnerships do not necessarily need to have all these features, but as our data shows, the more they have, the more likely the partnership seems to work.

CONCLUSION

The case reported in this chapter illustrates how the air service provider envisions changes and pushes the boundaries by actively establishing partnerships with the institutes of high learning, the government agencies, industry associations, and training partners, and at the same time building a learning culture for a resilient workforce. Evergreen turns Covid-19 from a risk into opportunities to strengthen partnerships with high levels of trust, commitment, and open participation to re-design learning and jobs, and create a resilient and sustainable future of their workforce. This is accomplished in part by co-creation of learning materials, experiences, and environments with partners with a focus on resilience and sustainability.

The findings identify important qualities that can be established as best practices for organisations to further forge their adult education partnerships and promote the wellbeing of their workforce during the pandemic. The development of sustained relational partnerships offers effective and creative methods to address evolving needs and problems brought about by changing circumstances. Through mutual benefits and open communication, partnerships are able to build social capital – networks, and shared values (Allison et al., 2006; Bourdieu, 1992; Kilpatrick et al., 2010; NCVER, 2007) and moral capital – mutual respect, tolerance and trust (Casey & Delaney, 2022) among partners and community members. Although some of the characteristics have been identified in earlier research, this study has enabled these important qualities to be further examined and defined. Partnerships in adult education that generate a learning ecosystem can be used to support co-creation and innovation. These abilities allow the organisation and its partners to tackle complex issues that are often too challenging for any single organisation and constantly adapt to change.

The COVID-19 pandemic presents a unique opportunity to reflect on business resilience. It has forced numerous changes in the way business has been conducted which, in turn, requires reskilling and upskilling of the workforce to meet those needs. Acknowledging the importance and benefits of a sustained relational partnership, organisations can take actively roles in building partnerships with the adult education sector to identify training needs, development new training programmes, upgrade training systems and methods, build learning culture and develop good career paths for employees. It is noted in the case the roles that government agencies play in driving collaborations and forging partnerships among diverse players in the ecosystem. In this vein, the findings can then be used by policy makers to strengthen an adult education ecosystem for a resilient workforce that is agile, globally competitive, and future ready.

ACKNOWLEDGEMENT

I would like to thank SkillsFuture Singapore Agency for funding this project. I am grateful to the useful inputs from the editors and my team members. Special thanks go to Dr Ilona Murphy, Ms Shannon Chan, and Associate Professor Helen Bound for their valuable suggestions.

REFERENCES

Allison, J., Gorringe, S., & Lacey, J. (2006). *Building learning communities: Partnerships, social capital and VET performance*. NCVER.

Billett, S., Ovens, C., Clemans, A., & Seddon, T. (2007). Collaborative working and contested practices: Forming, developing and sustaining social partnerships in education. *Journal of Education Policy*, *22*(6), 637–656. doi:10.1080/02680930701625288

Bourdieu, P. (1992). *The Logic of Practice*. Stanford University Press.

Braun, V., & Clarke, V. (2006). Using Thematic Analysis in Psychology. *Qualitative Research in Psychology*, *3*(2), 77–10. doi:10.1191/1478088706qp063oa

Casey, C., & Delaney, H. (2022). The effort of partnership: Capacity development and moral capital in partnership for mutual gains. *Economic and Industrial Democracy*, *43*(1), 52–71. doi:10.1177/0143831X19883007

Casey, C., Fiedler, A., & Fath, B. (2016). The European Company (SE): Power and participation in the multinational corporation. *European Journal of Industrial Relations*, *22*(1), 73–90. doi:10.1177/0959680115593653

Chang, V., & Gütl, C. (2007). E-Learning Ecosystem (ELES) – A Holistic Approach for the Development of more Effective Learning Environment for Small-to-Medium Sized Enterprises (SMEs). In Proc. Inaugural IEEE International Digital EcoSystems Technologies Conference (IEEE-DEST 2007), Cairns, Australia.

Chaskin, R. J. (2001). Building Community Capacity: A Definitional Framework and Case Studies from a Comprehensive Community Initiative. *Urban Affairs Review*, *36*(3), 291–323. doi:10.1177/10780870122184876

Chen, Z., & Hardy, S. B. (2023). Snapshot of the present, glimpse into the future: Impact of COVID-19 on higher education and adult training. *International Journal of Mobile Learning and Organisation*, *17*(1/2), 76–92. doi:10.1504/IJMLO.2023.128350

Chen, Z., Pavlova, M., & Ramos, C. (2021). A systematic approach to adult educators' professional development in Singapore: Challenges and future developments. *International Journal of Lifelong Education*, *40*(5-6), 455–470. doi:10.1080/02601370.2021.1978006

Chen, Z., & Ramos, C. (2022). Work satisfaction of adult educators in Singapore: An empirical analysis. *Journal of Vocational Education and Training*, 1–25. doi:10.1080/13636820.2022.2049624

Cook-Sather, A., & Luz, A. (2015). Greater engagement in and responsibility for learning: What happens when students cross the threshold of student-faculty partnership. *Higher Education Research & Development*, *34*(6), 1097–1109. doi:10.1080/07294360.2014.911263

Das, T. K. (2018). *Managing Trust in Strategic Alliances*. Information Age Publishing.

De Cooman, R., Stynen, D., Van den Broeck, A., Sels, L., & De Witte, H. (2013). How job characteristics relate to need satisfaction and autonomous motivation: Implications for work effort. *Journal of Applied Social Psychology*, *43*(6), 1342–1352. doi:10.1111/jasp.12143

Desjardins, R. (2017). *Political economy of adult learning systems. Comparative study of strategies, policies and constraints*. Bloomsbury. doi:10.5040/9781474273671

Desjardins, R., & Ioannidou, A. (2020). The political economy of adult learning systems—Some institutional features that promote adult learning participation. *ZfW*, *43*(2), 143–168. doi:10.100740955-020-00159-y

Ferrier, F., Dumbrell, T., & Burke, G. (2008). *Vocational education and training providers in competitive training markets*. NCVER.

Geary, J., & Trif, A. (2011). Workplace partnership and the balance of advantage: A critical case analysis. *British Journal of Industrial Relations*, *49*, s44–s69. doi:10.1111/j.1467-8543.2010.00827.x

Giddens, A. (1991). *Modernity and Self-identity*. Stanford University Press.

Gueguen, G., Boucher, P., & Torres, V. (2006). *Between cooperation and competition: The benefits of collective strategies within business ecosystems—The example of the software industry*. Gaelgueguen. www.gaelgueguen.fr/wp-content/uploads/GueguenPellegrinTorres.pdf

Hammersley, M., & Atkinson, P. (2007). *Ethnography Principles in practice* (3rd ed.). Routledge.

IATA. (2021*). The impact of COVID-19 on aviation*. IATA.

Kilpatrick, S., & Guenther, J. (2003). Successful VET partnerships in Australia. *International Journal of Training Research*, *1*(1), 23–43. doi:10.5172/ijtr.1.1.23

Kilpatrick, S., Johns, S., & Mulford, B. (2010). Social Capital, Educational Institutions and Leadership. In P. Peterson, E. Baker, & B. McGaw (Eds.), *International Encyclopedia of Education* (3rd ed., pp. 113–119). Elsevier. doi:10.1016/B978-0-08-044894-7.00426-7

Kochan, T. A., & Riordan, C. A. (2016). Employment relations and growing income inequality: Causes and potential options for its reversal. *The Journal of Industrial Relations*, *58*(3), 419–440. doi:10.1177/0022185616634337

NCVER (National Centre for Vocational Education Research). (2007). *VET regional partnerships at a glance*. NCVER.

Ong, Y. K. (2018). Tackling Inequality Will Always Be Work in Progress and All Singaporeans Have a Part to Play. *TODAY.*

Sztompka, P. (1999). *Trust: A Sociological Theory*. Cambridge University Press.

Watermeyer, R., Chen, Z., & Ang, B. J. (2022). 'Education without limits': The digital resettlement of post-secondary education and training in Singapore in the COVID-19 era. *Journal of Education Policy*, *37*(6), 861–882. doi:10.1080/02680939.2021.1933198

Chapter 2
Adult Basic Education Provision and Human Capital Development Perceptions of Adult Educators

Mziwoxolo Richmond Richmond Krexe
https://orcid.org/0009-0003-1447-0791
Walter Sisulu University, South Africa

ABSTRACT

This chapter raises an argument as to whether provision of adult basic education in the Eastern Cape Province of the Republic of South Africa can lead to bigger issues in the form of developing human capital which, in turn, will lead to inclusion of those once marginalised and excluded in the economic activities of South Africa. The main research question—To what extent does adult basic education and training (ABET) provision contribute to human capital development?—was pursued to probe the perceptions of educators in ABET centres and those in the education districts. A survey design, underpinned by the interpretivist paradigm, was used in this investigation, employing qualitative research method. One hundred and five (105) educators in the ABET centres and six (6) in the district offices participated in the study. The educators in ABET centres and those in district offices were purposefully selected. Data collection took place through questionnaires and interviews. The qualitative data were transcribed word for word for purposes of tracing any observable themes.

DOI: 10.4018/978-1-6684-6625-4.ch002

INTRODUCTION

Human capital development is part of human development which is usually determined by using a human development index. According to Harber (2010) the human development index is a composite measurement based on indicators such as life expectancy, adult literacy, proportions of enrolment in the different levels of education and the gross domestic product (GDP). Many people view human capital development as a function of the human resource division in big firms. Yet, the concept embraces opening the eyes of a person who could not read labels on medical containers, on food shelves in supermarkets and road signs to be able to read them and thus gain his or her freedom. This chapter follows the angle of human capital development as imparting people with new skills such that their livelihoods are improved. This is in the backdrop of Statistics South Africa's report of 2019 that approximately 18 million South Africans are vulnerable to poverty, or they are in need of state support.

BACKGROUND

Chikwe, Ogidi and Nwachukwa (2015:44) state that human capital is the stock of competencies, knowledge and personality attributes embodied in the ability to perform to produce economic value. It is attributes gained by an individual through education and experience. This chapter takes adult basic education provision as associated with human capital development beyond reading, writing and arithmetic but to be an enabler to trainability and helping people to acquire low and high order skills. In fact, Mongale and Masipa (2019:273) cite Ogundari and Awukuse (2018) who in their study concluded that the two measures of human capital, health and education have effects on economic growth, although the contribution of health is relatively larger than the impact of education. The focus of the chapter is to discover the experiences of educators in relation to adult basic education and training provision and human capital development in the Eastern Cape.

Eastern Cape is one of the nine provinces of the Republic of South Africa created after the 1994 democratic elections. It consists of six District Municipalities, namely, Cacadu, Amatole, Chris Hani, uKhahlamba (now known as Joe Gqabi), O.R.Tambo and Alfred Nzo (Eastern Cape State of the Environment Report, 2004). There are also two Metropolitan Municipalities, namely, Buffalo City and Nelson Mandela Bay. According to the Human Sciences Research Council (HSRC) (2004: 1), in collaboration with Whiteford (2004), approximately 57% of individuals in South Africa live below the poverty income line. HSRC (2004) further highlights that Limpopo and the Eastern Cape have the highest proportion of the poor, with 77%

and 72% of their populations living below the poverty income line respectively. The point is emphasised by a statement from the same report indicating that the poorest municipality in the Republic of South Africa is Ntabankulu in the Eastern Cape, where 85% of its inhabitants live below the poverty line. The report further reveals that out of the 10 poorest municipalities in South Africa, seven are located in the Eastern Cape. Statistics South Africa survey of 2014/15 (2019) shows improvement in the levels of poverty. The provinces with the highest headcount of adult poverty are Limpopo (67,5%), Eastern Cape (67,3%), KwaZulu-Natal (60,7%) and Northwest (59,6). The implication of these statistics is that the Eastern Cape is not only a predominantly rural province but also one of the poorest provinces in the Republic of South Africa.

One of the most renowned ways of extricating people from poverty and unemployment is capacity-building through education and training (Bhola, 2006: 231). Wolhuter (2001: 18) stresses the above-mentioned point when he avers that in the 1960s, education was seen as a panacea to all societal problems such as economic growth, eradication of poverty and unemployment, development, and stabilisation of a democratic culture. Capacity-building recognises and respects people's dignity and ability to fend for themselves, rather than to be dependent on hand-outs and other people's generosity and sympathies. In line with this statement, John Hopkins University (2002) cited by Indabawa and Mpofu (2006: 82) considers empowerment to be a person's ability to take effective control of one's life in terms of being well-informed and equipped with education, finance, and relevant skills to take decisions without external influence.

Bhasin (1992) cited by Indabawa and Mpofu (2006:82) defines empowerment from a women's empowerment perspective. He defines it as meaning among other things, the recognition of their contribution and knowledge, helping their self-respect and dignity, helping them to become more economically independent and self-reliant, reducing their burden of work, especially at home and promoting their qualities of nurturing, caring and gentleness. Indabawa and Mpofu (2006) believe that in the process of empowering people, adult education is a viable instrument that can be used at all times in all places. This view is confirmed by Nyerere's assertions in 1969 as cited by the institute of Adult Education (1975: 2), wherein he postulated that people's lives could only be improved by their own efforts and through their own understanding, and against a background of ignorance and poverty, this meant that adult education of all types was of vital importance for rapid development. Indabawa and Mpofu conclude by mentioning that literacy and adult education are a means for people to overcome poverty and exclusion, establish and reinforce democracy, achieve justice and comprehensive peace, enhance economic and social well-being, improve health, and ensure food security.

VIEWS OBTAINED IN THE LITERATURE

Branson, Garlick, Lam and Leibbrandt (2012:2) believe that the need to invest in human capital has been recognised in development economics over a long time. According to them, human capital typically includes both skills and health. The above-mentioned authors claim that there is a consensus that investment in human capital is good for both economic growth and the reduction of poverty and inequality, but there is much disagreement over the precise quantitative effects of human capital on the economic growth, poverty, and inequality and over the most efficient forms of investment in education. On the other hand, there is agreement that it is important for government to intervene to increase the quantity and quality of human capital produced. Groot and Van den Brink (2007: 65) view education and health as the two most important investments in human capital that individuals make as their economic value lies in the effects they have on productivity since both education and health make individuals more productive. Rosenbloom (2004: 3) claims that literacy and other basic skills imparted to adults and out-of-school youths through non-formal education programmes not only directly improve income generation, but also have a strong impact on family health status, children's educational attainment and sustainable management of local natural resources. The question that can be asked in relation to this paper is whether the latter author's claims are confirmed by the educators of the ABET programme in the Eastern Cape.

The Department of Education's Policy Document on ABET (1997) emphasises that ABET is both part of, and a foundation, for lifelong learning. Prinsloo (2000: 109) states that the understanding of literacy (an essential component of basic education) as a core basic skill that stands at the door to rational thinking, higher order skills and trainability is one that dominates policymaking and system-building in educational provision across countries. Aitchison and Harley (2006: 107) postulate that the importance of literacy in the workplace is ever increasing as the business world is ever changing and becoming more digital and electronic. These authors believe that having literate workers will imply that more work can be done through electronic processes. In South Africa, policymakers have the ideal of moving the pool of human resources in the country from a low-skill equilibrium to high-skill equilibrium (Prinsloo: 2000: 113). This chapter therefore sets out to establish whether ABET forms a foundation for higher skills and trainability of participants.

In some developing countries, a mix of education and training is available for skills acquisition, and there are multiple paths to skills development for a given population (Xiao, 2001: 1). Fitzsimons (2009: 1), when considering the reformulation of human capital theory, shows the emphasis that is put on the significance of education and training as the key to participation in the new global economy. Livingstone (1997: 2), concurring with the view expressed by Fitzsimons, states that throughout the post-1945 expansionary era, the simultaneous increase of school participation rates and earned incomes lent support to the view that more schooling would lead to higher productivity and macro-economic growth. Quiggin (1999: 3) adds his voice to the debate by stating that in the human capital theory, education is an investment that produces benefits in the future. Xiao (2001: 1) concurs with Quiggin (1999: 9) by asserting that human capital theory encapsulates the view that education or training raises productivity of workers by imparting useful knowledge and skills.

In the Eastern Cape Province, there has been an outcry about shortage of skills even though there is provision of adult basic education and training (Heather, 2003: xxxvi). In fact, Heather (2003: xxxvi) states that apparently, as much as 80% of the economically active population in the Eastern Cape are either semi-skilled or unskilled. The question of skills shortage is raised by Mapoma (2010:10) when he postulates that the shortage of suitable skills remains the key challenge in the Eastern Cape. This begs the question about the extent the provision of ABET contributes to human capital development in the light of the ideas and practices raised by the various scholars. So, the question: To what extent does provision of adult basic education and training contribute to human capital development? must be answered comprehensively in this chapter. The answer to this question would bring one closer to the achievement of the aim of this chapter. Furthermore, the Eastern Cape has a prismatic society that is more rural and traditional than urban and modern, so to what extent is the notion of skills development practicable and what form or shape does it take? Does adult basic education and training feature in the scheme of things in skills development in the Eastern Cape, and if so, how?

In attempting to answer the above-mentioned main research question, it would be very critical to answer fully and comprehensively each of the following sub-research questions?

- What does ABET provision's contribution to human capital development entail?
- To what extent does ABET provision contribute to human capital development?
- What stories can be told by ABET educators regarding ABET provision and human capital development?

In order to answer these questions satisfactorily, it would be important to formulate aims and objectives of this study based on the afore-mentioned sub-research questions. The aim of this study is to establish theperceptions of educators regarding provision of adult basic education and training and human capital development. In this regard, the following objectives would serve as the roadmap in unfolding the aim of the study:

- To find out what adult basic education and training's contribution to human capital entails
- To establish the extent to which adult basic education and training contributes to human capital development
- To hear the voices of the educators regarding provision of adult basic education and training and human capital development

This study aimed to uncover the extent to which people empowerment occurs through adult basic education and training. Some studies on adult basic education and training have been conducted in this province, however most of them focus on the functioning of ABET centres. A case in point is that of Krexe 1994, Nqabeni in 1996 and Magxala's study in 2008. The focus of each study entailed finding out the role of night schools in the provision of adult education, a case study of Centuli and Xhugxwala Literacy programme and on learner participation in adult centres in the Mthatha education district of the Eastern Cape respectively. These authors' interests were more on role of night schools in providing adult basic education, effects of literacy programmes on participating adults and factors that hinder or promote student participation, however, all these studies had no record regarding whether or not learner participation in ABET centres improves their learning. The current study would go beyond learner participation in adult centres and investigate what their learning achieves for them in the long run. Providers of ABET might be able to improve their practice because of the knowledge generated by this study.

In South Africa, a lot of studies have been undertaken. In the greater South Africa, several researchers have investigated different aspects of adult education. Lyster, Morphet, Clifford, Kerfoot, Castle and Hutton ((1992) produced a book on Adult Basic Education in South Africa: Literacy, English as a second language and numeracy. Rule (2006) wrote about the legislative framework, infrastructure and political will to implement an effective adult basic education and training. Aitchison reviewed adult education policies in South Africa with the aim of assessing the impact these policies had on the provision of adult education. Land (2021) wrote a paper on South Africa's adult educators in the community college sector: who they are, and how they viewed their training, their work, and their position. All these studies, except for the book by Lyster et al, do not address the effect of the adult education provided on the lives of the learners hence in this chapter there is a wish to explore the perceptions of the adult educators in terms of the extent to which adult education provision contributes towards human capital development.

THEORETICAL FRAMEWORK

This study was grounded on the Human Capital Theory. The human capital theory is one of the theories of development (Harber, 2010: 92). Harber (2010) specifies that one of the key social institutions believed to make a difference in the way societies operate and individuals behave is education. The afore-mentioned author further articulates the view that formal education has been linked to different theories of development because schools help to create the citizens and workforce of the future and therefore define the direction of development. This study sought to establish whether the above notion of human capital theory applies to the ABET Centres and Adult Basic Education and Training provision or not.

Harber (2010: 93) stresses that the human capital theory is based on the idea that the key to economic development is to see the increased education of the human workforce as a capital investment. The above author believes that education is not only a good investment for the individuals concerned, but that an educated population is necessary for industrial development and economic growth because such a population is more productive. Harber (2010) further highlights the fact that the skills and motivation for productive behaviour are imparted through formal education. It would be of interest to find out whether the skills and motivation for productive behaviour could also be imparted through adult basic education and training.

Verhogladova (2006: 253) highlights the following as important elements of human capital: intellectual capital (level of education, knowledge), fund on training and manufacturing (qualification, skills, experience), fund on health (psycho-physical and emotional characteristics), fund on economy-important information (about prices and earnings), fund on migration (mobility of human resources), motivation of economic activity and fund on free time (recreating and general cultural level of renewing human resources). He concludes by pointing out that there are three main factors that directly define the size of regional human capital, namely, number of economically active people in a population and its growth rate, index of educational level and state of health of the population. On this point, the South African Institute of Race Relations (SAIRR, 2014: 1), in its research report titled *The Eastern Cape: the worst province to live in*, found that in economic rankings built on indicators ranging from growth rates to unemployment levels, the Eastern Cape came last with a score of 18 compared to Gauteng, which came first with a score of 92 out of a possible score of 100. On social rankings, based on indicators ranging from malnutrition levels to matriculation pass rates, the Eastern Cape again came last. In education rankings, relying on indicators ranging from early childhood enrolments to the proportion of adults with a degree, the Eastern Cape tied at the bottom of the list with Mpumalanga, Northwest and Northern Cape and was regarded as the worst province in this regard. The SAIRR research report indicates the kind of work that still needs to be done to enhance human capital development in the Eastern Cape, hence this study also looks at the extent to which ABET provision contributes to human capital development.

According to Olaniyan and Okemakinde (2008:158), the theoretical framework "most responsible for the wholesome adoption of education and development policies has come to be known as human capital theory". Olaniyan and Okemakinde further highlight the work of Schultz (1971), Sakamota and Powers (1995), Psacharopoulos and Woodhall (1997) regarding the human capital theory as resting on the assumption that formal education is highly instrumental in and even necessary to improve production capacity of a population and, in fact, according to the human capital theorists an educated population is a productive population. Emphasising this point, Omojimite (2011) as cited by Mongale and Masipa (2019), points out that economic growth prospect in Africa is hindered by inadequate investment in education and health especially for the vulnerable and previously disadvantaged groups. This chapter would want to reveal the extent to which ABET contributes to the education of adults in the Eastern Cape and hence its impact on human capital development.

In this study, the assumption was that adult basic education and training contributes to human capital development in line with the basic underpinnings of this theory. The study intended either to confirm or refute the theory in the context of the experiences of practitioners in the adult basic education and training programme.

. The perspective of this study in relation to the human capital theory was that adult basic education and training programmes might not be ends in themselves but that they might be means to ends. The products of the programme must have acquired skills in this programme so that they become ready to embark on other skills development programmes as well as being empowered to participate in social, economic, and political activities with confidence and conviction.

RESEARCH DESIGN AND METHODS

The thrust of this study was to establish the perspectives of educators regarding adult basic education and training provision and human capital development. In this section, attention is paid to research design, population, sample and sampling procedure, data presentation and analysis and ethical considerations.

A survey research design was used in this study. In a survey, the investigator selects a sample of respondents and administers a questionnaire or conducts interviews to collect information on variables of interest. In the context of this study the researcher administered questionnaires and conducted interviews. Creswell (2009:145) gives a succinct statement of the role of a survey when postulating that it provides a quantitative or numeric description of trends, attitudes, or opinions of a population by studying a sample of that population and then a researcher can generalise or make claims about the population from the sample results. However, the researcher was more interested on the responses to the open-ended questions of the questionnaire rather than the quantitative aspect. The researcher underpinned the study on the interpretivist paradigm.

POPULATION

McMillan and Schumacher (2006: 119) define a population as a group of elements or cases, whether individuals, objects, or events, that conform to specific criteria and to which there is an intention to generalise the results of the research. In this study, the target population entails educators in the adult basic education and training programme both those in ABET centres and those who work in the education district offices.

SAMPLE AND SAMPLING PROCEDURE

The Eastern Cape Provincial Department of Education consists of twelve (12) education districts with a total of 2 950 ABET educators (Department of Education: ABET quarterly statistics, September 2020). For purposes of this sample, one hundred and five (105) participants were educators across twelve education districts and six (6) were ABET educators working in the district offices. The educators working in the ABET centres, on the one hand, were purposefully selected for purposes of administering questionnaires, and those working in district offices, were also purposefully selected for the interviews. The questionnaire return rate was 45.7%.

McMillan and Schumacher (2006: 126) describe purposeful sampling as a situation where the researcher selects elements from the population that are representative or informative about the topic of interest. They add that a judgment is made about which subjects should be selected to provide the best information to address the purpose of the research, because of the researcher's knowledge of the population. In the context of this study, the researcher ensured that the participants came from the six district municipalities of the Eastern Cape as listed in the introduction and background. The researcher delivered questionnaires to the ABET section of each district so that ABET officers could administer them at centres in their districts. The researcher encouraged the districts that are urban and rural in their constitution to ensure questionnaires reached both areas.

The districts had a clear rural/urban division so that the research results were not to be negatively influenced by the geographic location of the ABET participants. Out of the twelve (12) educators in the district offices of the Eastern Cape Department of Education, six (6) were selected for interviewing. One (1) ABET district educator was from the Buffalo City Metropolitan Municipality (BCMM) in the Amatole District and took care of the urban setting. The other five (5) educators came from O.R. Tambo, Alfred Nzo, Chris Hani, and Joe Gqabi District Municipalities in order to ensure fair rural representation. This was important to keep a balance between the rural and urban settings considering that most illiterate people are found in rural areas as revealed in the literature in the introduction and background of this study.

DATA-COLLECTION

Data collection took place by means of interviews and questionnaires

DATA PRESENTATION AND ANALYSIS

Tables were used to present the data. Qualitative data from the interviews of ABET educators were recorded mechanically using an audio tape recorder and were later transcribed word for word. Furthermore, other data from the open-ended questions in the questionnaires were treated together with the transcribed data with the aim of establishing whether there were observable themes or not.

INTERVIEWS

According to the educators, the ABET programme contained the training part which suffered due to lack of funding and resourcing, but the little that was offered made a difference to learners' lives. Skills such as health and hygiene skills, business skills, computer skills, handwork, gardening, sewing and to a small extent bead work formed part of the plan in ABET provision. The verbatim quotations from these educators demonstrated their views on skills training in ABET centres.

"Learners are trained in the Ancillary Health Care to become home-based care givers to patients who could not be kept in hospitals while suffering from diseases such as TB, HIV/AIDS, Sugar Diabetes and High blood Pressure. Furthermore, the adult learners are taught business skills such as business planning and budgeting and therefore can start informal profitable businesses ***(Educator 1).****"*

"In August each year, there is a Provincial gathering where learners exhibit and sell their handwork products such as shell and clay products, and this serves as a way of enhancing their business and entrepreneurial skills ***(Educator 2).****"*

"Although not all of the following skills are available in all the centres, some centres are able to provide one to three of the skills such as computer skills, handwork, gardening, primary health care skills and sewing **(Educator 3).***"*

"There is a move from the Department of Higher Education and Training to replace ABET with ADET (Adult Education and Training) and house it in the same directorate as the further education and training colleges. This move seeks to align what takes place in the ABET centres with what is happening in the Technical and Vocational Education and Training(TVET) Colleges so that the learners who pass ABET level 4 are able to proceed to FET Colleges to pursue skills of their choice ***(Educator 4)****".*

SUMMARY OF THE FINDINGS

The responses of the educators admitted to the low to medium-level skills that are offered in the ABET centres, but we cannot underestimate the value of those skills to people who had spent a large part of their lives with no skills at all. The majority of educators believed that ABET provision contributed to human capital development by:

- **Improving production capacity of people**

"Learners are trained in the Ancillary Health Care to become home-based care givers to patients who could not be kept in hospitals while suffering from diseases such as TB, HIV/AIDS, Sugar Diabetes and High blood Pressure. Furthermore, the adult learners are taught business skills such as business planning and budgeting and therefore can start informal profitable businesses."

- **Imparting literacy and other skills to adults and out-of-school youth**

Although not all of the following skills are available in all the centres, some centres are able to provide one to three of the skills such as computer skills, handwork, gardening, primary health care skills and sewing."

- **Providing relevant experience, training, and education**

None of the responses of the educators to the questions in the interviews touched on the experience, training and education and their effect on the learners.

- **Opening opportunities for social participation and economic development,**

"In August each year, there is a Provincial gathering where learners exhibit and sell their handwork products such as shell and clay products, and this serves as a way of enhancing their business and entrepreneurial skills."

- **Affording adults, a basis for trainability and higher skills training**

"There is a move from the Department of Higher Education and Training to replace ABET with ADET (Adult Education and Training) and house it in the same directorate as the further education and training colleges. This move seeks to align what takes place in the ABET centres with what is happening in the YVET Colleges so that the learners who pass ABET level 4 are able to proceed to TVET Colleges to pursue skills of their choice ".

The study has established that ABET provision assists human capital development by equipping learners with skills such as business, agricultural and life skills. The responses of educators have indicated that ABET provision contributes to skills development, although only to a small extent, in that ABET provides skills such as hygiene and health, business, literacy, agricultural, gardening, sewing and computer literacy skills. It is, however, important to point out that the provision of these skills in some public ABET centres is more a wish than a reality due to shortage of funds.

DISCUSSION OF THE FINDINGS

The finding that ABET provision improves the production capacity of the participants is confirmed by Fitzsimons (2009:1) who believes that the reformulation of human capital theory emphasises the significance of education and training as key to participation in the global economy. Other authors who have an affirmative view of this finding are Xiao (2001:1) and Quiggin (1999:9) who express the view that education is an investment that produces benefits in the future and that education and or training raises the production capacity of workers by imparting useful knowledge and skills. Olaniyan and Okemakinde (2008: 153) also confirm this finding by highlighting the work of Schultz (1971), Sakamota and Powers (1995), Psacharopoulos and Woodhall (1997) regarding the human capital theory as resting on the assumption that formal education is highly instrumental in and even necessary to improve production capacity of a population. In fact, according to the human capital theorists, an educated population is a productive population. The finding under discussion confirms the intentions behind introducing adult basic education and training in South Africa as to impart knowledge and skills so that human capital is developed. *A* learner equipped with one or all the above-mentioned skills feels the self-worth and gets motivated to participate in the projects of the community. The assistance that is provided by people trained in ABET centres to some members of the community enhances the value of these helpers to the community and hence improve their self-images. On the other hand, those that are helped feel accepted and loved instead of being neglected and despised.

The second finding entails that adult basic education and training imparts literacy and other skills to adults and out-of- school youth. The Department of Education (RSA 1997) and Prinsloo (2000) confirm this finding when they state that ABET is both part of, and a foundation, for lifelong learning and that the understanding of literacy as a core skill that stands at the door to rational thinking, higher order skills and trainability is the one that dominates policymaking and educational provision across countries. The significance of these skills cannot be underestimated. Imagine a worker who all his working life is being assisted in reading instructions to maintain the machine he works with, and through ABET acquires the literacy skills that enable him to read the instructions himself, the kind of relief, dignity, and freedom this would bring to this worker. Even when travelling the newly acquired skills help the recipients to enjoy their travelling as they read the names of the various places they pass through, and their lifeworld expands to a small extent.

The third finding that stresses opening of opportunities for social participation and economic development is confirmed by the White Paper on Education and Training (White Paper, RSA, 1995:18) where it is stressed that South Africa's performance, measured by international indicators of human development and economic competitiveness, is poor because in the past there was inadequate provision of basic needs, including education and training, to most of the population. The provision of adult basic education and training therefore opens new windows of opportunity if it can be ensured that the promised skills are delivered.

The last finding which entails affording adults a basis for trainability and higher skills is confirmed by Aitchison and Harley (2006:107) when they state that the importance of literacy skills in the workplace is ever increasing as the business is ever changing and becoming more digital and electronic. Acquisition of skills through adult basic education and training, namely literacy skills enable adults to access further skills that may be provided through workplace training.

CONCLUSION AND RECOMMENDATIONS

The purpose of this chapter was to establish the perspectives of educators regarding provision of adult basic education and training, and the extent to which such provision contributes to human capital development in the Eastern Cape. On the basis of the findings of this study, it can be concluded that ABET provision contributes to human capital development. However, there are aspects of ABET provision that need serious attention and remedy. In fact, taking ABET from the Basic Education Department to the Department of Higher Education and Training brought a bright hope in that vocational subjects such as Travel and Tourism, Applied Agriculture and Agricultural Sciences, Small, Medium and Micro-Enterprise and Information and Communication Technologies have been introduced as part of the training of educators and lecturers targeted to man the adult and community education and training centres. The skills obtainable in the ABET centres are low to medium-level skills. In some ABET centres, one or two skills are available and accessible, instead of a multiplicity of skills due to lack of willpower on the part of the bureaucrats. If the bureaucrats can remember what Nyerere emphasized regarding provision of adult education, they would step up their efforts to ensure that through ABET provision, no adult or out-of-school youth is excluded from participation in community projects, in social, political, and cultural activities and the economy in general. Nyerere believed that education of adults would hasten economic development instead of pinning our hopes on the education of children who will take 15 to 20 years to bring their skills to the economy. Nyerere's assertion goes very deep if rural development is taken with the seriousness it deserves. Empowering adults and out-of-school youth with agricultural and other relevant skills will enable them to use the various government grants they receive as working capital to start small scale economic projects instead of being solely dependent on such grants.

The main recommendation that emanates from this study is that skills that are offered in the ABET centres must be increased and they must be relevant to ensure that adults and out-of-school youth are not excluded in the economy of our country. Skills such as sheep-shearing, tree-pruning, castration of cocks, small stock and cattle, vegetable production and milk processing can divert the attention of many people from thinking that the only life for everyone is in the urban areas. These skills would ensure that rural people remain in rural areas but with conviction and confidence to establish income generating projects in these areas.

REFERENCES

Carver, D. F., Watson, J., & Jr Curtiss, J. (2018). *Ritual Killings in Ancient Rome: Homicide and Roman Superiority. Corado.* Colorado State University Library.

De Beer, F., & Swanepoel, H. (2015). *Community Development and Beyond issues, structures and procedures*. Van Schaik Publishers.

De Jong, W. (2015). "Makhosi a via (Chiefs Commit Ritual Murder)" Why ritual murders in Southern Africa should be seen as meaningful violence. *Africa Fus.*, *28*(2), 9–26.

Dlamini, K. (2011). *Southern Africa: Breaking the Science on Ritual Killings*. SAGE Journal.

Etilyob, E., & Omiegbe, O. (2016). Religion,Culture and Discrimination against People with Disabilities in Nigeria. *African Journal of Disability*, *5*(1), 1–6.

Guldbrandsen, O. (2002). The Discourse of Ritual Murder, Popular Reaction to Political Leaders in Botswana. *Social Analysis*, *46*(3), 215–233.

Johannessen, M. R. (2020). *Handbook of Research on Politics in the Computer Age*. University of South-Eastern Norway.

Kohl, J. (2018). A Murder, a Mummy and a Bust: The newly Discovered Portrait of Simon of Trent at the Getting. *Getting Research Journal*, *10*, PP27–PP60. doi:10.1086/697383

Masoga, M. A., & Rugwiji, T. (2018). A Reflection on Ritual Murder in the Biblical text from an African Perspective. Stellenbosch.

McConnel, C. (2002). *Community Learning and Development: The making of an Empowering Profession. Edinburgh Community Learning Scotland Merriam and Brocket (1997). The Profession and Practice of Adult Education*. Jossey-Bass Publishers.

Miller, C. (2008). The role of Adult Education in Community Development. Exploring the links. *International Journal of Lifelong Education*, *30*(4), 489–505.

Mokotso I.R (2015). A Sustainable educational response to the recent increased witch killing and ritual murder 'Liretlo' in Lesotho: Introducing Bosotho Traditional Religion in Lesotho School. *African Educational Research Journal, 3* (4), 209-220.

Moloto (2006). Ritual Killings Conference. South African Government.

OECD. (2019). *Community Education and Training in South Africa: Getting Skills Right*. OECD Publisher.

Rannditsheni, A. E., Masoga, A., & Mavhandu-Mudzusi, A. H. (2016). Some Perspectives on the Impacts of Ritual Murders in Vhembe District of South Africa: An Interpretive Phenomenological Approach. *Journal of Social Sciences*, *48*(3), 239–245. doi:10.1080/09718923.2016.11893586

Scholtz, H. J., Philips, V. M., & Knobel, G. T. (1997). *Muti or Ritual murder*. National Library of Medicine.

Stey. (2005). *Multi- murders form South Africa: a case report. National Library of Medicine*. National Centre for Biotechnology Information.

Wals, A. (2006). Action Research and Community-problem solving: Environmental education in an inner-city. *Journal Homepage.*, *17*, PP163–PP182.

Wikipedia. (2013). *Talk*. Community Education.

Chapter 3
The Ontological and Epistemological Connection Between Paulo Freire's Literacy Education and the CLING Project in South Africa

Zamalotshwa Florence Thusi
Durban University of Technology, South Africa

Sampson Tawiah
Durban University of Technology, South Africa

ABSTRACT

This chapter explores the link between Paulo Freire's ontological and epistemological philosophies and the community literacy and numeracy group (CLING) project in South Africa. The CLING project is based on the belief that literacy is about mastering reading, writing, and arithmetic skills. It also empowers individuals to reach their full potential and achieve success and fulfilment. The authors discuss how apartheid obstructed the education of black individuals, but Freire's ideologies and educational philosophies aimed to raise awareness and liberate individuals from illiteracy, economic struggles, and inequality. The authors emphasise the importance of critical literacy in promoting social justice. Using a qualitative approach, the authors gathered data from both primary and secondary sources and selected twelve individuals who provided information-rich insights. It was discovered that literacy education, including reading and writing, has helped marginalised individuals and empowered men and women.

DOI: 10.4018/978-1-6684-6625-4.ch003

INTRODUCTION: PAULO FREIRE LITERACY EDUCATION IN CONTEXT

Paulo Freire's approach to literacy education, as outlined in his book "Pedagogy of the Oppressed," centres around empowering marginalised individuals who are poor and uneducated. This involves transforming the social realities that contribute to their oppression, with learners playing an active role in the process. According to Suoranta *et al.* (2021), literacy education aims to restore self-esteem, trust, and potential in life. Freire uses education to raise awareness amongst the masses about the realities of oppression - including inequality, poverty, destitution, and illiteracy (Vittoria, 2018). His educational philosophy seeks to liberate individuals from their inferior status and humanise them, countering the forces of oppression. While oppression can alienate individuals from their humanity, Freire's pedagogy of the oppressed is revolutionary in that it fights for liberation, humanisation, and redemption (Pouwels, 2019).

Freire, born in Pernambuco in 1921, is widely recognised as a pioneer in literacy education for liberation. His contributions to critical pedagogy, popular education, and literacy methods have had a lasting impact that extends into the 21st century (Tygel & Kirsch, 2016; McCormack, 2020). According to Suoranta et al. (2021), his educational philosophies and ideologies have been adapted and embraced across diverse cultural, economic, gender, racial, and demographic boundaries. As a result, adult educators strive for broader socio-economic and political outcomes (Reder, 2020). At the time, the high illiteracy rate besieged the Northeastern region of Brazil in the 1960s. Of its population, about 72.6% could not read or write (Ferraro & Kreidlow, 2004, cited by Tygel & Kirsch, 2016). Thus, Freire epitomises that learning to read and write can indeed bring about transformation in human life. However, achieving this plight goes beyond learning vocabulary. Freire (1998:6) says it involves "word and action." He, therefore, emphasises that the cognitive dimension of literacy education must be a process of relationships between men and their world through reflection and action aimed at capacity building (Suoranta *et al.*, 2021).

Exploring the Concepts of Paulo Freire's Critical Pedagogy

According to Freire, problem-posing education requires a unique pedagogy that differs from the conventional banking education method. The learner and educator's roles, the curriculum, and the techniques used in this approach vary. He emphasises that problem-posing education allows learners to actively participate in learning and dialogue with the teacher as critical co-investigators (Freire, 1970). Freire believed that regardless of their level of knowledge or cultural background, every person can critically examine the world in a dialogical encounter with others (Freire, 1970). As a result, the focus of the learning process shifts from the teacher to the learner, bringing about a shift in power dynamics in the classroom and the broader social context (Aronowitz, 2012). However, Freire still emphasises the vital role of the teacher. He referred to adult educators as 'animators' responsible for driving learning (Freire, 1970).

Freire concludes that a teacher must possess the qualities of a 'revolutionary leader' (Freire & Macedo, 1998, p. 69) to be effective in their role. However, Freire demarcated between good revolutionary leaders and those who are authoritarian. Hence, the teacher's responsibility is to encourage learners to think critically about their reality and support them in solidarity. The democratic educator must prioritise the learner's critical thinking, curiosity, and autonomy (Freire & Freire, 2004, p. 33). This approach differs from authoritarian left-wing leaders who impose their ideas and views on people, such as those who come to tell people they are oppressed and exploited. Thus, intellectuals who merely memorise and read for hours without making connections to the world around them do not provide value to their students. They speak correctly about dialectical thought but think mechanistically, and their fear of taking risks prevents them from making personal connections (Freire, 2013).

Freire stresses the importance of initiating a creative dialogue with the community as a crucial aspect of a genuine revolution. Fear of people's expression and effective participation in power must be overcome. According to Harley (2012), dialogue is central to becoming more fully human, and the educator must promote it. However, talk is more than just people speaking to one another; it involves much more, as Freire indicates:

Dialogue characterises an epistemological relationship. Thus, in this sense, dialogue is a way of knowing and should never be viewed as a mere tactic to involve students in a particular task. ...In this sense, dialogue is an indispensable component of learning and knowing. (Freire, 1970, p. 17)

According to Freire, dialogue is the interaction between individuals through the lens of the world, with the intention of understanding and naming it. This involves identifying and solving problems, which is crucial for a liberating education. Learners need a secure and accepting environment to express their experiences to achieve this. They can then recognise oppressive situations and work towards ending them. Critical thinking is essential for dialogue, which is why problem-posing is necessary.

The problem-posing learning approach involves presenting learners with a problem through codes, known as codification, using the dialogical method. Freire states that these codes should be visual and dramatic and reflect everyday life experiences. The co-ordinator must listen to the individuals, challenge them, and pose problems related to the codified existential situation and their answers (Freire, 1970, p. 110). The codification presented should represent the learners' generative themes, which cannot be divorced from reality or men (Freire, 1970, p. 86). Therefore, the dialogue surrounding the fertile theme must be informed by the word used to read the world. Learners can name and transform the world through dialogue by speaking their words.

Engaging in meaningful dialogue is essential to have critical awareness and act to effect change in the world (Glass, 2001). This action is known as praxis, and it involves the oppressed individuals taking control of their lives to break free from the culture of silence imposed upon them by their oppressors. Freire believes praxis is rooted in a dialogical relationship fuelled by critical reflection and sustained intervention in the fight for liberation. True emancipation and freedom cannot be granted but must be achieved through the concerted efforts of the oppressed (Grundy, 2006; Thompson, 2001). Praxis is a political project committed to challenging capitalist relations of production and colonialism and ultimately achieving societal liberation (Darder, 2018, p.104). It is crucial to note that praxis is intrinsically linked to critical consciousness. Harley argues that...

The two activities fuse into one dynamic process in which learners act on themselves and their world, changing their consciousness and engaging with other people, organisations, institutions and objects around them (Harley, 2012, p. 279).

According to Freire, education can either be used as a means to conform to the existing system or as a way to promote the "practice of freedom" - the critical and creative engagement with reality and the pursuit of transformation in one's world (Freire, 1970, p. 34). This gave rise to the concept of "critical pedagogy" - a teaching approach closely tied to liberating oppressed individuals as historical agents with radical aims (Margonis, 2003). Its goal is to create a more equitable, humane, and fair world.

As Aronowitz (2012) explains, Freire's pedagogy is aimed at empowering the oppressed to confront their lives and break the cycle of psychological oppression through engaging in dialogue. However, according to Aronowitz, many projects claim to use the Freirean philosophy and methodology but are not doing so or are using what he calls "indeterminate" methods (p. 10). Some teachers may interact more with their students, structure class time as a dialogue, or allow students to express themselves without being corrected on their language skills. While these practices are commendable, they do not necessarily require Freire's methods. Aronowitz (2012) critiques these projects for ignoring the ontological purpose of Freire's radical humanism, which is to empower the oppressed.

Literacy Education in South Africa: Apartheid Era

In South Africa, education, particularly literacy education, was neglected due to apartheid oppression. However, with the large population needing primary education, literacy education became essential for youth and adult populations (Aitchison, 2003). As a result, promoting primary education for all became a priority for redress and liberation, leading to the development of post-apartheid educational policies. Adult education is the foundation for providing literacy and primary education for adults. In the 20th century, night schools were established to facilitate such initiatives (Aitchison, 2003). Unfortunately, providing primary education for black South Africans through night schools was short-lived due to the 1953 Bantu Education Act, which deemed any such provision of education illegal and punishable (Thobejane, 2013). For night schools to continue operating, they had to surrender their administration to the apartheid government. The following passage emphasises this reality:

The Bantu Education Act No 47 of 1953 was the cornerstone of apartheid education. One of the purposes of this act was to concentrate control of education for blacks in the hands of the State. One of the act's provisions meant that Church and night schools had to be handed over to the State or face diminished subsidy. Only the Roman Catholic Church could retain some control of its schools for several years until the cost became prohibitive (Aitchison, 2003:130).

The apartheid government had a negative mindset towards educating black individuals in South Africa. However, literacy education during that period was anti-apartheid and influenced by Paulo Freire's Pedagogy of the Oppressed. This led to protests against the apartheid education system, and the fight for education equality continues today (Aitchison & McKay, 2021). The phrase "aluta continua" still resonates with education activists in the 21st century. With millions of black South Africans lacking primary education and skills, researchers in the field of study play a critical role in promoting the country's social, economic, and educational development. This is essential in breaking the cycle of persistent economic dependency and being a tool for transformation in South Africa (Msila, 2007).

The education system in post-apartheid South Africa aimed to empower black citizens through literacy, financial literacy, and job skills training (Vally, 2022). The goal was for black South Africans to become self-sufficient, make sound decisions, solve problems, and plan for employment opportunities (Prinsloo, 1999; Thobejane, 2013). However, despite these efforts, many black South Africans still lack the education and skills needed for economic development. This is due to inadequate policy implementation and insufficient financial support for adult primary education

(Aitchison & McKay, 2021). It is crucial to continuously evaluate and restructure adult education institutions, practices, and policies to achieve educational goals. The constitutional rights of both young and old to primary education and skills training must be addressed, especially in today's challenging economic conditions (Rule, 2006).

The South African government has made significant efforts to combat illiteracy, particularly in impoverished rural areas, to improve the quality of life. However, despite these efforts, illiteracy remains prevalent in these areas due to the legacy of apartheid and its discriminatory education policies for black individuals (Rule, 2006). As a result, South Africa needs to perform better in literacy tests than other countries (Rule & Land, 2017). According to Rule and Land (2017), understanding the storyline in reading education can improve literacy performance. However, we contend that literacy education should encompass reading, writing, and skills training aimed at the economic advancement of underprivileged black Africans.

The CLING Project: A Historical Overview

The CLING Project was established in 2007 by a group of educational research units, including the WITS Education Policy Unit (WEPU), Centre for Education Policy Development (CEPD), and Education Policy Consortium (EPC). This initiative was part of the 3Rs Project led by CEPD, which focused on improving essential reading, writing, and arithmetic skills. The 3Rs Project received funding from the Embassy of the Kingdom of the Netherlands and ran for five years from 2007 to 2011. Its primary goal was to investigate why school children, particularly those from underprivileged 'black' communities, struggled with literacy and numeracy despite state resources being allocated. The project aimed to explore ways to provide quality education in these areas and make progress towards this goal.

The CLING Project was conceived in 2006 and launched in 2007 as a five-year research endeavour. Through documentary analysis, it was implemented across various sites at different times. The Freedom Park CLING site began in 2007 (though it was officially introduced in 2009), while the Siyandhani and Davhana areas in Limpopo commenced in 2012 (Gardiner, 2010). The project is currently under review to determine if it has concluded. The CLING Project was conducted in five locations, covering urban and rural communities. These included two sites in Limpopo, two in Gauteng (Freedom Park and Sebokeng in the Vaal Triangle), and one in the Eastern Cape.

At each site, the Community Researchers initiated the CLING Project, which rallied learners, supported community mobilisation, and helped school students with their academic work by conducting weekend classes, reading clubs, storytelling sessions, and setting up community libraries. Additionally, extracurricular activities like poetry and Hip Hop were introduced. Later, the CLING Project also offered opportunities for adult primary education and early childhood development (Baatjes, 2016). Classes for adult learners were designed to promote reading and writing skills for all age groups in the community (CLING, n.d.).

Purpose of the CLING Project

The CLING project is based on the notion that literacy encompasses more than just acquiring reading, writing, and arithmetic skills. It believes literacy is significant in humanity's emancipation and complete development (Baatjes, 2016; Baatjes, Kgobe & Sotuku, 2012). Various theories explain the learning process, suggesting that the most effective and stimulating learning occurs informally and incidentally in our daily lives (Foley, 1999). The CLING Project recognises that the most potent learning transpires when people fight against oppression, make sense of their experiences, and devise ways to overcome them. The project deliberately chose to engage in non-formal education in addition to informal and incidental learning (Baatjes, 2016, p. 15).

The CLING Project is premised on the belief that for a democracy to be healthy, citizens must be well-informed, critical, and actively participate (Baatjes, 2016; Čubajevaitė, 2015). As such, the project aims to investigate the impact and significance of participatory citizenship on democracy. It also acknowledges that literacy and numeracy require active participation and agency (Baatjes, 2016, p. 12).

Ties With Paulo Freire

When we first started our research, we found a document on the CLING Project by Gardiner (2010) online. To gain more insight, we also referred to a booklet on the project published by the Education Policy Consortium (EPC) titled "Umhlaba uyafufusa: Reflections on community participation in Education" by Baatjes (2016). It became evident that the CLING Project was based on the ideas of Paulo Freire. According to Michael Gardiner, the National Coordinator of the CLING Project, the project had a comprehensive understanding of literacy, including reading the word and the world and taking everyone's interests into account (Gardiner, 2010, p. 1). Baatjes (2016), who also worked with the project, supports this idea, stating that the project's definition of literacy was broader and focused on critical consciousness, participation in activities that lead to action and change for the better, and emancipation (Baatjes, 2016, p. 11).

The CLING Project used participatory action research (PAR) as a crucial methodology to examine oppressive conditions and effect change. Baatjes (2016) asserts that PAR is a valuable tool that supports the struggles of oppressed and marginalised groups, taking their side and promoting their interests. The CLING Project was thus dedicated to fighting against injustices in the communities it served, adopting a political stance that aligned with Paulo Freire's ideas of conscientisation and emancipation.

The CLING Project was founded on the belief that literacy is essential for the liberation and development of individuals (CERT, 2010, p. 11). This educational initiative emphasised the importance of critical consciousness, community participation, and practical action towards positive change and the emancipation of marginalised groups (Čubajevaitě, 2015). According to Baatjes (2016, p. 10), the project was genuinely transformative because it prioritised the struggles of the oppressed and was transparent about whose interests it served. Importantly, it recognised that marginalised groups possess valuable knowledge. By prioritising action, the project sought to understand and change the world (ibid).

Mapping the Theory of Critical Literacy in the Study

The power of critical literacy has been sustained by activism, with educators and young activists promoting literacy education to break free from social injustices. Critical literacy theory goes beyond cultural background and is practised through a deep understanding that holds value for learners. Anderson and Irvine (1993), as cited by Bishop (2014:51), emphasise the significance of critical literacy in this regard:

The importance of critical literacy being grounded pedagogically in a politics of difference offers learners, regardless of their class, race, or gendered subjectivities, opportunities to become 'border crossers.' Critical literacy is learning to read and write to become conscious of one's experience as historically constructed within specific power relations.

In order words, as from the above, critical literacy involves learning to read and write, enabling one of social responsibility. Thus, the literacy skills acquired can help one work with others to build a consensus of collaborative decision-making, identify problems, and take steps to solve them. Indeed, critical Theory fosters social practices that remedy social injustices (Bishop, 2014). It corroborates Freire's conception of literacy in understanding cultural identities and structures that seek to dismantle oppression, thereby enabling students in a shared critical transformation of a subjective social being (McLaren, 1992). Without a doubt, self-transformation cannot seize to exist without the modification of social structures that allow individuals to understand and work against facets of oppression. Citing Lewison, Leland and Harste (2008), Cheu-jey (2011:97) attests that;

Critical literacy practices encourage students to use language to question the everyday world, interrogate the relationship between language and power, analyse popular culture and media, understand how power relationships are socially constructed, and consider actions that can be taken to promote social justice.

Thus, critical literacy envisages a set of socio-political contexts geared towards identifying inequality of power relationships for setting a just course of action. According to Janks (2013), critical literacy involves more than just reading and writing but goes further to reading the world. The knowledge and skills students acquire must be instrumental in the success of a social change in the world they belong. Critical literacy, therefore, involves beneficial praxis in word and world, as indicated in terms by Janks (2013):

Critical literacy enables young people to read both the word and the world about power, identity, difference and access to knowledge, skills, tools and resources. It is also about writing and rewriting the world: design and re-design.

Speaking truth to Freire's ideology, critical literacy is linked to socio-political pedagogy and self-empowerment for life's fulfilment which, for some, has no realisations. Therefore, literacy's essential importance is encouraging social connectivity to allow for discussions in the socio-political sphere and for questioning and destabilising power (Janks, 2012).

The Study's Methodology

For this qualitative study, the researchers utilised both primary and secondary data. To access learners and facilitators who participated in the Community Literacy and Numeracy Group (CLING) Project, as well as members of the CLING Steering Committee and the Abahlali base Freedom Park community organising committee, the researchers used snowballing as a technique. This was necessary because it took time to locate participants for the study (Danglot et al., 2019). The participants helped the researchers identify other individuals who voluntarily participated in the study. All community members within the study's site were considered the study's population. A purposive sample of twelve information-rich individuals was chosen from this population, ranging in age from 20 to 70 years old and with regular employment.

The Connection Between the CLING Project and Freirean Ontological and Epistemological Philosophies

The overarching question this Study investigated is, to what extent did the CLING Project embrace the Freirean philosophy?

According to the secondary data in the literature review, Freire's epistemology is closely tied to his ontological ideologies. Freire believes that oppression dehumanises us, but it's our inherent nature to strive towards becoming more fully human (Freire, 1970). However, Freire also suggests that oppressed people may not even realise it, as their oppressors use education to conceal the truth. By treating learners as objects in the education process, rendering them passive recipients, Freire argues that this type of education is oppressive and akin to "banking education" or "domesticating education" (Freire, 1970, p. 44).

Freire suggests that problem-solving education, or liberating education, is crucial in the process of emancipation due to the inadequate education that students receive. As opposed to traditional banking education, this type of education emphasises the significance of dialogue and active participation of learners, promoting horizontal relationships between them and their educators (Gboku & Modise, 1999). Through dialogue, learners and teachers engage in honest discussions and debates about socio-political realities and theories, which enhances their knowledge (Bartlett, 2005). Consequently, through reflective dialogue, the masses are "conscientious," becoming aware of oppressive relationships and taking action to overcome them.

Through analysis of both primary and secondary sources, it has been highlighted that the CLING Project is closely linked to the philosophies of Paulo Freire. According to the project's National Coordinator, it was founded on a broad interpretation of literacy that values essential reading and writing (Gardiner, 2010). Baatjes (2016) also confirms that the CLING Project's definition of literacy is rooted in Freire's philosophy of critical consciousness, which leads to active participation in actions that promote positive change. Additionally, Baatjes et al. (2012) report that the CLING Project aimed to establish a vision for literacy incorporating participatory citizenship and developing a democratic environment. They argue that literacy should involve speaking out to transform reality and empower individuals to play a vital role in change. The research methodology employed in the project was based on Freire's concept of praxis, which emphasises critical reflection and action. This approach enabled a deeper understanding of social realities and the identification of activities that could foster positive change.

In 2012, Baatjes and colleagues conducted a project based on the Freirean methodology. Their goal was to promote conscientisation, or an increased level of awareness, through implementing activities in the CLING project. According to

Heaney and Horton (1990), conscientisation can only be achieved through learners' experiences and reflections, which enable critical thinking and heightened awareness.

Based on the preceding, Baatjes et al. (2012) intimate that CLING activities must be continuously reviewed to ensure their alignment towards achieving its objectives. However, the only problem identified was that the research needed to be more conceptual than practical, thus leading to Participatory Action Research (PAR) (Baatjes et al., 2012). Throughout the course of five years, the PAR promoted participatory methods of work. This was achieved through a reflective learning process, focusing on the various activities chosen as part of the community mobilisation strategy. The aim was to encourage active involvement and engagement from all participants.

The report further elucidated the trials and tribulations the CLING Project underwent in its five-year tenure operational activities as follows:

The implementation of the activities at each site differed given the dynamics and contextual realities within each of the communities ...Similarly, other areas, such as the urban / semi-urban communities of Evaton-North and Freedom Park, presented their contextual dynamics, which impacted the project (Baatjes et al., 2012, p. 27).

According to the report, the Freedom Park CLING group faced significant challenges due to the diverse political affiliations of its members. This created difficulties for the Community Researchers, and tensions persisted throughout the project's lifespan. These barriers hindered community involvement and organising, making the project inactive for eight months, from September 2009 to May 2010.

The second Synthesis Report of the Community Literacy and Numeracy Group (CLING)' written by the EPC & CLING Researchers, throw more light on the link of the cling to Freire's ideologies. Thus,

The methodology is based on Freire's notion of praxis (critical reflection and action), developing deeper understandings of the social reality and seeking activities that foster greater possibility for change (EPC & CLING Researchers, n.d., p. 6).

The report states that the PAR was introduced into the CLING Project to investigate the conditions of oppression and identify opportunities for resistance and change. The PAR was implemented because the organisers realised that;

It represents a radical epistemological challenge to the traditions of social science. PAR assumes that those most systematically excluded, oppressed, or denied carry specifically revealing wisdom about the history, structure, consequences, and fracture points in unjust social arrangements,... It propels into prominence the role of the oppressed as the architects of critical enquiry – the originators of knowledge for social change and collective revolutionary praxis (p. 6).

It is clear from the documentary analysis of secondary data that, as far as the National Coordinator and the 3Rs consortium partners who conceived the project are concerned, the CLING Project was designed and perceived to be based on the Freirean philosophy and methodology. In addition, primary data collected attest to the link of Paulo Freire's philosophy to the CLING project. With particular reference to the Freedom Park CLING project, the co-coordinator appears to have seen the project in this light, thus, suggesting that there was a degree of the evolvement of Freire's ideologies in that;

It also got involved now in the issues of the community and the problems of adult-based education because the understanding was that as we engaged in the discussions and so on…literacy was broadened. Initially, the experience was that literacy was learning how to read and write words, but as we engaged, the understanding was deepened; that you want to read and write so that you can be able to understand ukuthi izinto zime kanjani emhlabeni (how things look or stand in the world). So it was more about the world and the environment, what is happening around you, things like that. (Christopher)

The extract above indicates the level of understanding of the participants involved in the project. They believe that the project goes beyond reading and writing. It has the potential to emancipate them through productive activities. Thus, other facilitators seem to have become involved with the CLING Project through a local ABET provider, *Ikusasa Lethu,* who had students who were advanced in their years. Some had problems with their eyes as they could not see correctly. A participant who is a facilitator voiced out this challenge when interviewed as that;

The problem with the older adults was their eyesight; hence we had to take them to the local clinic to have their eyes tested and get them spectacles, and we realised that it was becoming too time-consuming… We got them from Joey, one of the NGOs around here that deal with older adults. We would go there, and Joey would give us those hours to teach them. (Jabu).

The above revelations indicated that attending to the needs of older people was time-consuming and did not make way for the project's primary purpose- learning and teaching.

On the issue of that taught in the classes, a facilitator mentioned that,

The people we had most wanted to learn how to write and count. We would even take them to the ATM so that they knew how to do that for themselves. We would also read stories for them. Others said SASSA says they must not deposit their money, so we also taught them how to make deposits. Some said they were not allowed by SASSA to deposit their money. So we will teach them that no money is better than any other; you are the one who decides on your expenses and saves the rest of your grant. (Nana)

Another facilitator interviewed emphasised that,

We taught them how to write their names; the X was not good. So we taught them how to sign their names and how to count.

The extracts above indicated that besides learning to read and write, the students were taught practical life skills such as writing their names, signing signatures and operating ATMs for financial transactions. Indeed, the participants are excited about their involvement in the CLING project as it helped them to advance their socio-economic lives. Moreover, the extent and content of the adult classes were explained by a coordinator of the project as follows:

The newspapers (Learn with Echo) that we were receiving from the University of KwaZulu-Natal were designed to teach adults. We would read those newspapers with them, and there would be some exercises and different topics discussed with them and izinganekwane (folklore). Bayazithanda izingane abantu abadala (Adults love folklore).

In the report, Čubajevaitě (2015) discussed the training that Community Researchers received. Specifically, she mentioned that the learning approach adopted by CLINGs in Gauteng began with the recruitment and initial training of CRs. According to her, the facilitators were trained in the Freirean methodology. Her report shows that the Freirean concept of critical consciousness influenced external education and training input. The training emphasised the communities' resourcefulness, highlighted the country's poor education, and advocated for quality education demands.

Contrary to expectations, the study found that there needed to be a more deliberate effort to pass down the Freirean philosophy to the facilitators. The facilitators mentioned attending various types of training, but they have yet to report receiving training specifically focused on developing their understanding of 'critical consciousness' in line with Freirean principles. Contrary to expectations, the study found that there needed to be a more deliberate effort to pass down the

Freirean philosophy to the facilitators. The facilitators mentioned attending various types of training, but they have yet to report receiving training specifically focused on developing their understanding of 'critical consciousness' in line with Freirean principles.

The coordinator spoke of 12-week training that the facilitators attended and 'ukufacilitator: ubafundisa kanjani abanti abadala' (were trained on adult education: how you teach adults), and Phaks and Nox went to an unspecified training 'in the Vaal organised by Jonathan [from ILRIG]...with the help of CERT'.

To fully understand the training program mentioned in the quote above, it is essential to clarify what skills were being taught. The education provided must meet the needs and goals of the community. According to Kerka (1997), popular schooling should be based on the needs and goals of the community. Facilitators must be trained to engage in a critical dialogue that blends political content with instructional practices and connects the issues with participants' real-life experiences. This highlights the importance of Participatory Action Research (PAR) in the project, a vital methodological element in mobilising, organising, and implementing activities for positive change. Horton and Freire (1990) argue that when there is a need for organising and mobilising, it should be a learning process for those involved, reflected in their changing language. As they collect and mobilise their speech, the contents of their address should change because they are learning from the people.

To achieve the ideal of the CLING Project, Community Researchers and facilitators, as well as project coordinators, must mobilise and organise. As per the CLING Draft Report 2014, the project began in each site with the Community Researchers recruiting learners and supporting community mobilisation. However, Baatjes et al. (2012, p. 31) noted hindrances to community organising and effective mobilisation and participation in Freedom Park. Given the Freirean influence, it is unsurprising that Participatory Action Research (PAR) was a crucial element of learning within the project. Through PAR, individuals research and construct knowledge about their social realities, apply it to create change, and develop agency to produce further change (Baatjes et al., 2012, p. 15). The scholars emphasise the importance of participatory methods in the project, as they have a proven track record of success in pedagogical projects aimed at bringing change to marginalised communities, particularly examining the effects of mobilisation and participation in education reforms. But unfortunately, PAR was brought in only later in the project, which seemed beneficial after that.

According to Čubajevaitě's (2009) research, learners and activists (known as facilitators) drew upon their experiences in community activism to enhance their learning and positively impact the CLING program. Hoag (1990) concurs thus,

In consciousness-raising and provoking critical reflection, the importance is attributed to the individual reality instead of analyses and theories produced elsewhere. Thus, though debilitating effects of the apartheid system, high numbers of illiterate adults, and growing disparity between schools in rich and poor communities might have been known to the learners-activists (brief information on the external input provided suggests that some aspects were discussed there), they would not be sufficient to mobilise for the process of conscientisation. Moreover, the context of the community, in which the learners-activists find themselves, facilitates their learning as conscientisation occurs among the oppressed / marginalised groups implying that with no context of oppression, challenging the held assumptions, critical consciousness would not happen. (p. 34-35).

In teaching literacy, Freire's methodology involves presenting learners with problem-solving activities that reflect their daily lives or experiences. The teacher/ facilitator's role is to challenge the learners and provide a safe space for dialogue and discussion facilitated through different themes. These themes are derived from the learners' lived experiences and social issues, using their words as the foundation for learning to read, breaking them down into syllables, and creating new words for further discussion. This approach enables learners to read and connect with the world around them. (Freire, 1970).

While Freire's philosophies offer many benefits, they are not without their challenges. One of the main difficulties arises when facilitators need to be adequately trained in the Freirean methodology or grasp its purpose and content. According to Bartlett (2005), a lack of understanding of Freire's ideologies has contributed to the struggles faced by adult literacy teachers in integrating students' knowledge. Furthermore, limitations in Freire's Theory of knowledge production have also played a role. Some challenges include considering learners' lived experiences and a tendency to maintain a traditional student-teacher approach. In some cases, teachers have yet to receive proper orientation regarding the purpose of the training, resulting in an emphasis on content knowledge instead of the skills required by the community. This has led to project facilitators needing to pay more attention to guide the learning process (Kerka, 1997) and students needing help to engage in meaningful discussions about political, social, and economic issues that reflect their real-life experiences.

In line with Aronowitz's (2012) observations, it is typical for program educators and administrators to claim that they are utilising and espousing the Freirean approach, even though their interpretation may be ambiguous. What the author deems to be indeterminate is a methodology that,

Sometimes merely connotes that teachers try to be 'interactive' with students; sometimes, it signifies an attempt to structure class time as, in part, a dialogue between the teacher and students; some even mean to 'empower' students by permitting them to talk in class without ritualistically correcting them...All these are commendable practices but hardly require Freire as cover (p. 257).

The main focus of Freire's methodology is to achieve emancipation through conscientisation, which involves reflecting on daily lived experiences and praxis/ action as a result. However, Aronowitz (2012) argues that the methodology is often used without the intention of achieving emancipation. In the case of the CLING Project, the methodology philosophy has been embraced by the national coordinator, the Freedom Park coordinator (to a lesser extent), and the 3Rs partners. However, the principles of the methodology have yet to be successfully applied in the community or classroom due to a lack of understanding and implementation.

CONCLUSION

In this study, we examined the extent to which the CLING Project embodies the philosophy of Freire. Through both primary and secondary data, we discovered a strong connection between Freire's ontological and epistemological philosophies and the CLING project in South Africa. We found that literacy education, including reading and writing, has helped marginalised individuals, inferior men and women. However, literacy education must go beyond these skills to truly free individuals from social, economic, and political oppression and achieve social justice. Freire's pedagogy of the oppressed serves as a tool for liberation, humanisation, and redemption (Pouwels, 2019). The CLING Project recognises that literacy is not just about reading, writing, and arithmetic but must also contribute to humankind's greater liberation and socio-economic development. Our analysis indicates Freire's ideologies and philosophies heavily influence the CLING Project. Therefore, the CLING Project recognises that literacy education is a means of liberation, conscientisation, and participation in productive activities for action and change in human life.

REFERENCES

Aitchison, J. (2003). Struggle and compromise: A history of South African adult education from 1960 to 2001. *Journal of Education*, (29), 125–178.

Aitchison, J., & McKay, V. (2021). A historical remembrance of Paulo Freire in South Africa: A tale of two activists. *Australian Journal of Adult Learning, 61*(3), 334–354.

Aronowitz, S. (2012). *Paulo Freire's radical democratic humanism: The fetish of method* (Vol. 422). Counterpoints.

Baatjes, B. (2016). *Umhlaba omutsha uyafufusa. Reflections on community participation in education: The Community Literacy and Numeracy Group (CLING)*. Education Policy Consortium.

Baatjes, I., Kgobe, M., & Sotuku, N. (2012). *Report of the CLING Project*. CLING.

Bartlett, L. (2005). Dialogue, knowledge, and teacher-student relations: Freirean pedagogy in theory and practice. *Comparative Education Review, 49*(3), 344–364. doi:10.1086/430261

Bishop, E. (2014). Critical Literacy:Bringing Theory to Praxis. *Journal of Curriculum Theorizing, 30*(1), 51–63. doi:10.4324/9781315635385

Centre for Education Rights and Transformation (CERT). (2010). *Annual Report, 2010*. CERT.

Cheu-jey, L. (2011). Myths about Critical Literacy: What Teachers Need to Unlearn. *Journal of Language & Literacy Education, 7*(1), 95–102.

CLING. (n.d.). *Community Literacy and Numeracy Group (CLING) Policy Brief.* Draft.

CLING Project. (n.d.) *CLING Findings and Methodology*. CLING.

Čubajevaitě, M. (2015). Transformative adult learning in new social movement – a case study from South Africa. *International Journal of Area Studies, 10*(2), 139–171. doi:10.1515/ijas-2015-0007

Danglot, B., Vera-Perez, O., Yu, Z., Zaidman, A., Monperrus, M., & Baudry, B. (2019). A snowballing literature study on test amplification. *Journal of Systems and Software, 157*, 110398. doi:10.1016/j.jss.2019.110398

Darder, A. (2018). *The student guide to Freire's 'Pedagogy of the Oppressed.* Bloomsbury Academic.

Foley, G. (1999). *Learning in social action*. Zed.

Freire, A. M. A., & Macedo, D. (1998). The Paulo Freire reader. New York, NY: Continuum.

Freire, P., & Freire, A. M. A. (2004). *EPZ pedagogy of hope: Reliving pedagogy of the oppressed.* A&C Black.

Freire, P. (1970). *Pedagogy of the Oppressed. New York, NY: Continuum. Freire, P. (1994). Pedagogy of Hope: Reliving the Pedagogy of the Oppressed.* Continuum.

Freire, P. (1998). Cultural Action for Freedom Paulo Freire. *Harvard Educational Review*, *68*(4), 1–12. http://www.thinkingtogether.org/rcream/archive/110/culturalaction.pdf. doi:10.17763/haer.68.4.656ku47213445042

Freire, P. (2013). *Education for critical consciousness.* Bloomsbury.

Gardiner, M. (2010). *CLING project activities.* CEPD. http//www.cepd.org.za/files/CLING_activities_May2010.pdf

Gardiner, M. (n.d.). *Making the best of local experience: Perspectives on community education and training centers.* CEPD. http//www.cepd.org.za/files/

Gboku, M. L., & Modise, O. M. (1999). Literacy work and the Freirean approach to literacy teaching: Lessons from the Botswana Literacy Pilot Project. *Australian Journal of Adult and Community Education*, *39*(3), 162–171.

Glass, R. D. (2001). On Paulo Freire's philosophy of praxis and the foundations of liberation education. *Educational Researcher*, *30*(2), 15–25. doi:10.3102/0013189X030002015

Grundy, S. (2006). *Curriculum: product or praxis?* Routledge.

Harley, A., & Langdon, J. (2018). Ethics and power in visual research methods. In R. Iphofen & M. Tolich (Eds.), *The SAGE Handbook of qualitative research ethics.* SAGE. doi:10.4135/9781526435446.n13

Hoag, C. N. (2009). *Social justice struggles in Freedom Park: Linking advocacy, research and community organizing* [Unpublished Masters paper, SIT Graduate Institute in Brattleboro, Vermont, USA].

Horton, M., & Freire, P. (1990). *We make the road by walking: Conversations on education and social change* (B. Bell, J. Gaventa, & J. Peters, Eds.). Temple University Press.

Janks, H. (2012). The importance of critical literacy. *English Teaching*, *11*(1), 150–163.

Janks, H. (2013). Critical literacy in teaching and research1. *Education Inquiry*, *4*(2), 225–242. doi:10.3402/edui.v4i2.22071

Kerka, S. (1997). Popular education: Adult education for social change. *ERIC Digest No. 185*.

Margonis, F. (2003). Paulo Freire and post-colonial dilemmas. *Studies in Philosophy and Education*, *22*(2), 145–156. doi:10.1023/A:1022280930241

McCormack, R. (2020) 'Freire's literacy: Reading and writing our worlds', *Fine Print*, 43(August), 31–499. https://search.informit.org/doi/pdf/10.3316/informit.308301161064629

McLaren, P. (1992). Critical Literacy and Postcolonial Praxis: A Freirian Perspective. *College Literature*, *19/20*(3/1), 7–27. https://www.jstor.org/stable/25111986%5Cnhttp://www.jstor.org/stable/pdfplus/25111986.pdf

Msila, V. (2007). From Apartheid Education to Revised National Curriculum Statement. *Nordic Journal of African Studies*, *16*(2), 146–160.

Pouwels, J. (2019). We are in need of each other. Paulo Freire and the role of conflicts in education. *International Journal of Social Pedagogy*, *7*(1), 1–15. doi:10.14324/111.444.ijsp.2019.v7.1.009

Prinsloo, M. (1999). Literacy in South Africa, An international hand book. Science Direct.

Reder, S. (2020). A Lifelong and Life-Wide Framework for Adult Literacy Education. *Adult Literacy Education: the International Journal of Literacy, Language, and Numeracy*, *2*(1), 48–53. doi:10.35847/SReder.2.1.48

Rule, P. (2006). " The time is burning ": The right of adults to basic education in South Africa. *Journal of Education*, *39*, 113–135.

Rule, P., & Land, S. (2017). Finding the plot in South African reading education. *Reading and Writing*, *8*(1), 1–8. doi:10.4102/rw.v8i1.121

Suoranta, J. (2021). Reinventing Paulo Freire's pedagogy in Finnish non-formal education: The case of life skills for all model. *Educational Philosophy and Theory*, *0*(0), 1–15. doi:10.1080/00131857.2021.1974839

Thobejane, T. D. (2013). History of Apartheid Education and the Problems of Reconstruction in South Africa. *Sociolinguistic Studies*, *3*(1), 1–12.

Thompson, J. (2001). *Emancipatory learning. NIACE Briefing Sheet*. NIACE.

Tygel, A. F., & Kirsch, R. (2016). Contributions of Paulo Freire for a Critical Data Literacy: A Popular Education Approach. *The Journal of Community Informatics*, *12*(3), 108–121. doi:10.15353/joci.v12i3.3279

Vally Salim, M. E. (2022). The Making of Post-Apartheid State Policies for Workers, Adult and Community Education and Training : Abandoned Possibilities. *Education as Change*, *26*, 23. doi:10.25159/1947/11366

Vittoria, P. (2018). Critical education in paulo freire: Educational action for social transformation. *Encyclopaideia*, *22*(51), 37–44. doi:10.6092/issn.1825-8670/8459

Chapter 4
Increasing Teaching Capacity for Supporting Students in an ODeL Institution:
Employing Letsema

Itumeleng I. Setlhodi
https://orcid.org/0000-0003-2644-9570
University of South Africa, South Africa

ABSTRACT

There is need to build teaching capacity in pursuance of strengthening instruction and support for improving learning, particularly for adult learners. To expound the enhancement of increasing teaching capacity for effective student support through letsema in an ODeL Institution, presenting transactional distance theory and narrating experiences, with emphasis on collective effort through letsema practice. The indigenous qualitative mixed method comprising autoethnography and conversational paradigms, underpinned the study, linking quality support and students' academic success in an ODeL context, consistent with the Africanisation of higher education and outlining the significance of core values inspired by the philosophy of ubuntu. Results suggest increased teaching capacity inspire collaborative letsema support approach, assuring mentorship opportunities, quality teaching, and informed learning towards increasing student throughput rate. Thus, affirming that the approach is suitable for supporting students. Hence the recommendation for implementing the approach in an ODeL context.

DOI: 10.4018/978-1-6684-6625-4.ch004

INTRODUCTION

The extent to which higher education institutions (HEIs) support students, determines their academic success as well as institutional excellence (Netanda, Mamabolo & Themane, 2017), particularly for students from deprived backgrounds. There is a growing understanding among researchers that a reduction in dropout rates, attrition, bridging the gap of under-preparedness and delayed completion of studies hinge on the procedures used to support students, particularly in open distance-eLearning (ODeL) settings. Overall, research conducted in HEIs confirms that supported students can increase their competence, gain knowledge, heighten their learning proficiency, improve their self-enhancement and, arguably, boost their chances of completing their courses within a specified period of time (Brookfield, 2017; Harris, Campbell Casey, Westbury, & Florida-James, 2016; Van Wyk, 2017). Other authors recommend that add-on of the aforementioned attributes depend on factors such as quality teaching, the provision of adequate resources, and learner-centric support (American Association of Community Colleges [AACC], 2012; Schrum, 2000). Pitsoe and Baloyi (2015) suggest that student support in an ODL context entails providing help to students, to enable them gain competence in their learning and ultimately succeed. In lieu of this chapter, student support entails guidance through a variety of online means and a collaborative *letsema* support approach, assuring mentorship opportunities that enables quality teaching, and facilitates informed learning towards increasing student throughput rate. The success of student support programmes is dependent on meaningful teaching offered in order to derive value from anticipated outcomes, thereby averting possible learning fallouts. This is echoed by Chen, Chen and Wang (2009), who argue that student support in distance learning spaces ought to include as many empowerment initiatives as possible. This can thus offer students an opportunity to direct their own pace of learning and achieve the envisaged outcomes (Setlhodi, 2019a). In this chapter, the argument is made that institutional values ought to underpin the principles informing the quality of teaching provided and the level of support students can access for effective learning that can yield improved results.

The foregoing suggests that teaching has to be improved, if HEIs are intent to deliver a cohort of critical thinkers who can comprehend and adapt to various learning strategies, have a set of values they subscribe to, and are able to reflect before taking the lead in directing their learning. Kumar (2008) notes that teaching and learning can be strengthened by specific values, which aim to increase learning competencies through the support provided. This meets the dual expectation of increasing teaching capacity to eliminate any competency gaps and improving students' academic success. Bezuidenhout (2018) expounds that the lecturers' competencies – particularly in an ODeL context – have a bearing on student support and achievement.

Most university lecturers in ODeL contexts, therefore, require intensified capacity-building programmes to improve their teaching and in turn offer requisite support to students. Such programmes should be geared towards enhancing the quality of student support which lecturers offer across various modules and programmes. For instance, interacting with students via online support platforms and using a variety of online platforms (such as familiar applications used in the social media, and other generic platforms that can be easily accessible) and varying collective measures for backing them, to offer effective and structured support. Collective effort – *letsema* (voluntary indigenous community endeavour emanating from interdependent, reciprocal and collaborative practices, bringing a strong sense of rootedness and characteristic of belongingness (Setlhodi, 2019b: 6) – is required to increase teaching capacity, and provide effective guidance and support – particularly in an ODeL context.

The chapter comprises the following sections:

- The context for student support in an ODeL context
- Theoretical framework
- Methodology
- Discussions, ending with the characteristics of a supportive, collaborative learning (*letsema*) within a technologically driven distance education environment.

THE CONTEXT FOR STUDENT SUPPORT IN AN ODeL CONTEXT

In ODeL settings, lecturers are expected to be intentional towards improving their practice, by capacitating themselves to eliminate competency gaps so that they can successfully rally informed and comprehensive support for students (Arinto, 2013). They can improve their teaching and offer effective support to students by working collaboratively, instead of individually (as is mostly the case in HEIs). Therefore, using collective effort to guide students increases the odds of improving those students' outcomes. Research shows that numerous benefits are related to lecturers and students taking ownership of their responsibilities and striving to achieve teaching and learning objectives by working together (Robichaux and Guarino, 2012; Ruys, Van Keer & Aelterman, 2012). Effective learning can further be facilitated by making available sufficient resources (e.g., learning material, virtual and contact sessions with students, specific module learning outcomes, connectivity for online tuition and interaction), including those accorded by the HEI, to augment lecturers teaching. Therefore, those charged with the responsibility of mediating learning (lecturers, tutors [be they e-tutors or face to face] and markers) and who offer instruction through feedback in an ODeL context, should have content knowledge as well as the requisite skills to use means accorded to them in utilising the available technologies to enhance learning. This can enable them to provide quality student support with a possibility of earning improved results and enhance academic achievement overall. The literature shows that online contexts offer better opportunities for learning, because they encourage group-focused scholarship, especially if it is managed accordingly, and are effective in promoting successful learner support (Baloyi, 2014; Bezuidenhout, 2018; Netanda et al., 2017; Van Wyk, 2017).

The preceding thus articulates the need for practical measures to be considered in ensuring students' cognitive growth within the HEIs. This could be achieved by using diverse student support modalities and technologically advanced instruction. An ODeL HEI in South Africa serves as a model case within the ODeL context, because of its complex, unusual online instruction modalities and learning platforms, comprising, tutor services, comprehensive support initiatives for learning and engagements with students, in an effort to utilise collective support modalities. *Letsema* is thus proposed as a means of providing holistic support.

Using *Letsema* to offer student support

Letsema represents an indigenous process of rallying efforts in support of a particular purpose or tackling a specific problem. Arafat (2016) defines *letsema* as a community-building initiative that serves to uplift livelihoods. Equally importantly, *letsema* is also used to support initiatives of common interest in formal and informal settings. It encompasses a commitment to coexist with others and cater for their wellbeing, in this context, supporting their learning endeavours (Setlhodi, 2019b). It represents interconnectedness and interchange through collaborative means, to advance a cause such as supporting students, in order to attain the envisaged learning outcomes in this instance. In practice, *letsema* is about influencing someone in a positive way, and bringing about desired change to improve an existing situation (such as, facilitating learning), underpinned by the values of *ubuntu* (Setlhodi, 2022). The intention behind this approach is to benefit everyone concerned, and to help better their situation (Boddy-Evans, 2017). Successful student support initiatives can be achieved when those providing such services are themselves willing to collaborate for supporting learning. Group effort is likely to offer success where there is effort towards a common purpose – this is what *letsema* entails. Thus, a collective effort on the part of lecturers, e-tutors, external markers and all those who provide learning support, will help to improve practices in an ODeL environment, particularly with consideration for needy students, who may lack sufficient learning resources. Through collaborative communication, the notion of *letsema* is used to encourage beneficial, resourceful acts of support. These, in turn, are informed by acts of *ubuntu* (benevolent praxis), where students are equally encouraged to team up for learning. In case of this chapter, *letsema* refers to collaborative efforts (such as various tutor models, and resources) to decentralise instruction, improve teaching and increase student throughput rates, within an ODeL setting. Letsema also relates to a sense of coherence in complementing teaching, for the attainment of success in throughput rate in this situation,

Efforts aimed at supplementing teaching capacity have to focus on ensuring that the instruction which HEIs offer is of a high caliber and is able to transfer critical thinking skills for students, strengthen their reflective skills, and advance their self-directedness to apply knowledge and achieve learning objectives. To increase capacity, training has to be provided. There is no unanimity concerning exactly what is involved in efforts to provide total learner support in an ODeL context, however, it would include the provision of resources, counselling, social support, mentorship and academic support, in an attempt to improve students' performance and completion rates (Harris et al., 2016; Netanda et al., 2017; Pitsoe & Baloyi, 2015).

Engaging mentorship

Mentorship is a structured support process, whereby an experienced and knowledgeable person (a mentor) is charged with the responsibility of assuming a leadership role in offering guidance, support, counsel and tutelage to a mentee or mentees (student/s). it entails mentoring of both students and secondary mentors in a complex multilayered online teaching environment. The mentor initiates the process by proposing a possible mentorship programme and sharing it with the mentee. In the case of students enrolled in an ODeL institution where virtual tuition takes place, the process may be extended to a collective of mentors such as the lecturers as primary mentors, whilst secondary mentors comprise tutors (face to face and e-tutors), including external markers, as well as peers (Setlhodi, 2018b). In an online setting, the structure of the mentorship process may comprise scheduled interaction with e-tutors, interactive contact online, the use of podcasts, digital support and peer mentorship, among others, with varying techniques being used to offer support from a collective of various sources.

Letsema appears to be ideal for providing student support in an institution that is increasingly positioning itself towards and charged with Africanising its tuition. For that reason, a sustained improvement in teaching capacity will foster the achievement of learning outcomes and improve learner support, particularly in an ODL environment. It therefore implies that secondary mentors themselves may well require a structured mentorship programme, which aims to capacitate these mentors to carry their role of mentoring students. [with the resources for teaching and learning organised to accord successful online support (Letseka & Pitsoe, 2014).

Their mentorship, therefore, is dedicated at improving their mentorship skills and enabling informed theoretical capacity.

ODeL institutions organise and reorganise their systems and resources to support teaching and learning, without necessarily requiring teachers and students to be in the same space at the same time (Letseka & Pitsoe 2014 ODeL institutions organise and reorganise their systems and resources to support teaching and learning, without necessarily requiring teachers and students to be in the same space at the same time (Letseka & Pitsoe 2014

THEORETICAL FRAMEWORK

This article is underpinned by the transactional theory of distance (Lichtenstein, Netemeyer & Burton, 1991), which refers to the virtual contact between students and lecturers in a distance education set-up. Institutions which offer learning via distance education, tend to experience teaching and learning challenges due to the remote nature of student 'contact' involved (Jowallah 2014, 189). The distant relationship between lecturers and students affects their interaction across varied communication channels, while the ability to self-direct and work autonomously forms the bedrock of the transactional theory of distance (Murphy & Rodriguez-Manzanares, 2008, 2). Moore (1991; 1993) maintains that transactional distance between learners and lecturers can be circumvented through a well-structured course design, greater student autonomy, and sound communication between the parties involved. This is inclusive of the nature of support meant for students in a distance education set-up.

According to Tait (2017), the application of transactional distance theory is suitable for tutoring and student support activities, as it works to ensure high throughput rates and for timeous completion of courses. Again, it also equips students with self-directedness and independence, enabling them to interact and cooperate with lecturers in an organised manner (Moore & Kearsley, 2012). Interaction and cooperation are vital components of *letsema*, as they encourage critical reflection amongst students particularly when learning in teams and motivate them to assume responsibility for their learning. Ensuring that all parties responsible (in the teaching process) provide the necessary support, devise means to join forces, coming together to assure that proper guidance and tutelage are offered the *letsema* way (Kaufman & Guerra-Lopez, 2013).

To that end, an appropriate and adequately structured course warrants sufficiently capacitated lecturers who are able to initiate dialogue (in a supportive manner) and offer targeted web-based tuition that affords students an opportunity to engage with online content (Zhang, 2003). Suitable collaborative support, underpinned by the principles of *letsema* and strengthened by the values of *ubuntu* (responsiveness, support, care and collaboration), in addition to greater reflection, will enable self-directedness on the part of students. All these factors can dovetail with academic initiatives geared at offering learners support to achieve their learning outcomes.

METHODOLOGY

An indigenous qualitative mixed method approach, using autoethnography and a conversational paradigm, was employed to expound the enhancement of increasing teaching capacity for effective student support through letsema in an ODeL institution, South Africa (Ellis, Adams & Bochner, 2011), for exploring ways for improving the quality of teaching and increase students' academic achievement in an ODeL institution. An autoethnography is a discipline of anthropology, used by individuals (auto) to mirror the culture (ethno) and values prevalent within a certain environment, before analysing and writing up (graphy) these phenomena, and relating them to the conduct of the sample under study. Thus, daily meaning and purpose are reflected in processes and products and expressed using the principles of autobiography and ethnography (Ellis et al., 2011; Gannon, 2017). The intention in this case was to improve methodology to suit the African context, avoiding the imposition of sterile and instinctive colonial research, which entailed going in, taking advantage of, frantically deserting participants, and then proceed to write about their culture, beliefs, and core values, inadvertently undermining them by doing so from a western perspective (Conquergood, 1991; Ellis, 2007).

Autoethnography ideally gives a realistic account of core values and inherent culture: in this context, of academic staff sometimes having to support over 20 000 learners by themselves, particularly in over enrolled modules. Occasionally, academics do require support with specific aspects of their work, so that, in turn, they can provide the necessary support to their students, amongst others by using conversational methods. The colloquial method, which is located within the paradigm of indigenous knowledge, is based on a culture of collaboration and reflexivity (Kovach, 2009). It is related to ethical practices (or a lack thereof), which rely on an indigenous mixed methods approach proposed by Botha (2011).

The focus is on indigenous participants, thus does not refer to the traditional qualitative–quantitative mixed method. For Botha (2011, 314), an indigenous mixed method approach implies the "merging of conventional qualitative research and indigenous research", to find a balance between western and indigenous methods of knowing, "so that more appropriate theories, practices and relations can be developed for their interrelation". Drawson, Toombs and Mushquash (2017) add that researchers should desist from using approaches disguised as indigenous research methods, while imposing colonial principles and arguably, lasing them with indigenous practices.

The attention should be on indigenous practices that have largely prevailed in Africa and are enculturated in this context, as well as efforts to seek tutelage from others in a manner that encompass traditional ways.

Culture, in this instance, includes the normative practices used to support students in an ODeL context in this instance. The conversational method is appropriate, because it can adequately uncover the means of fusing teaching in highly enrolled modules. It enables group's creation of open, comprehensive and deeper conversations particularly during collaborative engagements. For that reason, autoethnography can be used by one lecturer, with other support systems – the collective (such as e-tutors, external markers using real time synchronous tuition in a variety of available online platforms), employed to provide support for the greater good of the students and achieve a common purpose.

Ethical considerations must be kept in mind while applying reflexiveness, which is the ability to reflect (as a researcher) on one's own lived experiences when collecting data and interpreting them based on core values (Kovach, 2009). The moral intent permitting examining of own feelings, motives and reactions, whilst internalising reasons for applying this method and thus carefully evading any form of bias. The objective is to prioritise students and instil institutional core values, by supporting them while driven by the institution's value of 'shaping futures in service of humanity' within an African context. Both the autoethnographic and the conversational methods are presented, to illustrate their appropriateness within an ODeL setting (Van Wyk, 2017).

Autoethnography and the indigenous conversational mixed method

As an ODeL lecturer, I was daunted by the task of handling an over-enrolled module with over 20 000 higher certificate students by myself and having to employ collaborative processes within an ODeL environment. Supporting such high student numbers meant that, first, enabled a decision to take responsibility to plan for student support (individuals and groups). Second, having to liaise with tutors (face-to-face and e-tutors), as well as internal and external markers. Third, collaborate with a colleague by co-arranging video conferencing together even though he was responsible for another module. Fourth, taking responsibility to prepare routine support materials based on sections, which appeared to pose a challenge to students, as they did not perform well in them. Fifth, it was necessary to provide students with examination preparation support and give feedback for their assignments (through Tutorial Letter 201). Sixth, interacting with students (telephonically, via email and by permitting walk-ins). Finally, administering dedicated concessions to support learner who repeated the module more than three times, particularly those struggling to achieve the learning outcomes.

The learning culture in the module centres on writing assignments and then preparing for the examinations (formative and summative assessment), because it is a semester module. Soon after students completed their assignments, they had to prepare for their examinations. This left little time for actual teaching and learning, thereby putting pressure on lecturers to support students and put them at ease regarding achieving the learning outcomes of the module on time and be ready for the examinations. Inadvertently, effective support was compromised. To cope with the pressure, sometimes there was a need to be capacitated on an ad-hoc basis (by colleagues and administrators) on matters where I was lacking, such as tutoring via podcasts, which was a crucial component of the quest to effectively support students real time, particularly in situations where there was a need to respond to queries pertaining assignment feedback or preparations for the examinations. To this end, colleagues who could serve as my mentors were identified, particularly when it was essential, consequently, enabling me to carry out my responsibilities efficiently and support my students optimally.

Most of my students are from disadvantaged backgrounds, which make it difficult to learn in an ODeL environment because they often lack connectivity to engage with e-tutors online. This results in their overreliance on guidance from me, their lecturer. Most are not linked to tutors either, because they struggle to connect via information communication technologies (ICTs) or did not make the cut (only a limited number of e-tutors were available for the module). Only 14 e-tutors instead of 88 were allocated to me due to unavailability of sufficient pool to select from among other reasons, which made it imperative to employ high-powered and technologically advanced instruction and support platforms, as required by the institution. This further implied that most students depended completely on the lecturer, and partly benefited from feedback from external markers. Those linked to tutors (who also attend face-to-face sessions where feasible) are supported by the lecturer and by the external markers' intensive comments, provided as feedback on their written assignments. Markers are requested to give detailed comments when marking, because that is another means of tutoring and supporting students in a distance learning situation. Markers were required to conform to traditional ways of marking and giving feedback as a practice for student support in my module, thus ensuring the assimilation of these practices and institutional values. This is in line with my own socialisation regarding support given, as well as my observation of elders and seniors guiding others. Some students teamed up with their peers to learn together. Additionally, they receive support through interactive mediums of support, scheduled by the university. This made support a collective effort that formed part of the notion of *letsema*. Everyone is urged to take responsibility in assisting and supporting students by engaging in a common processes thorough tutor preparation (tutors' submitted lesson plans are reviewed); guiding students while marking (during the moderation process); encouraging students to take the initiative to direct their learning through bulk e-mails and short messaging services (SMS) on a periodic basis. Again, active interaction with students was normalised by urging them to contact me or their tutors (those who are linked) to seek help and maintain visibility on the institutions' learning platform for announcements and support (as is required practice at in my institution); through video conferencing; by encouraging those who can, to walk in for consultation (because I empathise with their learning difficulties and want them to excel); and by responding to emails (in the evening and over weekends). These are all ways of assuming social responsibility and are in keeping with responding when those in need reach out, similar to the Setswana adage "*go baya nokeng*" meaning, to help and support others. It is also in keeping with my institution's charter for transformation, which calls for commitment to the 11 Cs plus one (communication, conversation, conservation, community, connection, care, collegiality, commitment, cooperation, creativity, consultation plus courage) (Makhanya, 2011) and is embedded in the core values (ethical and collective responsibility, integrity, innovation and excellence, responsive student-centeredness, dignity in diversity) outlined in the institution's corporate strategy. My belief is that students should not be disadvantaged because of the shortfalls of inadequate planning of recruitment processes, thus complying with the institution's ethical code of practice, and ties well with the principle of *ubuntu*, which premises *letsema* (shared work, compassion, moral receptivity for the wellbeing of others).

Even though offering support can be onerous, the appreciative responses received from students, for going the extra mile in supporting them was reassuring. As a collective, the students assist and guide one another, which is a different form of *letsema*. Thus, tutors, markers and departmental administrators all help to facilitate an effective marking process (liaising with markers when not on campus), colleagues volunteer to assist with the moderation process, and many students show willingness to accept the help offered (via telephone or email) – even those in the deep rural areas.

Reflecting on the lived experiences of my students as they engage with myself, made me ponder how their problems affected their learning. Many experienced difficulties related to having to learn in a second language or hold down day jobs because some did not have the benefit of a privileged education. The use of technology remained a challenge for this cohort of students specifically, most of whom had limited resources. Although having to learn in an ODeL context is aggravated by language barriers and difficulties with technology, our students were courageous because they wanted to learn. They considered education to be a means of supporting their aspirations and improving their socioeconomic status. During consultation, one learner told me: "I have to acquire a qualification so that I can have a great head start to a sound career life." This underscores my view that student support should be provided via as many multi-faceted modes as possible, particularly in an ODeL context. Some students struggled with virtual submission methods, and thus resorted to writing by hand and posting their assignments. This contravened the ODeL principles of distant education instruction, engagement and submission. However, determination to use any means at my disposal to show compassion and support them, in keeping with the tenets of *ubuntu* enabled me to forge ahead, always striving for compassion. Compassion is a principle of *ubuntu*, and from it should come a willingness to engage in *letsema*, by enabling collective support for students in keeping with core values of compassion, consideration, community, connection, care, collegiality, commitment, cooperation, creativity, consultation, courageously and chronicling essential underlying practice to aid support.

Structural narrative analysis

Structural narrative analysis provided a reflective, innate culture for supporting an over-enrolled module in a department within an ODeL college of education (Larty & Hamilton, 2011). For a better understanding of the mixed method used, the transactional theory of distance was considered, to reflect on the core values of, and existing beliefs within, the institution. This is because theory transcends culture, therefore the structure of the analysis comes from narratives stated in the methodology (Barthes & Duisit, 1975). To plumb the depths of the analysis structure, an autoethnography and the conversational method were employed as indigenous paradigms, using transactional theory, which asserts that interaction (between lecturers, tutors and students) can, through virtual means, produce in-depth information (Patterson, 2008). Also employed were the enculturated practices of *letsema*, the values of *ubuntu*, the embedded institutional values and the 11Cs mentioned earlier. In explaining Barthes' work, Rcfrey (2012) outlines that analysis should be reflective of those narrations from which the narrative units come. Labov's narrative analysis model informs these units (also termed elements), which are, abstract, orientation, complicating action, evaluation, resolution and coda (UK Essays, 2013). These elements are founded (in this context) on the significance of having capacitated people through the application of values to the collective process of providing the necessary support.

Through this process, the bare bones of the narration are presented, using some (or all) of the elements needed to deduce themes (Wells, 2011, 6). The fact that collegiality is at the core of support (given the multiple helpful acts mentioned earlier) points to the basic process of *letsema* in an institution where technology is used to support students. *Letsema* is a way of urging others to action, conveying *ubuntu* values which endorse shared obligation (Setlhodi, 2019b) and instil institutional values. In this context, it enables collective effort to deal with the complexities of supporting and coordinating mentorship for a large number of students. The support team is orientated to ensure that each member follows a common approach in handling students' difficulties. The institutional values which guide the lecturers' practices and underpin their support are enculturated and have become the norm (emblematic of *ubuntu*). Students' difficulties are considered, and adequate measures put in place to ensure that they are supported, not only by ODeL systems but also by additional measures such as acts of benevolence and willingness to prepare them to write examinations. In an African context, it is expected of those providing tutelage to be considerate, kind towards, and caring of, those placed under their watch and guidance.

As this is an undergraduate module, most students struggled with submission issues and the use of technology even though special support was extended and offered as the need arose. Willingness by the markers to dutifully mark and give invaluable comments, tutors' continuous engagement with students, and their prompt email responses remained essential components of an efficient learning method. This corresponded with the Setswana axiom: "*Mabogo dinku a thebana*" (work is done better by collective/many hands make light work). Emergent themes were,

- cohesive support validating acts of *letsema*;
- overarching values informed by *ubuntu*; and
- a supportive culture and underlying ideals of commitment.

DISCUSSIONS

The significance of collective support for students in an ODeL institution is dependent on how such interventions benefit them. Zhang (2003) notes that offering support results in an improved learning of content, and the strengthening of performance (which yields better results). Involving the lecturer, tutors, markers and various platforms support the notion of an African approach (*letsema*) in tackling important issues related to learning. *Letsema* encompasses the African practice of volunteering one's services to help attain an objective (Modipa 2014; Ramagoshi, 2013). People who employ *letsema* work collaboratively to achieve a goal – in this context, to support students in achieving set learning outcomes. *Letsema* is underpinned by values such as motivation, responsibility, volunteering and accountability. People engaging in *letsema* are motivated to achieve a goal and assume responsibility to work towards attaining that goal. They hold one another accountable and are willing to go an extra mile by volunteering their services or going beyond the call of duty. In so doing, they practise *ubuntu*. Ramagoshi (2013) concurs, claiming that *letsema* practice, motivates people to undertake the notion of nation building and show integrity when working as a collective, by reflecting critical core values. The narration states,

"Everyone is urged to take responsibility in assisting and supporting students by engaging in a common processes thorough tutor preparation ...; guiding students while marking ...; encouraging students to take the initiative to direct their learning ... on a periodic basis"

The above is one act of cohesive support, thereby validating the employment of letsema practice and upholding critical values synonymous to African ways of living, engaging and socialising, which are underpinned by the value of ubuntu.

Ubuntu is a fundamental valuing of our shared humanity. It inspires acts of benevolence, such as markers giving detailed comments and references to which students can refer and gain better understanding. It involves tutors extending their scope to lecturing students online, of their own volition, and helping them to prepare for the examinations. *Ubuntu* in this context discusses acceptable relationships with others (Letseka, 2012). The focus is mainly on ensuring attainment of learning outcomes and in turn increase the quality of graduates beseeched by employment requirements. It relates to the interrelationships between people, and recognises people's existence and significance (here, engaging with students, identifying their need to learn, and providing support to enable such learning). Support extends to ensuring that students can transition from writing assignments to preparing for the examinations, within a limited time frame, and showing compassion while they are also enabled to cope within the unfamiliar ODeL setting. Khoza (2011) notes that the concerted efforts of *ubuntu* endorse collective support. In this chapter, for students who may be struggling due to socioeconomic reasons, connectivity problems and difficulties with the use of a second language. Such efforts are made possible by encouraging people to amass knowledge and seek to be capacitated when the need arises. Examples include lecturers, tutors or markers asking for clarification or upskilling themselves by attending workshops (j-router or online marking and student support), using the learning platform and other capacity-building workshops offered by the university), which links with the presented story, narrating that,

"...determination to use any means at my disposal to show compassion and support them, in keeping with the tenets of ubuntu enabled me to forge ahead, always striving for compassion".

Consideration of the needs of others also entails preparedness to seek help and develop one's capacity to advance practice and learn new and improved ways of supporting students, such as accruing mentors for informed improvement of practice as narrated.

"... sometimes there was a need to be capacitated on an ad-hoc basis ... which was a crucial component of the quest to effectively support students real time, ... colleagues who could serve as my mentors were identified, particularly when it was essential, consequently, enabling me to carry out my responsibilities efficiently and support my students optimally".

Willingness to reach out for help is crucial and often a hallmark of ability for self-immersion to one's responsibilities, taking charge of own development. Capacitated lecturers, tutors and markers have the ability to engage with students in an informed manner, thereby establishing a strong culture of support within the module offered. They also demonstrate embedded values in their practice as principles for attaining efficacy in one's work committing to continue perfecting ones craft by what Setlhodi (2019b) terms, 'sharpening ones cycle', thereby showing care for one's work, courage to reach out for help, consulting colleagues when there is a need, which can in turn encourage creativity and obligation in one's practice such as eagerness to also guide and support students.

Student support involves teachers knowing what they can do to guide students (Bates, 2014). They do not shy away from responding to students' queries, are responsive and committed to offering support, even volunteering their own time when there is demanded to do so. In turn, engaged students are able to take the initiative and direct their own learning. Van Wyk (2017) maintains that students who are adequately supported are enhanced to self-direct their learning and personal growth. they are further able to pace themselves (Setlhodi, 2019a). Self-directedness leads to the ability to reflect objectively on one's work (Garrett, 2011). If students are motivated to seek support whilst learning, it increases their learning competence and may result in them achieving set outcomes. The following characterises supportive, collaborative learning (*letsema*) within a technologically driven distance education environment:

- Lecturers, tutors, markers, mentors and all parties providing student support share knowledge and understanding, learn among themselves and accept responsibility for developing their students, by putting in place structured support mechanisms or developing their own.
- The value of *ubuntu* underpins relationships among those providing support and interacting with students by facilitating engagement, fostering support initiatives and practising core values associated with support.

- Coalitions, networks, partnerships, collaborations, collective effort and teamwork influence flexibility and lateral (peer) as well as vertical (professional) interaction, thereby encouraging voluntarism and willingness to go an extra mile for the greater good of students.
- Compassionate, cooperative support serves as a basis for increased learning competency, and encourages open-mindedness, self-reflection, independent thinking, active learning and self-directedness (a deep approach to learning).
- Demonstrating benevolence or willingness to help those who are struggling with language or connectivity or understanding the plight of those who are part-time students or are at a disadvantage due to socioeconomic difficulties, can enable students to achieve their learning outcomes and be competitive in employment.

CONCLUSION

This article showcased the significance of *letsema* in improving quality teaching and learning for students. It thus argues that the latter can be achieved by supporting students more comprehensively at all levels of learning. Greater support is likely to improve throughput rates in an ODeL contexts and bequeath values of compassion, cooperation, collegiality, care, and commitment, consistent with the Africanisation of higher education, as many previously disadvantaged students could have a chance at success. *Letsema* is both a community-building initiative inspired by collective effort and underpinned by the core values of *ubuntu*, to attain a set goal, as well as an underlying practice used commensurate with the Africanisation agenda. The transactional theory of distance demonstrated relevance in the virtual contact between teachers and learners in distance education, enabling courage for the creation of an environment that facilitates effective learning, to produce positive learning outcomes.

An indigenous qualitative mixed method, comprising autoethnography and the conversational paradigm, was used to reveal how a culture of support could be applied in practice, and the way core values could enable support of a large number of students. A structural narrative analysis was used as reflective, innate culture for supporting a highly enrolled module. The six elements of analysis were used to elucidate on how to theorise support through the orientation of those responsible, setting out actions to be taken, evaluating processes of support, repurposing support to enable collaborative learning, facilitating support mechanisms and agreeing to go an extra mile commensurate with *letsema* and *ubuntu* practice, with an aim to get students ready for their examinations and enable them to successfully achieve the learning outcomes. Incorporating the notion of *letsema* in supporting a highly enrolled module could help achieve the desired outcomes in an ODeL context.

Thus, the chapter finally outlined characteristics of collaborative (rooted in *letsema* practice) support in an open distance education setting.

REFERENCES

American Association of Community Colleges (AACC). 2012. *Reclaiming the American dream: Community colleges and the nation's future (21st century report)*. Washington, DC: AACC. Retrieved from https://www.aacc.nche.edu/aboutcc/21stcenturyreport/index.html (accessed 20 September 2018).

Arafat, M. A. N. (2016). *The rise of the local economy in South Africa: The five pillars of networking enterprise*. SesLocal.

Arinto, P. B. (2013). A framework for developing competencies in open and distance learning. *International Review of Research in Open and Distance Learning*, *4*(1), 167–185. doi:10.19173/irrodl.v14i1.1393

Baloyi, G. (2014). Learner support in open distance and e-learning for adult students using technologies. *Journal of Communication*, *5*(2), 127–133. doi:10.1080/0976691X.2014.11884832

Barthes, R., & Duisit, L. (1975). An introduction to the structural analysis of narrative. *New Literary History*, *6*(2), 237–272. doi:10.2307/468419

Bates, T. 2014. "Why learner support is an important component in the design of teaching and learning." Online Learning and Distance Education Resources. Retrieved from https://www.tonybates.ca/2014/08/26/why-learner-support-is-an-important-component-in-the-design-of-teaching-and-learning/ (accessed 30 October 2018).

Bezuidenhout, A. (2018). Analysing the importance-competence gap of distance educators with the increased utilisation of online learning strategies in a developing world context. *International Review of Research in Open and Distance Learning*, *19*(3), 263–281. doi:10.19173/irrodl.v19i3.3585

Boddy-Evans, A. 2017. "Julius Kambarage Nyerere – Father of Tanzania and initiator of *ujamaa*." Retrieved from https://www.thoughtco.com/julius-kambarage-nyerere-43589istory & Culture (accessed 17 March 2017).

Botha, L. (2011). Mixing methods as a process towards indigenous methodologies. *International Journal of Social Research Methodology*, *31*(4), 3–325. doi:10.1080/13645579.2010.516644

Brookfield, S. (2017). Teaching for critical thinking. In V. C. X. Wang (Ed.), *Adult education and vocational training in the digital age* (pp. 1–17). IGI Global. doi:10.4018/978-1-5225-0929-5.ch001

Chen, L., Chen, H., & Wang, H. (2009). Distance education in China: The current state of e-learning. *Campus-Wide Information Systems*, *26*(2), 82–89. doi:10.1108/10650740910946792

Conquergood, D. (1991). Rethinking ethnography: Towards a critical cultural politics. *Communication Monographs*, *58*(2), 179–194. doi:10.1080/03637759109376222

Drawson, A. S., Toombs, E., & Mushquash, C. J. (2017). Indigenous research methods: A systematic review. *International Indigenous Policy Journal*, *8*(2). Advance online publication. doi:10.18584/iipj.2017.8.2.5

Ellis, C. (2007). Telling secrets, revealing lives: Relational ethics in research with intimate others. *Qualitative Inquiry*, *13*(1), 3–29. doi:10.1177/1077800406294947

Ellis, C., Adams, T. E., & Bochner, A. P. (2011). Autoethnography: An overview. *Historical Social Research (Köln)*, *36*(4), 273–290.

Essays, U. K. November 2013. "Labov's model of narrative analysis." Retrieved from https://www.ukessays.com/essays/english-language/labovs-model-narrative-analysis-2563.php?vref=1 (accessed 13 September 2018).

Gannon, S. 2017. "Education, cultures, and ethnicities: Research and assessment methods." *Oxford Research Encyclopedia: Education*. Doi: . doi:10.1093/acrefore/9780190264093.013.71

Garrett, N. (2011). An e-portfolio design supporting ownership, social learning, and ease of use. *Journal of Educational Technology & Society*, *14*(1), 187–202.

Harris, P. J., Campbell Casey, S. A., Westbury, T., & Florida-James, G. (2016). Assessing the link between stress and retention and the existence of barriers to support service use within HE. *Journal of Further and Higher Education*, *40*(6), 824–845. doi:10.1080/0309877X.2015.1014316

Jowallah, R. (2014). An investigation into the management of online teaching and learning spaces: A case study involving graduate research students. *International Review of Research in Open and Distance Learning*, *15*(4), 186–199. doi:10.19173/irrodl.v15i4.1585

Kaufman, R., & Guerra-Lopez, I. (2013). *Needs assessment for organizational success*. ASTD Press.

Khoza, R. J. (2011). *Attuned leadership: African humanism as compass*. Penguin Books.

Kovach, M. (2009). *Indigenous methodologies: Characteristics, conversations, and contexts*. University of Toronto Press.

Kumar, A. (2008). Development education and dialogical learning in the 21st century. *International Journal of Development Education and Global Learning*, *1*(1), 37–48. doi:10.18546/IJDEGL.01.1.04

Larty, J., & Hamilton, E. (2011). Structural approaches to narrative analysis in entrepreneurship research: Exemplars from two researchers. *International Small Business Journal*, *29*(3), 220–237. doi:10.1177/0266242611401796

Letseka, M. (2012). In defence of *ubuntu*. *Studies in Philosophy and Education*, *31*(1), 47–60. doi:10.100711217-011-9267-2

Letseka, M., & Pitsoe, V. (2014). The challenges and prospects of access to higher education at Unisa. *Studies in Higher Education*, *39*(10), 1942–1954. doi:10.1080/03075079.2013.823933

Linchtenstein, D. R., Netemeyer, R. G., & Burton, S. 1991. "Using a theoretical perspective to examine the psychological construct of coupon proneness", in NA-Advances in Consumer Research Volume 18 (eds), Holman, R.H. and Solomon, M.R. Provo, UT: Associatin for Consumer Research, 501-508.

Makhanya, M. S. (2011). Speaking at the launch of the Unisa Charter on Transformation. University of South Africa., Retrieved from https://www.unisa.ac.za/static/corporate_web/Content/About/Executive%20management/Unisa%20Principal%20and%20 Vice-Chancellor/documents/PROF_MAKHANYA_CharterLaunchAddress.pdf, Retrieved August 30, 2018, from.

Modipa, M. E. 2014. "African values respect environment." Retrieved from https://www.iol.co.za/business-report/features/african-values-respect-environment-1668339 (accessed 30 October 2018).

Moore, M. G. (1991). Distance education theory. *American Journal of Distance Education*, *5*(3), 1–6. doi:10.1080/08923649109526758

Moore, M. G. (1993). Theory of transactional distance. In M. Keegan (Ed.), *Theoretical principles of distance education* (pp. 22–38). Routledge.

Moore, M. G., & Kearsley, G. (2012). *Distance education: A systems view* (3rd ed.). Wadsworth.

Murphy, E., & Rodriguez-Manzanares, M. A. (2008). Revisiting transactional theory in a context of web-based high school distance education. *Journal of Distance Education*, *22*(2), 1–14.

Netanda, R. S., Mamabolo, J., & Themane, M. (2017). Do or die: Student support interventions for the survival of distance education institutions in a competitive higher education system. *Studies in Higher Education*. Advance online publication. doi:10.1080/03075079.2017.1378632

Patterson, W. (2008). Narratives of events: Labovian narrative analysis and its limitations. In M. Andrews, C. Squire, & M. Tamboukou (Eds.), *Doing narrative research* (pp. 22–40). Sage. doi:10.4135/9780857024992.d3

Pitsoe, V., & Baloyi, G. (2015). Conceptions of success in open distance learning. In M. Letseka (Ed.), *open distance learning in South Africa* (pp. 91–104). Nova.

Ramagoshi, R. M. 2013. "The role of *letsema* in community struggles: Past and present." In Landman, C. (Ed.), *Hidden voices, untold stories and veiled memories: Oral history, representation and knowledge.* Proceedings of the Fifth Oral History Conference 2008, East London (pp. 49–57). ISBN 978-1-86888-736-1.

Rcfrey. 2012. "Structural analysis of the narrative." In *Annotations: Genre theory*. Retrieved from https://genretheoryannotations.wordpress.com/2012/02/15/structural-analysis-of-the-narrative (accessed 13 September 2018).

Robichaux, R. R., & Guarino, A. J. (2012). The impact of implementing a portfolio assessment system on pre-service teachers' daily teaching: Reflections on improvement, performance and professionalism. *Creative Education*, *3*(3), 290–292. doi:10.4236/ce.2012.33045

Ruys, I., Van Keer, H., & Aelterman, A. (2012). Examining pre-service teacher competence in lesson planning pertaining to collaborative learning. *Journal of Curriculum Studies*, *44*(3), 349–379. doi:10.1080/00220272.2012.675355

Schrum, L. (2000). Online teaching and learning: Essential conditions for success! In L. Lau (Ed.), *Distance learning technologies: Issues, trends and opportunities* (pp. 91–106). Idea Group., doi:10.4018/978-1-878289-80-3.ch008

Setlhodi, I. I. (2018). Mentoring in a web class for adult learners. In C. Fitzgerald, S. Laurian-Fitzgerald, & C. Popa (Eds.), *Student-centered strategies to transform adult learning in online environments* (pp. 206–220). IGI Global., doi:10.4018/978-1-5225-5085-3.ch010

Setlhodi, I. I. (2019a). The value of pacing in promoting self-directed learning. In F. Giuseffi (Ed.), *Self-Directed Learning Strategies in Adult Educational Contexts* (pp. 1–22). IGI Global., doi:10.4018/978-1-5225-8018-8.ch001

Setlhodi, I. I. (2019b). Ubuntu Leadership: An African Panacea for Improving School Performance, *Africa. Education Review*, *16*(2), 126–142. doi:10.1080/18146627.2018.1464885

Setlhodi, I. I. (2022). Values Centred Leadership: Insights from schools that underperform. *Open Journal of Social Sciences*, *10*(7), 10, 470–486. doi:10.4236/jss.2022.107036

Tait, A. (2017). European figures in distance and e-learning. *Journal of Learning for Development*, *4*(1), 5–11. doi:10.56059/jl4d.v4i1.197

Van Wyk, M. (2017). An e-portfolio as empowering tool to enhance students' self-directed learning in a teacher education course: A case of a South African university. *South African Journal of Higher Education*, *31*(3), 274–291. doi:10.20853/31-3-834

Wells, K. (2011). *Narrative inquiry*. Oxford University Press. doi:10.1093/acprof:oso/9780195385793.001.0001

Zhang, A. 2003. *Transactional distance in web-based college learning environments: Toward measurement and theory construction*. PhD. diss., Virginia Commonwealth University, Richmond, VA. Retrieved from https://wwwlib.umi.com/dissertations/fullcit/3082019 (accessed 28 September 2018).

Chapter 5
Unpacking the Interdependence of CET College Leadership:
A Systems Thinking Perspective on Organisational Change and Governance in South Africa

Lynette Lulama Mbatha
https://orcid.org/0000-0002-6351-0556
University of KwaZulu-Natal, South Africa

ABSTRACT

In the South African context, adult education is a critical component of the national skills development agenda aimed at improving the skills and employability of the adult population. Adult education takes many forms in South Africa, ranging from adult basic education and training (ABET) to technical and vocational education and training (TVET), community education and training (CET), and higher education. The South African government has significantly invested in adult education to reduce unemployment and poverty and increase economic growth. Leadership and management in adult education in South Africa face unique challenges, including a large and diverse learner population, scarce resources, and the need to balance the demands of various stakeholders. This chapter examines how various stakeholders understand the interdependence of the different parts of community education and training (CET) college leadership in organisational change, how change is managed, and how effective the organisational change is.

DOI: 10.4018/978-1-6684-6625-4.ch005

1. INTRODUCTION

Adult Education in South Africa has undergone massive changes in the post-apartheid era. These changes include policies that articulated good intentions for the sector, but the result on the ground and the effects of these policies on South African society show different results. For example, South Africa still experiences high illiteracy rates, skills shortages and unemployment. Really, what are we missing?

South Africa has developed the *White Paper for Post-School Education and Training* (RSA, 2013) to respond to the triple challenges facing South Africa: unemployment, inequality, and poverty. This policy document articulates one of its objectives: *"to prepare workers for the labour market and that everyone should be able to make a living for themselves and contribute skills to a developing economy"* (RSA, 2013, p. 8).

The introduction of the PSET model required the government to create structural and operational changes to how the adult education system would be managed. The legislative responsibility for Adult Education and Training (AET) was transferred to the Minister of Higher Education and Training through the *Higher Education and Training Amendment Laws Act, 2010* (Act No. 25: 2010

The *White Paper for Post-School Education and Training* (RSA, 2013) further outlines the country's aspiration to build an expanded, effective, and integrated post-school education and training system and to establish the CET system as a third institutional form alongside universities and TVET colleges. Currently, we are at a stage of transition from the Public Adult Learning Centre to CET Colleges.

It is envisaged that one million students will be enrolled at the CET colleges by 2030. This target places "an enormous responsibility [on] the entire CET College leadership" in South Africa (Davis et al., 2015, p. 333). To accomplish this prescription of the National Plan's target and for CET colleges to succeed, a new and exceptional calibre of leaders with a new way of thinking is required. For this reason, the Department of Higher Education and Training (2013) advocates that college leadership at the council and management level is vital for ensuring that the system transforms in the desired direction.

Effective leadership and management in South African adult education require understanding these contextual factors and a commitment to promoting social justice, equity, and inclusivity in education. Leaders and managers must be able to navigate the complexities of the South African education system, build strong partnerships with stakeholders, and implement innovative strategies to improve the quality and accessibility of adult education. They must also promote a culture of lifelong learning and professional development, ensuring that their teams have the skills and knowledge to meet the changing needs of learners and the economy. In summary, effective leadership and management in South African adult education require understanding the unique contextual factors shaping the field.

Having discussed the policy prescriptions, historical context related to CET colleges in South Africa and the relevance of this chapter, it is appropriate to locate this chapter and illustrate the governance and management structure in the CET colleges' organogram. This is done to highlight the relevant government stakeholders and their various levels of reporting and responsibilities within the CET colleges and to give background and justification for selecting respondents.

The National Plan for Implementing the *White Paper* for Post-School *Education and Training System* (DHET, 2019, pp. 38-39) stipulates that.

public community colleges will be the responsibility of the Department of Higher Education and Training (DHET), which will oversee the clustering of the PALCs to form the colleges, as well as the expansion of the system. Community colleges will be governed by councils, including ministerial appointees and community representatives. Still, they will also have representation from the local government, other post-school educational institutions and local businesses. At the same time, management and administrative responsibility for each community college will rest with a principal.

This organogram (Figure 1) below depicts the structure of the CET colleges in South Africa.

This chapter is located on the second level of the above structure, with the

Council is responsible for the oversight of college operations and the welfare of students and staff. They are also responsible for overseeing college policies that are developed in the interest of the college and aligned with national legislation (DHET, 2019, p. 39).

CET College and Administration (CETCA) are also responsible for the administrative role of the management governance and take operational decisions that filter down to the CLCs. CLCs and satellites are delivery sites and are where implementation takes place and where the 3,4 million (or 59%) of youth "Not in Employment, Education or Training" who are referred to as NEETs (RSA, 2013, p. 7) will be located. The CLCs are managed by centre managers, and supervisors oversee the day-to-day running of the satellite centres.

Figure 1. CET College Institutional Structure

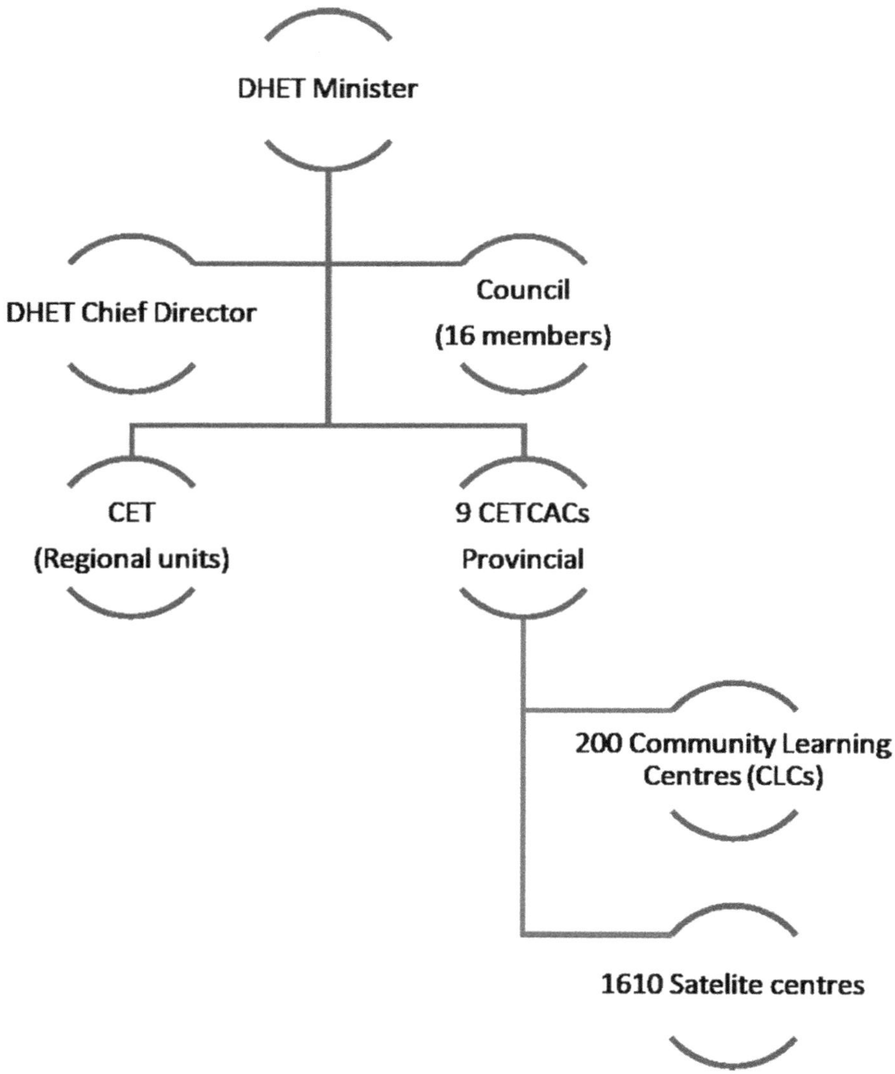

2. THEORETICAL UNDERPINNINGS

The chapter employs systems and transformational leadership theories. System theory is commonly used to understand the interrelationships of the systems and to get a holistic picture of all the interrelated parts of the system. Transformational leadership theory can identify the need for change, gain the agreement and commitment of others, and create a vision that guides change and embeds the change. Both approaches advocate for continuous improvement, organisational learning and feedback loops. The role of leaders in an open system involves monitoring inputs, throughputs, output and feedback loops and making changes where necessary to increase organisational effectiveness or goal achievement.

Transformational leadership theory has four concepts as follows. **Idealised Influence (II)**—this concept perceives leadership as charismatic, and followers seek to identify with and emulate the leader. **Inspirational Motivation (IM)**—these leaders inspire followers with challenge and persuasion, providing meaning and understanding. They articulate a compelling vision of the future, and followers want to meet and demonstrate commitment to goals and shared vision. **Intellectual Stimulation (IS)**—leadership is intellectually stimulating, expanding the followers' use of their abilities. These are new ideas and creative problem solutions, and the leader gets followers to look at problems from many angles. **Individualised Consideration (IC)**—followers and colleagues are developed to create higher potential opportunities in a supportive climate. Interactions with followers are personalised, and the leader spends time teaching and coaching.

Systems theory complements the transformational leadership theory. The systems theory as an organisational theory has concepts such as **system within a system** that comes with the three elements—input, throughput and output—and the environment and feedback loop. The other concept is **systems thinking,** a framework for seeing interrelationships rather than things and patterns of change rather than static 'snapshots.

Often, leadership decisions cause many complex and unforeseen reactions. Therefore, systems theory accepts an ability to understand interactions and relationships in complex, dynamic systems that leaders are surrounded by and embedded in (Senge, 2006). Systems theory further encourages leaders to use such concepts as continuous incremental improvement, organisational learning, and feedback loops. Ackoff (1999) stated that a transformational leader must understand a system's nature and how the transformation of a system differs from a transition. He further argued that a system is transformed when the type of system is thought to be changed; therefore, a transformational leader can produce or encourage and facilitate the production of a mobilising vision of a transformed system. Equally important is that the leader must be able to inspire, organise, or effectively pursue that vision and maintain it even when sacrifices are required. Hence, Briggs et al. (2012) have argued that systems theory is suited to explain leadership practices and actions in a specific school or university.

Visionary and courageous leaders are needed to: challenge the prevailing paradigm; sacrifice personal and organisational interests for systemic benefits; enhance inter-organisational collaboration; and advocate for change. People in leadership roles need not be traditional heroic, charismatic individuals; leadership can and should be distributed throughout organisations over time. Workers at all system levels can be transformational leaders by challenging basic assumptions about how education is delivered; mobilising around a shared vision of equity and efficiency; and elevating all stakeholders' values, vision, mission, and morals. An organisational culture that embraces such leadership is critical. Using multiple methods, this chapter aimed to establish how leadership is distributed and how this contributes to the effectiveness of change management in the two CET colleges.

Given the above explanation and understanding of transformational leadership and systems theories, it is clear that leaders in organisations may benefit from understanding and applying the systems approach to transform the organisations. This will give them a better understanding of how the different parts of the organisation connect and interrelate. The understanding will result in applying the necessary skills to optimise the whole. Organisations are effective if they are led effectively. Therefore, leaders must think about relationships between and among departments instead of thinking about them as independent components. Figure 2 below reflects the three concepts, showing how the two theories interface with these concepts.

Figure 2. The interface of change management and leadership theories

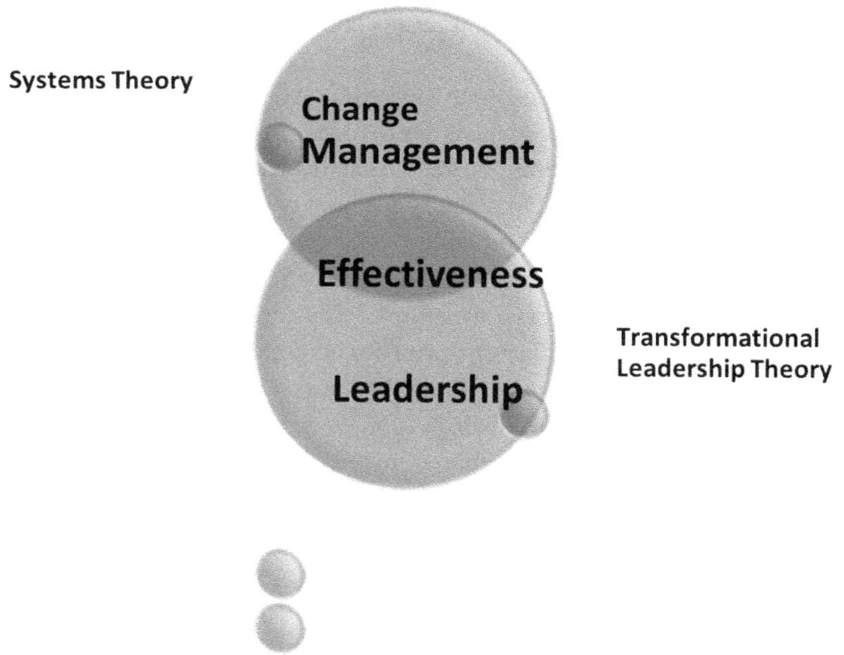

3. RESULTS AND ANALYSIS

The primary data source is my doctoral thesis submitted in fulfilment of a doctoral degree at the University of KwaZulu Natal PhD study on the experiences of CET college stakeholders on the leadership of organisational change management. The study was located in two provinces. This research study used four data generation techniques. Purposeful sampling was used, and the data was collected from those in governance and leadership structures. The arguments presented in this chapter have adequately offered contextual factors which resulted in the claims made below.

Figure 3. Data presentation

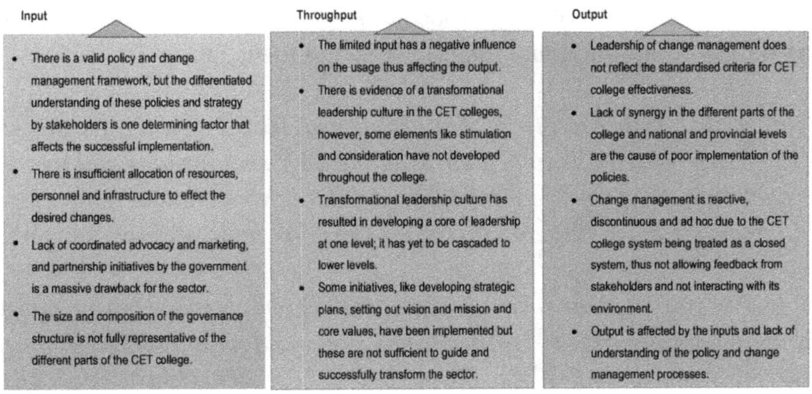

Similar data was used for this chapter, and the results are discussed below using examples from the data.

3.1 Policy, Strategy, and Change Management as Enablers

To facilitate change management, it is imperative to have a framework that includes policy, strategy, and change management principles. Such a framework would guide decision-making, clarifying the reasons behind the specific course of action and identifying the when, how, and by whom implementation should be evaluated. Policies and strategies play a crucial role as inputs for both change management and systems theory. The respondents agreed that there are policies and frameworks to manage the transition from PALCs to CETs. Below are some examples showing the respondents' support for the statement:

There is a clear framework in place and the framework regarding the governance and administration of these institutions, so there is clarity in how things should happen, so the framework is in place. (Interview Participant 10)

It is evident, and there is also a clear sector plan which determines imperatives in line with the NDP that describes where they should be by 2030. (Interview Participant 2)

I think we've got excellent policies with good intentions. (Interview Participant 9)

Some primary stakeholders also concurred with the above views about the availability of robust policy frameworks. The primary stakeholder shared a picture similar to the above statements but also alluded that provincial strategies have unrealistic targets and are not understood at the CLC and satellite levels. Below are revealing quotes from individual interviewees and focus group discussions:

The targets could be more realistic; they are very high, and we did raise this with the branch when they were still conceptualising the CET sector plans and the colleges cannot reach those targets. We were told we don't have a choice; the college must see that they reach those targets. (Interview Participant 3)

As a college, we need a clear strategic plan. It is overemphasised in some parts. It is unrealistic in other factors, and Minister has suggested a total review of the targets as the current ones will never be achieved in 5 to 10 years. Minister acknowledged that the plans were done without a budget and thus targets were thumb sucked. (Interview Participant 6)

Here are some of the statements picked up from focus group discussions relating to the CLCs and satellites level:

There are documents given to us, but because of the amount of work, we have not read them, and as a result, we cannot say what they are saying. (Focus Group 2)

We are bombarded with policies but can't implement them because we don't understand them. The whole process is messed up. (Focus Group 1)

A few of those interviewed at the college level indicated that nothing is guiding them. Interview Participant 1 commented, "There is no guideline; we are on our own, to be honest". Another interviewee alluded to the notion that:

Things were not clearly stated, and a lot was not right. Us and DHET were trying to find our feet, and we would ask DHET questions, and they would not give us answers and say, 'sisaqala, bekezelelani kuzolunga [translated to English as we are starting, hang in there, and things will get better]. (Interview Participant 6)

The function came from provincial education departments; for some reason, each province did whatever it wanted with what it wanted in the sector. The common factor is that each province was running the sector through circulars. They were reactive and will issue circulars to address issues as they unfold. There was no solid base with policies, although there was an ABET Act. It was at a superficial level in a way. There weren't policies that grounded or guided the space. As the head office (DHET), we had to backtrack to ' establish policies and ensure that policy frameworks were in place so that we talk the same language across the colleges and provinces. (Interview Participant 10)

3.2 Governance and Management Structure as Part of CET Enabling Environment

Successful implementation of change in organisations requires a wide range of governance and management structures, leadership behaviours and competencies. As mentioned earlier, introducing the new CET model in South Africa required the government to create structural and operational changes to how the adult education system would be managed. The stakeholders presented their views on the size, shape, competencies and responsibilities of the council and college management.

The findings revealed that the governance structure (council) in colleges did not mirror the composition, meaning that both councils did not have the full complement of members. It was established that not having a full complement was due to resignations and difficulty recruiting people with the required expertise. Colleges were unable to fill the donor representative portfolio. Failure to recruit a donor meant that even with no resignations during the term, the council was non-compliant as they did not have a full council. Lack of track record and understanding was raised as a significant reason for not recruiting and maintaining council members.

We have no donor, regardless of our efforts to find one; we have tried all means within our power, including approaching the Chamber of Business. This is a national problem; all councils in South Africa do not have donor representatives—the challenge is a lack of sector understanding. They do not see the value in participating. They won't be interested if they are unsure of 'what's in it' for them. (Interview Participant 6) the stakeholders perceive that the colleges' senior management is incompetent, and it is insinuated that their understanding of the sector is limited.

Leadership doesn't know what they are doing. The shoes are too big for them. They appointed people who have never been in AET, and they think college is TVET. They left out people there since the beginning, and we are led by people who don't understand the sector. (Focus Group 1)

This finding raises concerns about whether the contribution made by the leadership is meant to assist the sector in transitioning and achieving its mandated objectives.

3.3 Leadership Style, Behaviours, and Skills of Those in Governance and Management Structures

College leadership at the council and management level ensures the system transforms in the desired direction. Hence it became essential to determine what leadership styles, behaviour and skills the college leadership and management adopted.

Significant differences exist between the two questionnaires in that followers rated the leaders differently from how the leaders rated themselves. A picture that emerged is that a combination of transactional and transformational leadership was evident among the colleges' leadership. Transformational leadership scored higher than transactional leadership, although the difference is not significantly high.

You need leaders who love the community and who have passion and patience. Who are proactive and hardworking. (Interview Participant 3)

We need leaders who know the system and are hands-on with issues—the list is endless.

I think the required leader is a person who can change with time. (Interview Participant 1)

We need leaders that can collaborate with others. Collaborative planning and responsibility are required, demanding collective accountability, and I think our management needs to strengthen in that area. (Interview Participant 10).

4. IMPLEMENTATION OF THE DESIRED CHANGE

To initiate significant changes in an organisation, there needs to be a reason for the change, followed by strategic planning and setting the organisational vision, mission, objectives, values, and principles. Establishing what needs to be changed is made possible by diagnosing the problem and understanding the policy imperatives and the environment.

Only 48% of respondents indicated curriculum and programme offerings as the significant change in the sector. However, they could not identify the main problem to be addressed and possible solutions considered to solve the problem. Below are statements that summarise the essence of what was said:

The aim is to move from basic education to higher education. This was because they [the government] realised that basic education did not address skills and thought. After all, skills are the main focus of Higher Education. (Focus Group 2)

DHET officials must go to CET colleges and centres to give a clear directive. This needs to be clarified. Otherwise, it will affect the implementation. (Focus Group 1)

I think we have to look deeper at the social challenges in the first place. In my view, this will help us to find out the 'common denominator'- [meaning what is common and is the root cause] and focus CET college towards addressing those. Check what led to the need, and find the common factor determining the vision or focus for change. (Interview Participant 1)

However, there is no capacity to implement the changes. Data revealed only an 18 per cent high capacity to transition from PALCs to the community college model. Figure 4 below shows varying views on the capacity level to clarify a need or reason for moving from PALCs to the college model. Thirty-six percent of respondents said there is full capacity and 18% said there is a high capacity, while 37% and 9% said there is moderate to low capacity, respectively.

4.1 How CET Leadership Managed and Contributed to the Implementation of Desired Change

4.1.1 Transformational Leadership Elements

4.1.1.1 Idealised Influence (II)

This element addresses whether a leader maintains subordinates' trust, faith, and respect; exhibits dedication to them; appeals to their ideals, hopes and dreams; and acts as a role model. Five of the 30 participants were perceived as less favourable in this element.

Figure 4. Clarity on mandate, vision, and mission

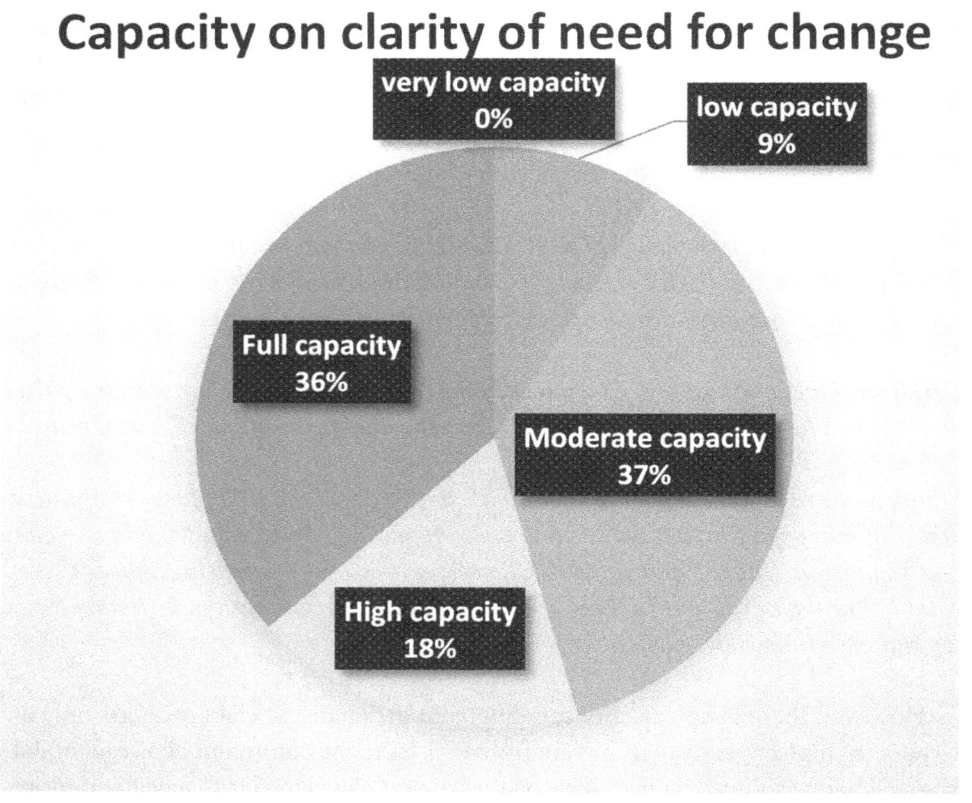

… indicated that she practices an open-door policy. She advised letting her subordinates feel free to ask for assistance and input. She allows them to find solutions, and she does not come across as her way is the only way, and she says this helps accomplish several things. (Interview Participant 8)

4.1.1.2 Inspirational Motivation (IM)

This element of transformational leadership pertains to how leaders articulate a compelling vision of the future and make others feel their work is significant. Participants from the focus group discussions felt that they were not fully aware of the vision and mission of the college. Other participants did not want to respond to the question, and some participants were unclear about the meaning of the term 'vision'.

4.1.1.3 Intellectual Stimulation (IS) and Individualised Consideration (IC)

This transformational leadership element relates to the degree that leaders expand the followers' use of their abilities and creativity by questioning assumptions, reframing problems, and approaching old situations in new ways. Individualised consideration is the fourth and final element of transformational leadership. It focuses on whether leaders pay special attention to each follower's needs, supporting the follower, mentoring and coaching. During the focus group discussion, most participants expressed negative feelings that their managers pay no particular attention to their needs.

Management and Council are not close to us. They are too far, and they don't see our pain. They make promises and do not fulfil them...the leadership doesn't know what they are doing. The shoes are big for them. (Focus Group 1)

No one has been trained since they took over, and we are eager to see what they are coming up with for centre managers and educators. (Focus group 2)

I pay attention to my subordinates' well-being by constantly observing if they are still coping. To prevent people from taking sick leave, one must always monitor their well-being. (Interview Participant 8)

However, in focus group discussions, responses differed from the views of the college leadership. Subordinates were categorical that "they do not get immediate support for the programmes they initiate". Further probing of the subordinates about working relationships revealed that collaboration, sharing ideas, teamwork, and core values are not encouraged. Most participants expressed negative feelings during the focus group discussion, noting that their managers paid no particular attention to their needs.

Among the four elements of transformational leadership, the followers perceive their leaders to be high on idealised influence and inspirational motivation, with 76% and 82%, respectively, and low on intellectual stimulation and individual consideration, with 41% and 58%, respectively. However, leaders rated themselves an average of 90% across all four elements. Yet, when they were asked (in Interview question 2.2) to describe their leadership styles, many interviewees could not respond to this question. Those who did respond made it clear that transformational leadership behaviours were prevalent in the college. The same is evident with the transactional leadership elements, where leaders scored themselves higher than the followers. It was noticeable that there were low scores in the laissez-faire element, with 29% by the followers and 50% by leaders.

4.1.2 Transactional Leadership Elements

4.1.2.1 Contingent Reward (CR)

This is the first of the three elements of transactional leadership. It focuses on the active and positive exchange between leaders and followers, whereby followers are rewarded or recognised for accomplishing agreed-upon objectives. Thirty percent of the participants perceived their leaders noticeably less favourably in this element, and most responses were from the followers

I send personalised emails to my subordinates to acknowledge their contribution. During face-to-face meetings, I share their contribution with the rest of the team, and I hope that it will motivate others to make meaningful contributions. (Interview Participant 7)

4.1.2.2 Management-by-Exception (ME)

This element of transactional leadership focuses on whether leaders tell others of the job requirements and watch for deviations from rules and standards, take corrective action and intervene only if standards are not met. The data shows that 92% of leaders strongly support this element, telling their followers about the job requirements and monitoring them continuously. However, only 64% of followers are in agreement.

People appreciate communication, such as communicating with them on things that affect our operations. Then give feedback on how the district has done, provide support, and intervene where possible. (Interview Participant 9)

Management cannot just come when it's time for evaluation, but they must be involved throughout by sharing expectations and standards of performance. They must also support us throughout the process. (Interview Participant 4)

4.1.2.3 Laissez-Faire (LF)

This is the last element of transactional leadership, and it measures whether leaders require little of others, abdicate responsibilities and avoid making decisions. Data revealed that there is agreement from both followers and leaders as they are shown relatively less favourably for this element, which means that leaders avoid making decisions.

5. MEASUREMENT OF ORGANISATIONAL CHANGE MANAGEMENT OF THE CET SYSTEMS

Pedraza (2014) alluded to the importance of consensus on the criteria for measuring organisational effectiveness because no one size fits all. This section will explore three areas: What criteria measure CET college models' effectiveness? Who is responsible for measuring CET colleges' effectiveness and how they are doing in their roles? How successful or effective are the CET colleges?

5.1 What Criteria Are Used to Measure the Success/Effectiveness of Organisational Change Management of the CET Colleges?

The chapter revealed that the six clusters of strategic levers in the National Implementation Plan are the critical success factors for the realisation of the CET college vision and, therefore, the success measures for the CET college's effectiveness. Below is a list of the strategic levers or success factors listed in the implementation plan (DHET, 2019) and identified as the measures of success.

- Qualifications, Programmes and Curriculum
- Advocacy and Stakeholders' Engagement
- Partnerships and Linkages
- Funding and Financing
- Institutional Planning and Development
- Monitoring, Evaluation and Research

Each of the strategic levers contains different elements. For example, the Qualifications, Programmes, and Curriculum cluster have the following components: a) increasing youth and adult access to community education and training opportunities; b) ensuring the delivery of responsiveness programmes that cater for the diversity of students and articulation outcomes; c) improving the youth and adult success in community education and training programmes and qualifications; and d) improving the quality of provision in CET colleges.

The *National Policy for the Monitoring and Evaluation of CET Colleges* (DHET, 2016) revealed the following areas as three listed below as focal areas for monitoring and evaluation:

a) Education, training, and development (teaching and learning management, student enrolment, and admission, qualifications, programmes, and curriculum; supply, adequacy, and quality of teaching and learning support materials; lecturer demand, supply, quality, development, and support; student performance; examination and assessment; student and community support; strategic partnerships and linkages)

b) Planning, institutional development and support (functionality of the council; functionality of the academic board; functionality of the representative student council; functionality of other committees of council; advocacy and community mobilisation; infrastructure development, acquisition, and maintenance)

c) Financial management capacity and systems (annual reports and audited financial statements)

Figure 5. Criteria to measure success from questionnaire participants

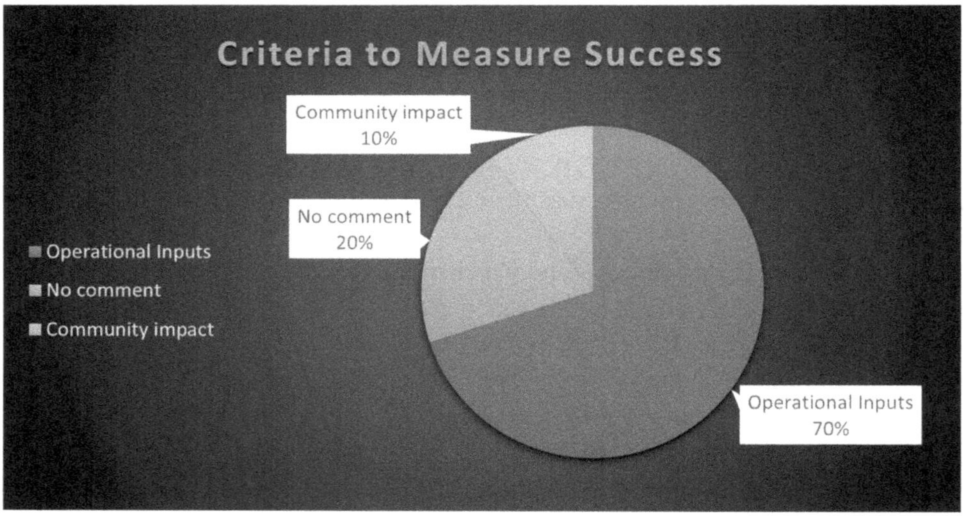

The finding in this chapter suggests that only 10% of the questionnaire participants mentioned community impact as a criterion to measure success. This is significant to this chapter because it impacts the colleges' mandate to bring about social change in communities.

The measurement of CET college effectiveness must be based on their impact on their communities. I think they [CET colleges] use traditional measurement tools such as throughput or pass rate. (Interview Participant 1)

Surprisingly, participants from the focus group discussions responded negatively and said that there were no criteria to measure the success or effectiveness of the organisational change management of the CET college model because there was nothing to measure. When probed further, both focus groups' participants alluded to the non-availability of resources. This was consistent with the 70% of the interview participants who stated lack of operational inputs as the measure of success,

What transpired is that those who agreed to the existence of measures were council representatives and those in management positions. At the same time, the other 45% who objected were secondary stakeholders. When probed further, one of the participants of the organisational effectiveness questionnaire argued that *"DHET and CET want to claim when there is a success but don't want to take responsibility when there are failures."*

I conclude that only one out of the six strategic levers is used to measure CET colleges' effectiveness. This indicates a lack of understanding of what needs to be measured and poor performance on those entrusted with this responsibility since they are unsuccessful and unable to contribute to social change or to fulfil their mandate or vision.

5.2. How Successful or Effective are the CET Colleges in Organisational Change Management?

Pedraza (2014) has stated that organisational effectiveness measures big-picture performance across various criteria. Financial performance, long-term planning, internal structure, and adherence to core values may all be critical components in understanding organisational effectiveness.

The qualitative data obtained from the interviews had varied views on the meaning of effectiveness. Some participants viewed effectiveness or success as the pass rate of learners; others considered effectiveness to reflect meeting community needs or achieving the organisational vision and mission. Most interview participants declined to comment on the success and effectiveness of the CET colleges, which suggests they are unhappy with the college's effectiveness.

I can answer that question passionately and say we are successful since we have an unqualified audit. But when it comes to other means of reaching the community, we are far from it. (Interview Participant 7)

They [CET colleges] perform way below 40%. This [referring to change management] is taken as a game. Until someone at DHET takes the implementation of policies seriously, there will be no improvement. (Focus Group 1)

All participants agreed that there should be concerted efforts to strengthen the M&E sector. Some even suggested collaboration with universities to develop a comprehensive monitoring tool. Such suggestions and proposals for collaboration with universities are a phenomenon that has been around for a while. Aitchison (2003) has mentioned that universities play a significant role in adult education and have been identified as critical stakeholders in the *National Implementation Plan* of the CET college model.

6. DISCUSSION

This chapter showed that leaders do not view the CET college holistically, or there is no holism. The conclusion is that the college is viewed as a closed system with no feedback loops. An implication of this is that CET colleges are not open to their environment and thus cannot receive and give feedback. This creates an environment where stakeholders need to be more valued and engaged. Even the leaders in the subsystems do not view CET colleges holistically. As a result, change management needs to be more active, and ad hoc.

CET college must adopt a more inclusive and collaborative approach by encouraging and utilising feedback to create a culture of engagement and empowerment. Leaders must think about relationships between and among departments instead of thinking about them as independent components. Leadership that is visionary, courageous, competent, and passionate about the sector—committed to the job, sector and community and people that s/he leads—are needed to challenge the prevailing paradigm.

From the above is that a system is always more than the sum of its parts and that a system also forms part of a larger whole or system. Leaders may benefit from understanding and applying the systems approach to transform their organisations.

Senge (2006) agreed that for organisations to be led effectively, leaders must think about relationships between and among departments instead of thinking about them as independent components. A lack of understanding of the subparts of the CET college model/system (community, local municipalities and general businesses) is detrimental to its success.

The contribution to organisational change involves three major components. The first one is to rally support from all role-players, creating a conducive organisational culture and setting internal work processes that support the successful implementation of change. These factors explain the relatively good correlation between understanding what to change, the actual change, and the calibre of leadership.

The chapter found that CET college leadership needs to understand what needs to be changed. If the diagnosis only identifies one of several problems, the changes may fail to achieve the desired outcome. Therefore, a change in one part of a system will eventually affect other components, and reactions to the change may cancel out the consequences.

I argue that managing change requires transformational leadership skills and mindsets. This argument is supported by Yukl (2013), who emphasises that leading and managing change is one of the most important and challenging responsibilities for leaders. The broad picture that emerged from this chapter was that transformational leadership is not broadly inherent in CET colleges. The current chapter found that Idealised Influence and Intellectual Motivation were positive. Still, the contradiction is that they failed to rally support for change, and the few that were negative are significant and are from those in lower levels of management. This indicates that these leadership behaviours have yet to cascade throughout all CET college management levels.

Another important finding was that Inspirational Stimulation and Individualised Consideration overwhelmingly received negative responses from participants, much weaker support than the other two elements. These elements of transformational leadership pertain to how leaders articulate a compelling vision of the future and make others feel their work is significant, as well as a leader's interest in another's well-being, consideration of individual ability and preference, and promoting involvement in the group. Therefore, the need for a shared vision suggests a weak link between the understanding and interpretation of the policy and change management. This finding has important implications that may be explained as a failure by the leadership to manage and contribute to change management.

However, because the findings were unable to demonstrate 'contribution to social change' as a metric of success, it did not support previous research by Baatjes and Mathe (2004) and the OECD (2019), which advocated and made a strong case for effective institutions that will contribute significantly to citizens' well-being. This implies they have no linkage or synergy with the mandate for the CET college model. This chapter supports the conclusion that the CET college model/system subparts must be better understood.

These findings support Pedraza's (2014) conclusion that highly effective organisations excel in five areas: leadership, decision-making, structure, people, work processes and systems, and culture. Because this chapter could not demonstrate any of the benefits above, the CET colleges were deemed unsuccessful. These findings further concur with Pedraza (2014), who concluded that highly effective organisations exhibit strengths across five areas: leadership, decision-making and structure; people; work processes and systems; and culture. This chapter has not shown any of the strengths mentioned above, thus deeming the CET colleges ineffective.

The findings support Todnem's (2005) assertion that organisational change management is reactive, discontinuous, and ad hoc. The most plausible cause is a lack of leadership abilities to drive the change management process, which results in a lack of understanding of how to implement and manage change properly.

7. CONCLUSION AND RECOMMENDATIONS

In conclusion, one needs to reflect on how to bridge this gap. Evidence suggests that the South African Adult education system has excellent policies, strategies and change frameworks. What is needed is to ensure a shared understanding and interpretation of these frameworks by all stakeholders, especially those entrusted with the implementation. One way is to engage meaningfully with all subsystems of the CET system to ensure an equal understanding of the interdependence of each subsystem. Also, ensure that each subsystem contributes meaningfully to the Adult Continuing Education and Training (ACET) sector to reduce unemployment, poverty, and inequality, improve social cohesion, and achieve social justice.

Therefore, the findings of this chapter could contribute to informing a leadership style and change management framework that could ensure that this new model does not flounder like past programmes and interventions in adult education; instead, that these institutions are meeting their intended objectives as set out in the national policy and are deemed fit for purpose. Leadership and management in adult education must adapt to the needs of learners, instructors, and staff. Leadership theories such as transformational, servant, and situational are identified as best practices for communicating, motivating, and empowering teams.

Adult education leaders and managers must prioritise a learning culture for learners and staff. Adult education programmes often collaborate with various stakeholders, including instructors, learners, funders, and community partners. Leaders and managers in adult education must be able to build and maintain positive relationships with these stakeholders while also managing competing interests and priorities. Leaders and managers in adult education must operate with high ethical standards, ensuring that their actions align with the values and principles of the sector.

Strong leadership and management influence are needed if the change is to succeed and be effective. For this reason, the leadership and management need to support and remain accountable through the organisational change process. The leadership must be prepared to sacrifice personal and organisational interests for systemic benefits, thus enhancing inter-organisational collaboration and advocating for change.

I recommend that governance structures suitable for CET colleges, rather than replicating the TVET college governance model, are set up to include representation of the communities in which the CET colleges are located. This will ensure that the community's needs are considered and that the colleges' strategic plans respond to the community's needs. For the sector to partner, they need to embark on advocacy initiatives. This can be done by ensuring that transformational leadership behaviours are embedded at all levels to embrace stakeholder involvement and humanness.

While an unqualified audit opinion is essential for financial accountability, more is needed to indicate success in achieving the intended impact of CET colleges on the community. A shift in focus is necessary to prioritise community impact as a measure of effectiveness and success. Therefore, there is a need to develop more effective and relevant criteria for measuring CET colleges' success and improving policy implementation and evaluation processes. I suggest that performance measures/ or measures of success include the impact the CET colleges make on employability and poverty. One way is through meaningful engagement with all subsystems of the CET colleges to ensure an equal understanding of each subsystem's interdependence. Also, ensure that each subsystem contributes meaningfully to the ACET sector to reduce unemployment, poverty, and inequality, improve social cohesion, and achieve social justice.

The findings suggest that CET colleges are implementing a generic change management programme due to a lack of careful diagnosis of the respective CET college's problems. Based on these findings, the chapter recommends adopting a 'go slow to go fast' approach. This suggests that more time should be spent preparing for change so that when change is implemented, there is synergy and the process for change is seamless. The implication is that sufficient time should be spent on creating conditions for change by building a coalition, communicating and sharing the vision and ensuring that all stakeholders understand and share the same vision and are meeting towards a common goal. The second recommendation is that a silo mentality in the sector should be avoided. There should be synergy within the CET sector. Change may become slow if the silo mentality in planning is not eliminated.

7.1 Change Management Process for South African CET Colleges

Based on the research findings from this chapter, I recommend the following proposed three-phase change management process for CET colleges in SA.

7.2 The First Phase: Setting the Scene

This phase must include a detailed analysis of the problem using the soft systems methodology. Checkland (1995) argued that its aim is to improve social concerns by activating a learning cycle, ideally never-ending, in the people involved in the situation. Part of this phase should also include identifying vested stakeholders. The policy experts must determine cause and effect relationships between and among stakeholders to ensure that all the stakeholders are clear and understand the interdependence of the different parts of the CET college from the onset. This phase also is where the anticipated issues in the interpretation of the policies are identified and clarified to ensure clarity in the implementation phase.

7.3 The Second Phase: Planning for a Change

The change agents should spend more time in this phase to ensure that it is realistic and that the change management plan has considered the CET college contexts. The regional directorate should drive the planning for change, and it should involve all relevant stakeholders. A communication and feedback loop is necessary to encourage interactions and adaptation to environmental changes. There are several more detailed activities needed to ensure that all inputs to achieve the purpose are in place, and these are:

1. Conducting a thorough needs analysis followed by setting clearly articulated strategic goals and missions with realistic and measurable targets, timelines, and quality criteria so that these can be measured and evaluated against the identification and appointment of project stakeholders.
2. Agreeing on project scope and understanding the KPIs.
3. Creating a communication plan. The communication plan is crucial because having clear communication helps the upper management get frequent updates. The team involved in the change process feels management heeds their feedback and concerns.
4. Detailing and substantial allocation of resources (financial, human resources, and infrastructural) to facilitate and manage change.
5. Selection of pilot sites. Pilot sites must combine different contexts and be managed by permanent full-time staff.

7.4 The Third Phase: Implementing the Change Plan

This phase should follow the steps defined in the previous stage. The change agents should empower the teams to take proper steps to attain the pre-set goals. During the change implementation process, it is common to expect barriers. The change agent must pay attention to them (include additional and continuous training and upskilling), have a well-planned organisational structure, adopt new systems to accommodate new techniques, and update job descriptions relating to new workloads. When required, adjust the change process—record learnings and adapt the change process to fit into the CET college requirements. It is better to make slight changes than keep the same plan and fail to execute it. Changes must also be incorporated

Figure 6. Llm proposed change management process for CET colleges

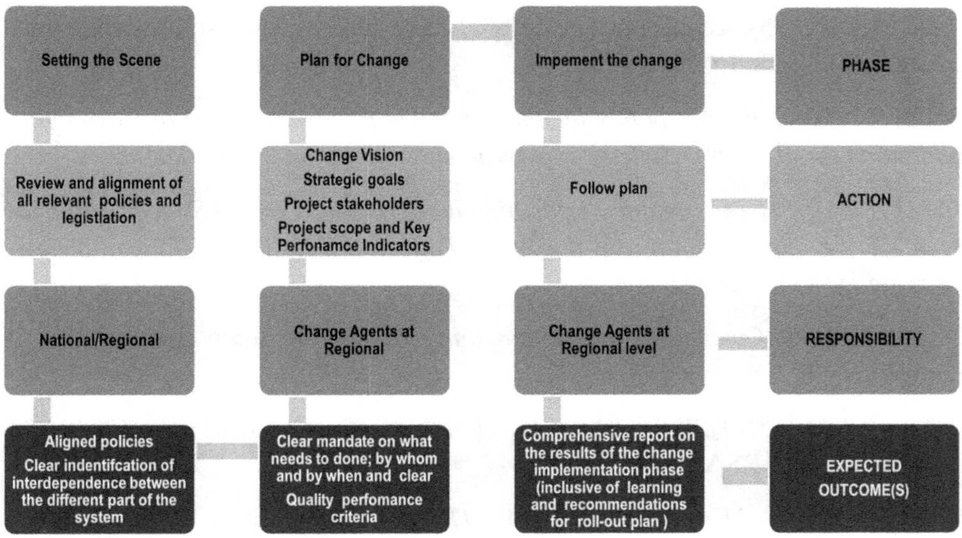

into the organisation's culture, which means the goal has been reached. Incorporating the principle of continuous learning and improvement will help to involve further changes, as there is always scope for improvement.

While the pilot is proceeding, other PALCS will continue operating as usual until the change management's final evaluation report, followed by a wide rollout, which is dependent on the results of the pilots. Below is the graphical representation of the three phases.

REFERENCES

Ackoff, R. L. (1999, June/July). A Lifetime of Systems Thinking. *The Systems Thinker, 10*(5).

Aitchison, J. (2003). Brak! - Vision, mirage and reality in the post apartheid globalisation of South African adult education and training. *Journal of Education*, (31), 47–74.

Baatjes, I., & Mathe, K. (2004). Adult education and social change in South Africa (1993-2004). *Changing class: Education and social change inpost-apartheid South Africa*, 393-420. HSRC Press.

Briggs, A. R., Morrison, M., & Coleman, M. (2012). *Research methods in educational leadership and management*. Sage Publications. doi:10.4135/9781473957695

Davis, A. D. (2015). A conceptual model of systems thinking leadership in community colleges, 333-353. Springer.

DHET. (2016). *National policy for the monitoring and evaluation of Community Education and Training Colleges. Government Gazette No.39867*. DHET.

DHET. (2019). *The Community Education and Training College System: National Plan for the implementation of the White Paper for Post-School Education and Training System*. Pretoria: DHET.

OECD. (2019). *Community Education and Training in South Africa*. (OECD Publishing)

Pedraza, J. M. (2014). *What is organizational effectiveness How an organization could achieve it?* RSA.

Senge, P. (2006). *The fifth discipline: The art and practice of the learning organisations*. Currency, Doubleday.

Todnem, R. (2005). Organisational change management: A critical review. *Journal of Change Management*, *5*(4), 369–380. doi:10.1080/14697010500359250

Yukl, G. (2013). *Leadership in organisations*. Pearson.

Chapter 6
Assessment of Indigenous Language Archive Preservation in South Africa

Nkholedzeni Sidney Netshakhuma
https://orcid.org/0000-0003-0673-7137
University of Cape Town, South Africa

ABSTRACT

The purpose of the study is to assess the role of indigenous language archives preservation by the Selected provincial archives with the view to promote socio-economic wellbeing of marginalized societies. The indigenous language archives are necessary to establish the socio -economic wellbeing of their communities and individuals. These rights of using indigenous language archives materials for education curriculum was denied during the period of the apartheid system in South Africa. People feel recognised when their archival materials are recognised by the Provincial Archives.

INTRODUCTION

This study assessed the preservation of indigenous South African language archives in the Selected Provincial Archives to recommend the best practices to promote the socio-economic well-being of marginalized societies in the province. This is the case study limited to the provincial archives of South Africa, not their entire South Africa provincial archives. The study assessed the role of indigenous language archives preservation by the Selected provincial archives with the view to promoting the socio-economic well-being of marginalized societies. The marginalized societies in

DOI: 10.4018/978-1-6684-6625-4.ch006

this case study are referred to as indigenous people segregated by the South Africa apartheid segregation policies.

The researcher assesses whether the Provincial archives preserve indigenous knowledge culture, traditions, and norms records in South Africa. The preservation of indigenous language culture is significant to the transformation of society in South Africa. A community may fill honored when their archive materials are preserved by local archives.

A close look at the indigenous languages archives highlights that indigenous languages are underrepresented in the provincial archives of South Africa. Very little research has been written on archiving initiatives of indigenous language archives in the Selected province of South Africa. This study fills gaps in the literature on indigenous language archives in Southern Africa. More research is required on the impact of language and culture on archives management.

HISTORICAL BACKGROUND

The Selected Province is located in the eastern part of South Africa., bordering Eswatini and Mozambique. The Selected rovince Under the direction of the provincial archivists, the Selected provincial archives provide leadership in the coordination of archives services throughout the province to promote the socio-economic well-being of marginalized societies. The Selected provincial archives mandate includes the preservation of the South African indigenous language archives. The enactment of the Mpumalanga Archives Act No 14 of 1998 Section 3 (g) promotes the empowerment and upliftment through archival usage of indigenous people (Mpumalanga Archives Act 1998). This implies that indigenous language archives may be used for curriculum development for school activities. Therefore the Selected Provincial Archives may collaborate with the Department of Education to ensure that archives materials became part of the educational system The article is organized as follows: historical background of South African indigenous language, research methodology, the problem statement, literature review on indigenous languages, data analysis, discussions, and recommendations.

SOUTH AFRICAN INDIGENOUS LANGUAGE

The apartheid enacted racial laws to exclude community initiatives to collect indigenous language archives by the National Archives of South Africa (Bhebhe 2021). The apartheid government ensured that indigenous language archives were not collected by the State Archives (known as the National Archives of South Africa)

(Netshakhuma, 2021). In Australia, the loss of indigenous language archives is closely associated with the violation of indigenous lands, the destruction of a land claim, and the involuntary incorporation of indigenous people (Shephard 2016). South Africa's transformation from the apartheid system to a democratic state in 1994 requires an archives institution to collect and preserve indigenous language archives. South Africa's transformation which led to the adoption of the Constitution of the Republic of South Africa Act No. 106 of 1996 and the National Archives and Records Services Act No. 46 of 1996 led to the recognition of indigenous language archives (Ngoepe and Nkwe 2018, p. 134).

Collection and preservation of language archives are part of the right of indigenous peoples to their land and cultural and economic self-determination. Language retention is a human rights issue. Therefore, cultural transformation requires government commitment to human rights. Language revitalization program depends on the situation in which the language finds itself.

To minimize conflicts that come as a result of the indigenous languages, the Constitution of the Republic of South Africa Act No. 106 of 1996 recognized eleven languages. Language documentation encodes more than just linguistic information (Holton 2012). The South African Centre for Digital Language Resources (SADilLar) supports research and development in the domains of language technologies and language-related studies in humanities and social sciences(https://sadilar.org/index.php/en/about.). The SADilar has a digitization and digital humanities program to develop a language program. This implies that the promotion of indigenous language promotes the socioeconomic well-being of marginalized individuals through the use of language. Language archives connect users such as language communities, linguistics, and researchers (Burke 2021). Culture influences the type of records preserved by communities. Issues of inclusion and exclusion of language archives contribute to the promotion of a democratic state (Van der Merwe 2015). The Bill of human rights enshrined in the Constitution of the Republic of South Africa recognized indigenous languages (Satgoor 2015, p. 97). Language preservation includes information related to marriage and other cultural artifacts. Language documentation had a long and diversified history in South Africa.

RESEARCH METHOD

A quantitative approach was used by the research to collect data. Structured interviews and questionnaires were used to collect data. The quantitative data were collected together, using both questionnaires and interviews. applied for this research. Data were analyzed and interpreted in a statistical format. The 20 participants were recruited as they were affiliated with the Selected provincial archives under being records managers of various ministries or departments and municipalities in the province. The population was deemed to be uniform because the researcher believed the participants sought to enhance the collection and preservation of indigenous language archives, all of which support the Selected provincial archives mission. It was appropriate for the researcher to obtain first-hand information from respondents. The researcher visited participants to distribute the questionnaire. Interviews were also conducted in addition to the questionnaire. Data collection was collected in December 2021. The limitation of the collection of data was that member of the community was not included in the sample despite that they are archives material that needs to be preserved by neither National nor provincial archives

PROBLEM STATEMENT

The review of the literature shows limited collection and preservation of indigenous archives by the National Archives of South Africa to promote the socioeconomic well-being of marginalized communities (Schellnack-Kelly 2019). The collection of indigenous language archives. There is limited knowledge about indigenous language archives in the public domain relevant to language, tradition, culture, and history (Netshakhuma 2021). This is despite the national and provincial archives' mandate to collect indigenous records of enduring value including indigenous language (Mpumalanga Archives Act 1998).

Indigenous language archives are on the verge of disappearing because communities and departments were not transferring their indigenous language archives to the Mpumalanga Provincial Archives. The fundamental issue for archiving in South Africa is ensuring that indigenous language archives previously denied being collected and preserved by the national archives are collected and preserved by the provincial archives (Netshakhuma 2021). The collection and preservation of language archives should be done in collaboration with community members.

The research is of the view that information communication technology is an enabler to preserve the indigenous language.

Research questions

Answers to the following questions were provided in this study

1. Do the Selected provincial archives of South Africa play a role to preserve indigenous language archives?
2. There was any collaboration between the Selected Provincial Archives with the community to preserve the indigenous language?
3. Does the Community aware of the South Africa Copyright Act of 1978 on the preservation of indigenous language archives?

4. Do indigenous language archives are accessible to indigenous people?
5. Does Information Communication technology plays a role to preserve indigenous archives?
6. What archives management skill/training do the archivists and community possess?

LITERATURE REVIEW

Little archival science literature emerged from South Africa that interrogates the issue of language archives; therefore, it is necessary to draw particularly on the United States of America and Australian scholarship to understand the significance of language archives. The Archive of the Indigenous Languages of Latin in America (AILLA) at the University of Texas at Austin is a digital archive with a South American languages archives collection to address indigenous people's lack of access, ownership, and control over the documented history, focusing on principles of participation, cultural respect, and representation (Seifart, Drude, Fianchetto, and Gasche 2008). Several specialized language archives were established to work with indigenous people to identify indigenous language archives use for education purposes. The Open Language Archives Community (OLAC) is an international partnership of institutions and individuals to establish a worldwide virtual library of language resources to guide both non –indigenous archivists and indigenous communities. OLAC was founded in 2000 as an international partnership of institutions and individuals to preserve indigenous language archives. This collaboration of international organizations is based on the Dublin Core metadata. OLAC developed standards and processes for the management of online language resources. OLAC developed an encoding scheme known as OLAC Language for language identifiers. These initiatives provide a platform to access regional language data.

Indigenous communities in Australia engaged in language revival crave any extant records or documentation to assist in expanding their understanding of their language heritage. Archive materials have different significance to the community. Most institutions do not apply standardized metadata to describe indigenous language archives (Balogun and Kalusopa 2021). This is so because language archives are not recognized as a national heritage by most institutions. Hence Standardization is a key element to develop digital language archives. It is necessary to develop standards to facilitate search modes enabling different user groups to search various databases (Hindal and Wyller 2004).

The lack of an indigenous language archives policy in the national sphere of government to guide the collection and preservation of language archives was cited as the major challenge. The study by Bow (2019) recommended organizations adopt a policy on the collection and preservation of indigenous language archives. South Africa National Archives lack strategies for the long-term preservation of language archives(Matla 2019, p. 96). South African institutions lack policies to guide the management of records (Matlala 2019, p. 103). An integrated national framework needs to be supported with infrastructure, policy, funding, staff, and resources (Ormond-Parker 2012; 208). Digital language archives should be built upon national policy on language archives management. Languages archives are an essential component of an ethical and effective response to language endangerment (Nathan 2012 p. 287).

ROLE OF ARCHIVES INSTITUTIONS IN THE PRESERVATION OF INDIGENOUS LANGUAGE ARCHIVES

The role of archives institutions is a concern not only to archivists but to linguistics, and language practitioners responsible to preserve the language archives. This is because language archives are unique and often systematic to promote the socio-economic well-being of marginalized communities. The concern is that collections of language archives not be found in any archives (Withers 2017). The role of national archives is to preserve national records with cultural, historical, and social values that are not understood by communities (Lopang Venson, Ngoepe & Ngulube 2014, p. 58; Chilcott 2019). These national records may be used to promote the socio-economic well-being of marginalized individuals and communities. The creation of language archives designed to legitimize community archives that have been neglected by the state archives has proved to be a potent form of research, promoting a diverse society and fostering community identity among groups marginalized by elite groups (Dittmar & Entin 2016: p.3). The review of the literature shows that European archivists contribute to a representative and just society by establishing racial, ethnic, and community-based repositories (Jimerson 2007; p. 266). The language development archives represent an assertion of racial pride and an effort to secure the power that comes from being able to explain the collective story of suffering and achievement. Indigenous records constitute the cultural capital of the history and culture of a nation.

Archive institutions were criticized for not collecting indigenous communities' archives. and for being incapable of finding a place to preserve historical records. Hence, their role is to develop societies by safeguarding and contributing to individual and community memory (Shepard 2016). Archives play a role to disseminate information to various community members for educational purposes. Archive materials may be utilized for educational foundations, general education, sociology, distance education, educational leadership and management, and information and communication technology.

Archives are well-positioned to support the multicultural identities of societies. This implies that all ethnic groups should get their voices in the archives. The inclusion of an archives program is necessary for the Mpumalanga province where there are Swatis, Ndebele, and Tsongas tribal groups. Each ethnic group should have their voices in the archives materials to be interpreted and analyzed. So the issue of constructing archives intersects with the issue of rebuilding memory and identity (Ormond-Parker 2012). Constructing archives is the form of the construction of political narratives and political positions. In Australia, local Aboriginal culture and histories are embedded in local language archives that have, since the 1960s, involved a substantial uptake of technologies (Ormond – Parker and Sloggett 2012). Communities establish archives with the view of attracting indigenous people to learn about their culture, tradition, and culture.

COMMUNITY INVOLVEMENT

Most national archives did not collage with communities to collect indigenous language archives to promote the socio-economic well-being of such marginalized communities. (Thorpe & Galassi 2014 p. 91). A study conducted by Jones & O'Neill (2014. p. 121) recommends archivists participate in community engagement with the view to collecting indigenous language archives. There is a need for organizations or individuals who want to collect indigenous language archives to develop policies and frameworks for the collection of indigenous language archives. This statement is alluded to by Reid and Howard (2016, p. 196) who said that most organizations lack a formal policy on community engagement to collect indigenous language archives. A lack of formal policy highlighted by various studies in their effort to get out of the archives and into the community as a strategy to forge community connections and establish community awareness on the collection and preservation of indigenous archives(Nicholls, Booker, Thorpe, Jackson, Girault, Briggs & Jones 2016; Wasson, Holotn, and Ruth 2016).

National archives may collaborate with indigenous people with the view to providing networked access to indigenous language archives (Timms 2009). By this, the researcher means that the archives involve indigenous people in the indigenous language archives collection. Engagement with indigenous communities is a means to identify records of archival values (Chilcott 2019). The emergence of participatory archive frameworks offers language archives to engage with the community on the preservation of indigenous archives materials (Wasson, Holton, & Roth 2016). Engaging language community members in the documentation of language expand archives collections (Trilsbeek and Konig 2014). Community members are in the best positions to insert archives materials metadata.

COPYRIGHT LEGISLATION

The significance of legal and policy frameworks in the creation and preservation of language archives cannot be overemphasized (Okello-Bura 2011). Understanding the legal framework on the right of ownership is important during the collection and preservation of indigenous language archives (Garaba 2014, p. 3). This is so because of traditional protocols and procedures for some materials not to be collected by communities. Most organizations struggle to comply with a legislative framework because most of their staff are not trained on the requirement of the legislation. (Pereira 2018 p. 225). The South Africa Copyright Act of 98 of 1978, and the Constitution of the Republic of South Africa No.108 of 1996 have an impact on the collection of indigenous language archives because of restrictions to collect certain records to adhere to cultural protocols (Satgour 2015, p. 101). The Berne Convention in 1886 brought the protection of language archives (Fabunmi 2007).

South Africa signed international treaties and conventions to create an avenue for the rapid development and valuing of intellectual property. South Africa Copyright Act of 1978 gives the owner of archives, musical compositions, books, or pieces of information, the right to decide what others can do with them. Hence, archivists have a role to play in caring for and providing access to other people's copyrighted work. Copyright exceptions enable information access to indigenous language archives (Mungai, Dorvlo, Nuwagirya & Holmner 2020, p. 572). This is so because most users of copyrighted materials are not aware of their dependence on law and policy for access to information and for gaining knowledge. However, archives are underutilized because of unclear intellectual property ownership (Shepard 2016). This promotes a situation where indigenous people lack to share information with the archives institutions. Issues of rights and access to information are fundamental matters for negotiation between researchers, indigenous people, and their communities. Indigenous people are integrated into the curation of archival materials. The involvement of indigenous language speakers may transform language archives from repositories' of static objects into sites for ongoing dialogue and exchange with living communities.

The provincial archives are to apply for the exemption concerning the South Africa Copyright Act No. 98 of 1978 to ensure that certain information is accessible to various stakeholders. Copyright exceptions enable researchers to use copyrighted works to promote information access (Wanjiru-Mungai, Dorvlo, Nuwagirya, and Holmer 2020). WIPO provides a balanced intellectual property system to promote innovation and creativity for the social, cultural, and economic development of all countries (WIPO 2019).

ACCESSIBILITY OF INDIGENOUS LANGUAGE ARCHIVES

The review of the literature shows that archives materials are not collected and accessed by indigenous people in Australia (Thorpe and Galassi 2014 p. 96). The same applies to indigenous archives materials that were not collected by the National and Provincial Archives of South Africa because of the apartheid legislation. In South Africa, like in Australia, indigenous people seek access to land, in certain cases, control over indigenous language archives (Netshakhuma. 2021a). The reason for the establishment of language archives is to make archives accessible to various stakeholders (Shepard 2016). This is because language documentation is of less value if is not accessible. Accessibility to archives promotes access to knowledge of human society, promotes democracy, protects citizens' rights, and enhances human rights violations. Multi parties have the right to access archives materials (Gilliland and McKemmish (2014).

ARCHIVES MANAGEMENT SKILLS

A study conducted by Ngoepe and Katuu (2017) found that African archivists lack archives management skills to preserve indigenous language archives because of limited qualifications in archives management offered by South African universities. There are limited institutions of higher learning offering qualifications in archives and records management. This statement is alluded to by Rakemane and Mosweu (2021) who stated that staff lack of skills in archives management is a challenge to collect and preserve indigenous language archives. Baro, Obaro, & Aduba (2019) emphasized professional's archivists to equip themselves with archives management skills. Empowerment of communities with skills in archives and records management is a strategy used by the organization to equip archivists. Archivists strive for collections management under his supervision (Strom, 2012). Most archives materials are created on a digital or electronic platform which requires them to be retrained on the digital platform. Archive materials creation is influenced by technological advancement. Archival skills are necessary to equip professionals to deal with digitization and archiving of content.

INFORMATION COMMUNICATION TECHNOLOGY AS AN ENABLER TO DIGITIZE LANGAUGE ARCHIVES

There is little recognition of information communication technology as an enabler to enhance the accessibility of traditional custodial archives (Upward, McKemmish, and Reed 2011, p. 206). Digital archives for community heritage groups need to be viewed as an extension of the archives management system. (Beel, Wallace, Webster, Nguyen, Tait, Macleod, and Mellish 2017). Digitization initiatives lack adequate digital preservation infrastructure in Africa (Balogun and Kalusopa 2021, 178). An archivist in Africa is faced with the problem of preserving archives materials in their institution repositories (Olatokun 2008). Lack of organizational plan, low awareness on preservation of language archives, absence of budget dedicated to language archives. Technological obsolescence is a challenge for the preservation of language archives in Southern Africa. Information communication technology assists to make the existence of language archives online. The research conducted by Rakemane and Mosweu (2021, p. 44) stated that the adoption of information communication technologies is of little use if indigenous language archives are not collected and preserved by either national or provincial archives. The challenge faced by archival institutions is to prove the originality, authenticity, and reliability of electronic records (Ngoepe and Katuu 2017) and to make archives materials available to various stakeholders (Marowa 2015). There is always a physical threat, hardware, and software format changes, standards, accessibility and findability, functionality and usability, digitalization, or records capture (Pinnick 2017). Digital platforms assist postcolonial communities to own their stories, thereby contributing to positively identifying formation and empowerment.

DATA ANALYSIS

Data analysis is based on the interviews and questionnaires conducted with selected participants. Results were presented in line with the research questions

Table 1. Role of the archives in the preservation of indigenous language archives

Do the Archives play a role to preserve indigenous language archives?	
Number of participants (15)	No
Number of participants(5)	Yes

20 participants were asked about the role of the Selected Provincial Archives in the collection and preservation of indigenous languages archives with the view to promoting the socio-economic well-being of marginalized communities or individuals. The majority of participants (15) answered that the Selected provincial archives did not establish an archives management program to preserve the indigenous language archives.

The fact that the majority of participants are not aware of the indigenous language archives, shows a limited number of archives institutions collecting, and preserving archives materials. This was influenced by the fact that the Mpumalanga provincial archives did not employ language practitioners and linguistics to establish indigenous language archives sections. Some of the participants were of the view that the Human Rights Commission in South Africa would play a role to promote the role of language even in archives institutions by ensuring that archival materials are preserved and disseminated to various stakeholders.

Table 2. Community involvement

There was any collaboration between the Archives with the community to preserve indigenous language archives	
Number of participants (17)	No
Number of participants (3)	Yes

Twenty (20) participants were asked about the role of the Selected Provincial Archives in collaboration with communities to preserve indigenous language archives with the view to promoting the socio-economic being of marginalized communities. So, most participants (17) stated that there was less collaboration between the Mpumalanga Provincial Archives and with communities. The community engagement program will stimulate the incorporation of archives on education programs/.

The Selected Provincial Archives lack a community consultation framework with the community. The community consultation framework will play a role to build community relationships. The participants (17) interviewed stated that they are not aware of the role of either the Provincial archives or the community in the preservation of indigenous language archives. Participants (17) cited a lack of community engagement policy within the departments as the challenge to collect and preserve archives materials.

Table 3. South Africa copyright act no. 98 of 1978 compliance

Does the Community aware of South Africa Copyright Act No. 98 of 1978 on the preservation of indigenous language archive	
Number of participants (14)	YES
Number of participants (6)	NO

The twenty (20) participants were asked whether they were aware of the requirement of the South Africa Copyright Act of 1978 on the preservation of indigenous language archives to promote the socio-economic well-being of marginalized communities or individuals. The majority of participants (14) states that they were aware of the existence of the South African Copyright Act of 1978 legislation and its implication for the collection of indigenous language archives. While few of the participants (6) stated that they were not aware of such legislation requirements. Few of the participants indicated that the National Archives and Records Service Act No. 43 of 1996 and the Constitution of the Republic of South Act No. 106 of 1996 are the only law that they were aware of. From the above responses, the ability of the participants to recognize the legal requirement for copyright would mean that they will benefit from its potential. Such copyright benefits include ensuring and promoting legislative compliance, protecting the rights of stakeholders, and meeting legal requirements when selecting indigenous language archives for preservation.

Table 4. Accessibility of indigenous language archives

Do indigenous language archives accessible to indigenous people	
Number of participants (14)	YES
Number of participants (06)	NO

The purpose of this theme was to investigate the accessibility of indigenous language archives preserved by organizations with the view to promoting the socio-economic well-being of marginalized communities and individuals. The 20 participants were asked to identify the factors affecting the accessibility of indigenous language archives in the archives repository. The majority of participants (14) state poor physical conditions, lack of budget, and physical conditions may affect the availability of indigenous archives in the institutional repository. This implies that the Selected Provincial Archives need to dedicate a specific budget to the collection, and description of the indigenous archives materials.

Table 5. Information communication technology as an enabler in the digitization of language archives

Does information communication technology plays a role to preserve indigenous archives	
Number of participants (20)	YES
Number of participants (0)	NO

The fact that the National and provincial archives did not collect language archives implied that such records were not preserved in the institutional repository. Language archives are still preserved by individuals in their own space. This makes it a challenge for education departments to design education curricula using archives materials.

The future of preserving indigenous language archives lies in the ability to adapt information communication technology. 20 participants were asked about the role of information communication technology in the preservation of indigenous language archives. All participants acknowledged that information communication technology plays an essential role to preserve indigenous languages. The results show that the Selected provincial archives lack advanced information communication technology to preserve language archives in an electronic environment. The reason is that some of the storage media are outdated and the equipment is no longer available on the market. The constraint against the preservation of archives materials is inadequate funding. The Selected Provincial Archives receive no additional core funding to embark on a project to collect indigenous language archives to add to their collection. Most archives institutions in South Africa used manual systems to preserve archives materials. This implies that institutional memories collected by a particular institution may not be shared with the rest of the world. Hence there is a need to preserve indigenous language archives for educational purposes, history, and memory of the nation.

It was important to confirm if the study participants possess skills or training that enable them to collect and preserve indigenous language archives. Archivists need archives and digital management skills to collect indigenous language archives. The participants (20) were asked if they had any skills or training in archives management. The majority of participants (15) said that they did not have any training in archives

Table 6. Archives management skills

What archives management skills/training do archivists possess?	
Number of participants (15)	Lack of skills/ training
Number of participants (05)	They have skill/ training

management that helps in the collection and preservation of indigenous archives. The 5 participants who said they had archives management skills were referring to library and museum concepts. The researcher believed that those who have demonstrated little knowledge about archives management used ideas developed from their educational background not related to archives management. Their educational background might have taught them the significance of archives management. None of the archivists received any formal qualifications in archives management. Employing staff without appropriate qualifications has always occurred and increased (Shipp 2016). In South Africa, formal archives management qualifications are offered by the University of South Africa, the University of Limpopo, the University of Kwazulu Natal, and the University of Cape Town. Archives management training provides an overview of the required knowledge that help the community and archivists preserve indigenous archives.

DISCUSSION

The results of this chapter point to the fact that there were several problems associated with the collection and preservation of indigenous language archives. The findings were structured according to the theme of this research emanating from the research questions. Based on data collected from the Selected provincial archives, organizations were not playing their role to collect indigenous language archives. This implies the Selected Provincial Archives to develop a framework to collect indigenous archives. The establishment of a collaboration project between the Mpumalanga Provincial Archives and the community enhances a collection of indigenous archives. The study found that the Selected Provincial Archives did not invest in information communication technology to ensure the long-term preservation of archives materials. This implies that indigenous language archives were not preserved on electronic records management systems. This is despite that the National Archives of South Africa developed digital recordkeeping guidelines that address the creation, management, and preservation of electronic records. The guideline developed by the National Archives of South Africa covers aspects of the digital management environment in line with the US DoD 5015.2. The national archives of South Africa have a role to assist organizations to preserve archives materials. The Mpumalanga provincial archives are to collaborate with both the SADilar and the community to preserve the indigenous language.

One of the study's finding point to the development that there is an increasing willingness for the institution of the archive to involve the community in archives management project. This collaboration is significant for both archives and the community since both are trying to preserve and legitimize their role and influence in society. Concerns of representation and selectivity are significant to the community. Communities did not fully participate in archives activities. The National and Provincial archives did not formulate an archives forum to promote sharing of information and the involvement of the community in the identification of indigenous language archives that need to be collected by archives institutions. It is the role of National and provincial archivists to build relations with communities by ensuring that the community participated in the archives management program.

The study found that most participants were aware of the South Africa Copyright Act No. 98 of 1978 and its implication for the collection of indigenous language archives. Before archivists embarked on the collection of indigenous language archives, they are supposed to demonstrate competency or basic legal background in copyright archives management. Copyright legislation is a key factor in identifying the type of indigenous language archives that need to be collected and preserved by the Selected Provincial Archives. This implied that provincial archivists and records managers are to be trained on the Copyright Rights Act of 1978. Furthermore, the current South Africa Copyright Act of 1978 should be amended to provide adequate and specific guidelines for the collection and preservation of language archives.

Archivists are required to advance their skills at the archives management level. The researcher found that the archives management skills of the participants were at a basic level. The basic level implied that the respondents had no formal archives management qualification, and did not have a system in place. This implies that language archives require specialized skills and knowledge to manage archives materials.

The fact that the National and Provincial Archives did not collect data related to indigenous archives' language implies that indigenous archives were not available to various stakeholders. Therefore, archivists are required to understand indigenous languages. This is so in South Africa has more than 11 official languages. This implies that human rights concerning the quality of education were not considered by the National and Provincial Archives.

The study found a lack of indigenous language archives systems preservation in South Africa. It seems that archives were not playing their role to collect and preserve indigenous archives.

RECOMMENDATION

It is evident from the findings above that a framework will establish a conducive environment for the collection and preservation of archives materials in the Mpumalanga Provincial archives that need to be preserved and documented. The Mpumalanga Provincial Archives need to establish an Indigenous Unit to distribute information through Indigenous networks and meet with relevant community groups to discuss how the archives can collect Indigenous language.

The Selected Provincial Archives should come up with a strategy to coordinate, collaborate, collect, and preservative of archives. Among the objectives of such initiatives would be to raise awareness and advocacy, training on the collection and preservation of indigenous language archives. This should be conducted at a strategic, technical as well as on community level

The Selected provincial archives must undertake a project to collect indigenous archives history in South Africa to promote the socio-economic well-being of marginalized communities and individuals. This is so because the indigenous language archives were ignored by the national archives systems during the apartheid period. During the apartheid period in South Africa initiatives were done to preserve only the Afrikaans language. This statement is alluded to by De Vaal-Senekal, De Kock, and Putter (2018) who stated that the Afrikaans Language Museum was established to preserve and promote only Afrikaans as a written language, recognized as an official language, and conduct research. Furthermore, national and provincial archivists must promote various stakeholders to access archival materials.

CONCLUSION

In conclusion, there is a need to recognize Selected Provincial Archives role on collection and preservation of indigenous language archives. The Mpumalanga Provincial Archives need to ensure that objectives in terms of Mpumalanga Provincial Act No. 14 2008 Section 3 (g) which states that " promote the empowerment and upliftment through archival usage of previously disadvantaged people and groups". The provincial archives need to develop an implementation plan for language archives to promote the socio-economic well-being of marginalized individuals. Language archives need to be collected from various indigenous language in South Africa. Archives need to be made accessible and transferable to different indigenous archives. South African government planned national language networks with indigenous languages. These enrichments can be new sources to enrich archives repositories.

AREAS FOR FURTHER STUDIES

This study can be replicated in another province in South Africa. A study can be conducted to assess whether provincial archives are complying with the National Archives and Records Service Act 43 of 1996 regarding the collection of marginalized communities to promote the socio-economic development. This study is supported by the National Insitue For the Humanities and Social Sciences.

REFERENCES

Balogun, T., & Kalusopa, T. (2021). A framework for digital preservation of Indigenous Knowledge System (IKS) in repositories in South Africa. *Records Management Journal*, *31*(2), 177–195. doi:10.1108/RMJ-12-2020-0042

Balogun, T., & Kalusopa, T. (2021). A framework for digital preservation of Indigenous Knowledge System (IKS) in repositories in South Africa. *Records Management Journal*, *31*(2), 176–196. doi:10.1108/RMJ-12-2020-0042

Baro, E. E., Obaro, G. O., & Aduba, D. E. (2019). An Assessment of digital literacy skills and knowledge-based competencies among librarians working in university libraries in Africa. *Digital Library Perspectives*, *35*(3/4), 172–192. doi:10.1108/DLP-04-2019-0013

Beel, E. D., Wallace, D. C., Webster, G., Nguyen, H., Tait, E., Macleod, M., & Mellish, C. (2017). Cultural resilience: The production of rural community heritage, digital archives, and the role of volunteers. *Journal of Rural Studies*, *54*, 459–468. doi:10.1016/j.jrurstud.2015.05.002

Bhebhe, S (2021). Proposed independent organizational structure for memory institutions in Zimbabwe and South Africa. *Collection and Curation*.

Bow, C. (2019). Diverse Socio-technical aspects of a digital archive of Aboriginal languages. *Archives and Manuscripts*, *47*(1), 94–112.

Burke, M. (2021) Collaboration with language Community Members to Enrich Ethnographic Descriptions in a language Archive. *Proceedings of the Ist International workshop on Digital Language Archives*. HDL. http://hd1.handle.net/2142/111706

Chilcott, A. (2019). Towards protocols for describing racially offensive language in UK public archives. *Archival Science*, *19*(4), 359–376. doi:10.100710502-019-09314-y

De Vaal-Senekal, P., De Kock, C., & Putter, M. (2018). Challenges in the Archives of the Afrikaans Language Museum, Paarl, Western Cape, South Africa: A case Study. *Atlanti*, *28*(1), 195–205. doi:10.33700/2670-451X.28.1.195-205(2018)

Dittmar, L & Entin, J (2016). Introduction: Archives and Radical Education. *Radical Teacher. A Socialist, Feminist, and Anti- racist Journal on the Theory and Practice of Teaching, 105*, 1 – 6.

Fabunmi, A. B. (2007). The roles of librarians in Copyright Protection in Nigeria. *International Journal of African & African American Studies, V1*(1), 84–93.

Garaba, F. (2014). Preparing collections for digitization: The case of religious archives in Pietermaritzburg, Kwazulu – Natal, South Africa. *Verbum et Ecclesia 35*(1). http://dx.doi.org// ve.v35i1.1319. doi:10.4102

Gilliland, A., & McKemmish, S. (2014). The Role of Participatory Archives in Furthering Human Rights, Reconciliation, and Recovery. *Atlanti: Review for Modern Archival Theory and Practice*, *24*, 74–88.

Hindal, S., & Wyller, H. E. (2004). The Norwegian Archive, Library and Museum Authority – Our role in a society based on knowledge and culture. *Library Review*, *53*(4), 207–212. doi:10.1108/00242530410531820

Holton, G. (2012). Language archives: They're not just for linguists anymore. *Language & Conservation Special Publication*, *3*, 105–110.

Jimerson, R. C. (2007). Archives for all: Professional Responsibility and Social Justice. *The American Archivist*, *70*(2), 252–281. doi:10.17723/aarc.70.2.5n20760751v643m7

Jones, M., & O'Neill, C. (2014). Identity, records and archival evidence: Exploring the needs of Forgotten Australians and Former Child Migrants. *Archives and Records (Abingdon, England)*, *35*(2), 110–125. doi:10.1080/23257962.2014.951032

Marowa, I. (2015). Archives as extended memory of communities: The case of Dandawa Chiefdom in Hurungwe District, Zimbabwe. *ESARBICA Journal*, *34*, 104–116.

Mungai, W. M., Dorvlo, S. S., Nuwagirya, A., & Holmner, M. (2020). Influence of copyright exceptions and limitations on access to information in Kenya, Ghana, and Uganda libraries. *Library Management*, *41*(6/7), 565–577. doi:10.1108/LM-03-2020-0052

Nathan, D. J. (2012). From preserving language Resources to Serving Language Speakers: New Prospects for Endangered Language Archives. *Language Documentation and Description*, *12*, 187–208.

Netshakhuma, N. S. (2021). Incorporation of indigenous archives into Limpopo archives repository: a case of Venda indigenous archives. Global Knowledge, Memory, and Communication. doi:10.1108/GKMC-05-2020-0064

Netshakhuma, N. S. (2021a). Accessibility of Land Claims Records at Kruger National Park of South Africa. T. Robin (ed) Indigenous Research of Land, Self and Spirit. IGI Global. doi:10.4018/978-1-7998-3729-9.ch010

Ngoepe, M., & Katuu, S. (2017). Provision of Records Created in Networking Environments in the Curricula of Institutions of Higher Learning in Africa. *New Review of Information Networking*, *22*(1), 1–12. doi:10.1080/13614576.2017.1297731

Ngoepe, M., & Nkwe, M. (2018). Separating the wheat from the chaff with the winnowings fork: The eeny meeny mo appraisal approach of digital records in South Africa. *Records Management Journal*, *28*(2), 130–142. doi:10.1108/RMJ-09-2017-0027

Nicholls, S., Booker, L., Thorpe, K., Jackson, M., Girault, C., Briggs, R., & Jones, C. (2016). From Principles to Practice: Community consultation regarding access to indigenous language material in archival records at the State Library of New South Wales. *Archives and Manuscripts*, *44*(3), 110–123. doi:10.1080/01576895.2016.1239116

Okello-Obura, C (2011) Records and Archives Legal and Policy Frameworks in Uganda. *Library Philosophy and Practice (e-journal)*, 9.

Olatokun, M. W. (2008). A survey of Preservation and Conservation Practices and Techniques in Nigerian university libraries. *Libres Library and Information Science Research Electronic Journal*, *18*(2), 1–18.

Ormond-Parker, L., & Sloggett, R. (2012). Local archives and community collecting in the digital age. *Archival Science*, *12*(2), 191–212. doi:10.100710502-011-9154-1

Pereira, R. (2018). Assessing the implementation of the National Archives and Records Services Act at Eduardo Mondlane University in Mozambique. *ESARBICA Journal*, *37*, 222–239.

Pinnick, J. (2017). Exploring digital preservation requirements: A case study from the National Geoscience Data Centre (NGDC). *Records Management Journal*, *27*(2), 175–191. doi:10.1108/RMJ-04-2017-0009

Poole, A. H. (2020). The information work of community archives: A systematic literature review. *The Journal of Documentation*, *76*(3), 657–687. doi:10.1108/JD-07-2019-0140

Rakemane, D., & Mosweu, O. (2021). Challenges of managing and preserving audio-visual archives in archival institutions in Sub-Saharan Africa: A literature review. *Collection and Curation*, *40*(2), 42–50. doi:10.1108/CC-04-2020-0011

Reid, H., & Howard, V. (2016). Connecting with Community: The Importance of Community Engagement in Rural Public Library Systems. *Public Library Quarterly*, *35*(3), 188–202. doi:10.1080/01616846.2016.1210443

Satgour, U. (2015). Celebrating libraries in 20 years of democracy: An overview of library and information services in South Africa. *IFLA Journal*, *41*(2), 97–111. doi:10.1177/0340035215585100

Schellnack-Kelly, I (2020), Decolonising the archives: languages as enablers and barriers to accessing public archives in South Africa. *Archives and Manuscript. 40* (3), 291 - 299.

Seifart, F., Drude, S., Franchetto, B., & Gasche, J. (2008). Language Documentation and Archives in South America. *Language Documentation and Conservation*, *2*(1), 130–140.

Shepard, A. M. (2016). The Value–Added Language Archive: Increasing Cultural Compatibility for Native American Communities. Series: Emergent Use and Conceptualization of Language Archive. *Language Documentation and Conservation*, *10*, 458–479.

Shipp, N. J. (2016). Do I really need specialist qualifications to work as a professional in a gallery, library, archive or museum? *The Australian Library Journal*, *65*(4), 280–287. doi:10.1080/00049670.2016.1233604

South African Centre For Digital Language Resources. (n.d.). *Index.* SADILAR. https://sadilar.org/index.php/en/about

Strom, M. (2012). The Congressional Archive: A breed apart. *Journal of Library Administration*, *52*(3-4), 332–340. doi:10.1080/01930826.2012.684531

Thorpe, K., & Galassi, M. (2014). Rediscovering Indigenous Languages: The Role and Impact of Libraries and Archives in Cultural Revitalisation. *Australian Academic and Research Libraries*, *45*(2), 81–100. doi:10.1080/00048623.2014.910858

Timms, K. (2009). New Partnerships for Old Sibling Rivals: The Development of Integrated Access Systems for the Holdings of Archives, Libraries and Museums. *Archivaria*, *68*, 67–95.

Trilsbeek, P., & König, A. (2014). Increasing the future usage of endangered language archives. In D. Nathan & P. K. Austin (Eds.), *Language Documentation and Description* (Vol. 12). Special Issue on Language Documentation and Archiving.

Upward, F; McKemmish, S and Reed B (2011). Counterpoint Archivists and Changing Information Spaces: A Continuum Approach to Recordkeeping and Archiving in Online Cultures. *The Journal of the Association of Canadian Archivists (Archivaria) 72.*

Van der Merwe, R. (2015). Collections create connections: Stitching the lives of marginalized women on the national memory canvas. *Museum Management and Curatorship*, *30*(4), 268–282. doi:10.1080/09647775.2015.1043022

Venson, L. S., Ngoepe, M., & Ngulube, P. (2014). The role of public archives in national development in selected countries in the East and Southern Africa Regional Branch of the International Council on Archives region. *Innovation*, *48*, 44–64.

Wasson, C., Holton, G., & Roth, S. H. (2016). Bringing user-centered Design to the Field of Archives. *Language Documentation and Conservation*, *10*, 641–681.

WIPO. (2019). *WIPO and the sustainable development goals: innovation driving human progress*. WIPO. Https://www.wipo.int/edocs/pubdocs/en/wipo_pub_1061.pdf

Withers, D. (2017). Ephemeral Feminist Histories and the Politics of Transmission within Digital Culture. *Women's History Review*, *26*(5), 678–691. doi:10.1080/09612025.2016.1166887

KEY TERMS AND DEFINITIONS

Apartheid: This is a political system of separating groups in terms of color and race in South Africa. the system was established in 1948 by the National Party of South Africa. It ended in 1993 before the transition to democracy in South Africa

Indigenous Language Archives: These are archives created by ethnic groups of the Ndebele, Tsonga, and Swazis based in the Mpumalanga Provincial Archives.

Marginalized communities: These are ethnic groups such as Ndebele, Tsonga, and Swatis in the Mpumalanga province neglected during the apartheid period in South Africa

Mpumalanga Provincial Archives: This is one of the nine provincial archives established in South Africa

Chapter 7
The Contribution of Community Education Towards Minimising Ritual Murder in the Community for Good Social Order

Avhurengwi Samson Mabade
Walter Sisulu University, South Africa

ABSTRACT

An individualistic education can hardly minimize community-based problems; hence, community education could play a magnificent role towards reducing community-based problems. Although the literature about community education appears to be in abundance, the literature about community education and community-based problems seems to be few. For this study, the researcher's aim is to strengthen and sustain a responsibly coherent community to minimize ritual murder through community education. The researcher adopted a participatory action research approach to involve community members in the fight against ritual murder in their community. The researcher employed qualitative techniques to collect data. Twenty-two (22) participants were selected purposively. The participants formed a focus group that had discussions and interviews. The study concluded that ritual murder is a serious community-based problem threatening communities. Community education is recommended to modernize culture and tradition for reducing ritual murder.

DOI: 10.4018/978-1-6684-6625-4.ch007

BACKGROUND AND MOTIVATION TO THE PROBLEM

This chapter provides ritual murder as one of Community-Based problems. Ritual murder seems to be one of Community-Based problems in most of the African countries more especially in rural areas. This practice entails the killing of the most vulnerable people including people with disabilities, women, and children. The literature about ritual murder is available but the critical and crucial part towards the solution to the problem seems not enough, more especially the solution by community members themselves. It is crystal clear that the solution to the problem is amongst community members themselves. The majority of people in the rural community appear to be still at the level of general knowledge. These people still believe that human body parts could contribute significantly towards the improvement of the quality of their lives irrespective of work and education achieved. In rural community, most of the people seem to be left on their own trying to reinvent a wheel in a time-wasting fashion. If one wants to reinvent an organization to meet challenges, one should start by the people who make up that organization. Therefore, community members should be empowered to be critical enough. A critical thinker identifies and challenges any assumption as well as myth. Salisbury and Roberts (2012), this killing is motivated by the belief that human body parts can be used for medicinal purposes and supernatural powers that bring prosperity and protection. In countries such as Nigeria, Uganda, Swaziland, Liberia, Botswana, Tanzania, Namibia, Zimbabwe and South Africa, such killing is rife or predominant.

Ritual murder and related human rights abuses occurs in African countries because the majority of people still believe that the use of charms and the performance of ritual sacrifice can fortify them spiritually, enhance their fortunes in business and during elections or protect them from harm, disease, poverty, accident, death or destruction (IHEU,2010). The researcher agrees with Salisbury and Roberts (2012) and IHEU (2010) that the majority of African people do not believe that education could improve their lives rather than ritual killing of other people. It is crystal clear that the level of education could also contribute towards the ritual killings. Therefore, this remains the responsibility of the community members themselves to reduce this pandemic of ritual murder. In Britain, a boy was killed for muti purpose and genitals were removed. That boy was taken from Nigeria so that the practice could occur away. Although it is not easy to investigate such cases, so many Nigerians were arrested in 2003 in connection with the ritual murder of this boy (Encyclopedia,2021). People believe that drinking blood and practicing cannibalism can help them to achieve power and immortality. African belief is complex and mysterious. African people have illusion about their beliefs. Vast factors contribute towards this practice of killing people for a number of beliefs such as robbery and luck. The robbers' belief that ritualized waste or water which was used to wash the dead body could be used for stealing purpose. It is believed that if such water could be mixed with muti and sprayed in the bedroom, people would deadly sleep. Therefore robbers could break into the house and steal whatever is in the house (Masoga and Rugwiji, 2018). For this study, it is community education that can change the level of thinking and the decision-making process. In each community, educated people are and some of them appear to be the perpetrator of the problem. Community education is fundamental of working on the pressing problem of a particular community to promote good interpersonal relationships. This needs critical people because in most cases, the perpetrators are some of community members. Therefore, community activities can assist other community members to change their mindset and start to see other people as they deserve to live and enjoy the benefit of a particular community.

In early April 2023, six-year and nine-year boys disappeared in Soweto and the Community started to look for the children till they found their bodies with some missing parts. The Community organized itself so that the perpetrators could be found. Due to the Community's support to the police, the perpetrators were apprehended. Unfortunately, all the perpetrators were related to the children. Those were crystal clear ritual murders. In February 2023, a child disappeared for more than three weeks until the body was found by community members with some parts missing that showed a clear ritual murder. Due to the community's unity, the perpetrator was apprehended and brought to the record. Therefore, the body of the diseased could only be discovered where community stands responsibly as a coherent community.

After all occurrences, family members remain traumatized with fear and sometimes they blame themselves. In most cases, the perpetrators are not arrested although they are known to the community. Ritual murder has negative impact to both the family and community. More than 117 cases of ritual murder were reported in Vhembe District by 2016 (Rannditheni, Masoga and Mavhandu, 2016). Police who should protect the community members appear to be the relatives of the people implicated in this practice of killing people. The perpetrators are related to the police in many ways. Despite, the relationship of the perpetrators and the policy, community can still benefit from community-based education from myriad perspectives. Community education can empower community members on the report ways and communication with other community members. Communication is crucial in each community to share any activity in the vicinity. Below are some of the beneficial effects of Community-based education and activities.

(Organisation for Economic Co-operation and Development, 2019)

CLARIFICATION OF CONCEPTS

Community

Community refers to a group of people who share something in common. This can be defined by the shared attributes of people and the strength of connections among them. This includes people who feel some sense of belonging or interpersonal connection. Community may be huge and diffuse, or niche and tightly connected (De Beer and Swanepoel 2015). Community refers to the quality or character of human relationships and social group but always share a bounded geographic territory. A group of people who have a common interest, purpose or objective who learn to acquaint themselves with one another over time through a gamified information system (Johannessen, 2020) For this study, community refers to a group of people living together, sharing the same culture and tradition. The people share common beliefs, values, norms and customs. They live in the same geographical territory and also include the surrounding areas.

Community Education

Community education is a philosophical concept based on a partnership between the community and education where each views the other as a valuable resource in developing community, improving community's lives and developing a common process toward the end of individualised education. This includes public participation in education for decision-making and the community school as a delivery system of educational services. The people of the community participate in programmes designed to fulfil their educational needs, while promoting more effective use of public education facilities and other public facilities, for the purpose of providing recreational, cultural and other related community services. The programmes and activities are developed in dialogue with community as participants. The purpose of community education and development is to develop the capacity of individuals and groups of all ages through their actions, the capacity of community, to improve the quality of their lives and develop the ability to participate in democratic process (McConnel and Charlie, 2002).

According to Merriam and Brocket (1997) Community Education refers to any formal or informal action-oriented or problem-solving education that takes place in the community. The seeds of the solution to a community-based problem are contained with that community. For this study, community education refers to planned or unplanned activities that can improve the quality of lives of the community members. This type of education can be facilitated by the educator of the adults or adult educator. Community education occurs through awareness campaign, project and/or workshop approaches. This also occurs through community meetings that include participatory action. Community education contribute significantly to worthwhile public decision-making process.

Ritual Murder

Ritual or muti-murder is a form of human sacrifice practised by some African tribes. The murder is carried out after body parts are removed while the victim is still alive. The body parts are used for medicinal purposes. The human body is said to be very powerful (Schotz, Philips and Knobel, 1997) and (Stey, 2005). For this study, ritual murder refers to the killing of a person after such person would have hidden in an isolated place for quite a few days. This killing happens after body of a person would have cut off when crying calling the relatives.

Community Development

Community development refers to the improvement of community in relation to personal, social and economic issues in a particular community. Adult and community education can raise awareness in the community about social, economic, and political issues affecting the community (Miller,2008) Community development is the educational process by which people change themselves and their behaviour and acquire new skills and confidence through working in cooperation. This is a method to bring about desired change initiatives are taken by local people (de Beer and Swanepoel, 2015). For this study, community development refers to the ability of the community to deal with the problems affecting their community including ritual murder that is cultivated by economic and political factors. If community could have knowledge and skills to solve these problems, therefore, this is a community development. Community needs to be empowered by community education to balance between fairness to an individual's needs with the fairness to community's needs. The change of people's behaviour is serious community development.

COMMUNITY APPROACH TO STRATEGIC PLAN

It is imperative for community to understand how to approach a problem when it surfaces hence community approach strategic plan cannot be separated from community education. The researcher found it crucial to engage the Community towards strategizing to achieve solutions to their problems. It is however critical to come to the right strategy that could be magnificent towards arriving at the appropriate solution to the problem. The right type of strategic planning helps people and the

Community to know where the Community is going and a game plan to get there. Community members have to understand their culture, Community's strengths and weaknesses and then design an approach that would work best for them. Traditional strategic planning approaches and processes appear not adequate more especially in the democratic culture. They could design something remarkable and desirable predilection to explain. The question remains, what can Community do to turn things around?

Although there is several strategic planning, Agile Strategic Management planning appears to be employable in the community in order to turn everything around. This could help Community to achieve its goals hence it requires genuine leadership. It leverages the power multi-disciplinary teamwork, iterative design and improvement and a continuous focus on top priorities. This strategy entails developing and adjusting strategies, products, services and operations as needed on live data and new insights. This strategic plan encourages that every Community member should receive live input and make adjustment, tap into the best ideas of others, work together to coordinate and execute, understand the community's focus and its top priorities and fully engaged and productive. This is used in goal setting, strategy development, product and service and process improvement (Willden, 2017). For this study, this strategic planning could help community members to work together and listen to each community member's ideas for the improvement of interpersonal relationship as well as the quality of the lives of each Community member. The lives of Community members should remain top priorities in each Community. This is possible if the leadership has capacity to develop and lead capacity in the Community.

This encourages a shift from the traditional method of dealing with or addressing Community-based problem to a new paradigm which includes a synergistic approach that involves active participation of Community members themselves. This empowers community to be proactive in improving their current situation. It gives community a sense of ownership and builds sustainable programmes that are more feasible. This enhances a transformation brought about by man which leads into the transformation of man himself. Therefore, the transformation which is brought about by community will lead to the transformation of community members themselves. This transformation could be attained and sustained if participatory action research is adopted. Participatory action research is half academic research and half reality. Action research is an approach which needs active participation of the people affected by the problem. In action research the researcher facilitates the whole process of research as an academic or scholar. The people involved, identify the problem themselves in their particular Community. Community members would come with the strategies that could help them to deal with the problem. The strategies can be in the form of programmes that should be supported by Community members.

The strategies or plans that Community draws should also have marmalade at the corner with coffee stains for the development and growth of the programme. Action research is an integrated part of a strategy for the development of strategic plan by people themselves to deal with Community-based problems. The central traits that are emphasized are Community Education and Community-based problem.

What is a community-based problem in a particular Community is not obviously a community-based problem in another Community? This also implies that the strategy that can be used effectively in a particular Community for the same Community-based problem cannot be obvious effective in another Community solving the same problem. In this occurrence, an individual education is not enough to deal with Community-based problem, but Community education is an appropriate type of education to deal with Community-based problem. Community-based problems differ from one Community to another. For example, one Community could be predominated by crime in the form of house breaking while another could suffer from crime in the form of child and woman abuse or ritual murder. This is often taken as the mobilization of people as well as building their confidence. The researcher adopted Action Research Approach to allow active participation of community members. The researcher employed qualitative technique for the data collection. The collected data from the participants and literature was concluded and presented with recommendations.

Community-based problem is one of the worldwide problems which need serious attention by all community members affected. In this instance, an individual education is not enough to address Community-based problem but Community education instead. Community education is the ultimate result of action learning. In the traditional method of dealing with Community-based problem, the researcher would do everything in his study without serious involvement of community members themselves. Participatory action research involves community's voice and painting a more accurate portrait of the situation.

Wikipedia (2020), Community refers to community of individuals with common problem or issue as well as common interest or goal. Participatory action research in community-based problem encourages collaboration of formally trained researcher partner from an area of expertise with community members who are fully committed to produce results usable to the community. Community members participate in the research and develop outcomes that can be used to make changes in their community. Community members are involved throughout the research process, which is from design phase, data collection, data analysis, dissemination and action. In the traditional method of research, the researcher would never try to know the community personally, and provide a report of information that the researcher collected (Janice, Burns and Deanna, 2011)

Community-based participatory action research includes those affected by a community-based problem in collaboration with someone who has research skills to conduct research on and analyse the problem with the aim of developing strategies to resolve the problem. Community-based participatory action research replaces the traditional research which relies on the academic researcher. Community members refer to those directly affected by the problem and they should be asked what they need. The researcher recruit members of the community affected because they are familiar with and known by the community. The community members work with the researcher as colleagues, participate in the conception and design of the project, data collection and data analysis. The community members could participate in reporting the results of the project or study (Centre for Community Health and Development,2020). The people affected by the problem decide to address that problem. They explore, discuss and negotiate as people affected by the problem. Community members generate ideas and develop plan that would help them to solve their problem. They implement the plan and evaluate the effectiveness of the plan. The effectiveness of the plan would result adoption of the plan or the development of another plan. This process develops in a spiral way till the people affected would be satisfied. During the whole process, all participants develop learning with real understanding of the situation. Community members recognize the problem identified, collect evidence, organize and analyze the information (Wals, 2006).

People in an affected community are more likely to talk and give straight answers to researcher known to them and know that they are in a similar situation than someone not known in the community. People who have experienced the effects of the problem may have ideas and information about the problem studied. People who are deeply affected by the problem may participate actively and they know what is important when they see or hear the problem. These people are likely to develop felicitous programme to develop aspiration amongst community members.

Findings may receive more community support because community members know that the research was conducted by people in the same situation as their own. Action research is often used to address social problems but can also be used to address the environmental issues, health issues and political issues as well as economic issues (Centre for Community Health and Development, 2020).

DESCRIPTION OF THE PROBLEM

Ritual murder is the killing of people with the intention of removing their body parts. A number of ritual murders is implicated with the idea of human sacrifice for religious reasons. However, religion is used in different contexts of beliefs such as Satanism and Vamparism. Although it involves religion, it has psychological, psychosexual, and cultural elements. This is assumed as occult belief systems. The word occult means hidden and cannot be investigated with easy. This practice is influenced by an over desire to personal transformation, self-deification, and healing. Although ritual killings involve old people, teenagers could happen to be perpetrators due to Satanic cults more especially in Europe and United States (Encyclopaedia, 2021)

Ritual murder refers to the killing of a person for the purpose of harvesting the body parts for the use as traditional medicine or muti. Ritual murder is a pandemic because it is inevitable. This is a form of sinful practice by a vast number of African tribes (Masoga and Rugwiji,2018). In Nigeria, people with mental illness are killed as part of ritual practice that emanates from meticulous beliefs that the body parts of the disabled person could make a person rich and blessed. Hence people with negative belief about the mental ill people claim that their hands are unclean. People with albinism are killed because people believe that their body parts could be used for wealthy purpose (Etilyibo and Omiegbe,2016)

In Southern Africa, the belief that female parts provide supernatural powers that bring good fortune or make criminals invisible to police and other authorities is predominant. In Eastern Africa, they believe that the breast and woman's private parts enhances business aspiration, man's private parts are believed to increase virility while the tongue can smooth one's path to a lover's heart. That is a love potion. The perpetrators target vulnerable members of community such as the poor, women, children, people with disabilities and albinos whose families do not have access to higher offices of justice because the local police happen to be bribed. Ritual killings or muti-killings are committed for the purpose of taking human body parts which are used to prepare charms and other traditional medicines. These charms are believed to have supernatural powers greatly enhanced if the organs or parts are removed while the victim crying. These body parts are sold at a haggle price of R3000 (Dlamini, 2011).

Ritual murder is politically and economically motivated. Although ritual murder is related to indigenous healing, body parts are mixed with medicine for economic and political strength. The ancestors need to be informed before any ritual murder, therefore amongst perpetrators, there should be close relative to the victim. It is believed that the body parts should be removed while the victim is screaming to alert the ancestors. A hand or a tongue can cost as much as $500 on the black market. The suspects are mostly egocentric, superstitious and opportunistic people in the community. Throughout Southern Africa, such occurrences of ritual murder and mediating forces of Kings and Chiefs are known phenomena (de Jong, 2015).

RESEARCH DESIGN AND METHODOLOGY

The researcher adopted a participatory action research approach within a critical paradigm. Action Research is half academic research and half reality. Critical paradigm aims towards the empowerment of the participants. For this study critical paradigm focuses on the empowerment of the community to deal with community-based problems including ritual murder. The focus group was established after several meetings of community members at the Chief's kraal. The purpose of the meetings was to discuss on going ritual murders in the community which were morally unacceptable. The focus group was established including three traditional leaders, three church leaders, two policing staff, five Civic organization members, three educators, two traditional health practitioners, two business practitioners and two community policing forum. Twenty-two (22) participants were purposively selected for the study. The purpose of selecting these participants was to find their perceptions and to ascertain strategies that can be adopted to minimise ritual murder in the community. The researcher employed qualitative technique including focus group discussions and interviews for data collection. Each focus group member used his/her means of transport to a particular selected school. The discussions and interviews were conducted in the afternoon from 16h00-18h00. The purpose of conducting discussions and interviews in the late afternoon was to find the most convenient time to the participants. The focus group discussions and interviews were based on identified themes. The findings were discussed and synthesized by the focus group. The recommendations were made that the suggested strategies should be implemented after presenting them to community although there was a room for further study. Their feedback was reported as a participatory action research.

FINDINGS FROM THE COMMUNITY

The findings from the discussions and interviews of the focus group were recorded on the audiotape and then transcribed by the researcher. The participants used their know-how to discuss their perceptions in a focus group. The feedback is discussed below in different themes:

The Participants' Knowledge About the Problem Understudy

The focus group reported occurrences of ritual murder in their community including the surrounding areas in Vhembe District of Limpopo Province of South Africa. Ritual murder is unbearable in most of the communities. Taking very few occurrences of this nature into consideration, the readers would agree that this is a community-based problem and there is a need of worthwhile contributions to make.

In 2012, a man from Mphagane community was ritually murdered and none of the implicated people was arrested. In 2013 a man from Kharadza community was ritually murdered and nobody was arrested, and a woman was ritually murdered from Makuleni community the same year. In 2014, a man was ritually murdered in Khakhu Thondoni and a child was ritually murdered in Maname the same year and no arrest was successful. In 2015 two boys were ritually murdered from Mabulo community and an old man from Maname was also killed and arrest of the implicated people. In 2019, a boy was ritually murdered from Sheshe community and another boy from Tshixwadza community, no one implicated was arrested. In 2020, a man was ritually murdered from Khakhu and no arrest of the implicated people. In this practice, most of the people implicated appear to be the relatives of the Victim. In one occurrence, both parents of the victim were implicated. When community members wanted to assist them, they told the community to refrain from searching. In another case a mother of the victim told community that what should be done if one does not get married. Some of the questions instigated suspicion to community members.

In 2021, a boy was ritually murdered from Niani community, and no arrest was successful during the writing of this chapter. In March 2021 in Phiphidi area of Thohoyandou, a woman escaped from a ritual murder. The woman was raped first and the perpetrator tried to remove her womb. During the interviews of the Victim by the media, it was terrifying. The perpetrator, the boy wanted to remove her private parts while she was screaming. Based on the incidences above, the researcher was quite satisfied with such pertinent occurrences to confirm these as one of community-based problems which need community itself for mitigation. Community should develop mechanics of intelligence to deal with community-based problems.

In 2022 September, a nine-year-old boy disappeared and looked for the whole night till he was found in a pit toilet in Khakhu village. That was after the Community had searched in most areas including the same pit toilet, but they could not find him. The boy indicated to have been dropped there after he was hidden the bush for such a long time, but he was brought to the pit toilet due to Community outcry. Community members protested so that the perpetrators could be arrested but the police indicate that the evidence was not enough even though the boy indicated to show them the perpetrator amongst Community members. Many Community members were arrested instead of the perpetrators. If it were not Community search, the boy could have been murdered because after a month in the same year an old lady from Tshiheni village alleged to be consulting Khakhu Clinic but disappeared in the same country. Unfortunately, Community search was not successful, and the old lady disappeared and was never found either dead or alive. On the 12th of May 2023, a man disappeared in Tshifume village of Khakhu area, and the community stated searching the following day. The man was found after five days in the vicinity of the orchard where people pass by every day. The victim could not utter a word, but he was taken to hospital where he spent three weeks with speaking. Unless community can step up to the mark, this problem would remain a serious community-based problem.

Victims of Ritual Murder

Participants identified people who are likely to be the victims of the problem as mentioned below:

- Children
- Old people
- Mentally deranged people
- Impaired people
- People with albinism

Contributing Factors Towards Ritual Murder

According to the participants, some of the traditional leaders still believe that body parts of a person can assist them to attain dignity and respect in their communities hence some of them do not participate actively in the fight against ritual murder. Where public decision-making process is not yet improved, community violence surfaces. It is only through community education where decision-making process can be improved to bring amicable and harmonious solution to the problem. For this study, laziness and lack of perseverance appeared to be one of the contributing factors. There are young people who do not want to work hence there are so ambitious. The businesspeople on the other hand expect to be richer without hard work and proper planning of their business. They think that body parts of human being can attract many customers so that they can get rich. In addition, people who used to consult traditional health practitioners when they need advice on matters related to their business, they fall into this temptation of ritual murder. When law enforcement agency to take to respond to ritual murder, this also promotes ritual murder when people think that law enforcement is not active. Load shedding is also contributing because most of the people who disappeared for mutilation, they disappeared when there is no electricity.

In conclusion, traditional leaders, traditional health practitioners, politicians, farmers, and church leaders appeared to be the promoters of ritual murder for respect, love and dignity while businessmen seemed to be the promoting ritual murder for wealth. Most of them do not murder themselves, instead they pay people to murder people for body parts. The law- enforcement agency's delay on reacting on this problem, results community violence.

Suggested Strategies That Can Be Used to Minimise Ritual Murders in the Community

In the discussions and interviews, participants ascertain that all community structures including the Traditional leader's sub-council, should conduct awareness campaign against ritual murder in their community to condemn that level of thinking. In addition, community workshops must be established on community development and Human Rights for in-depth understanding of each community member. Some of the workshops can contribute towards the modernisation of culture and tradition that promote ritual murder. Again, projects that can assist community members to share the resources in that community in this regard cannot be underestimated, the lives of community members could improve that can ultimately minimise the murder of people for wealth purpose. Community education in the form of awareness, project and workshop is of paramount importance in the fight against community-based problems including ritual murder. The participants emphatically advised one another that community members must be encouraged to be critical to all religion in their community because there appears to be certain religion that promote ritual murder. Community members must be sure of the significance of that religion to each individual and the community at large. However, it is imperative to each community to establish Community Policing Forum (CPF) that could add its effort to the policing effort to be more effective and efficient every day for the benefit of the entire community. Each community should also have a forum of traditional leaders and traditional health practitioners for discussing culture and tradition of that community. In all community meetings, ritual murder and quality life of community members should be on the agenda for discussion. However, community must also invite law enforcement agency in its meetings to be educated on the law issues so that whatever community members do should not be against the law. Community members could know the procedure of reporting ritual murder and how to make a follow up. Community members ascertain that this problem can be minimised if law and justice could be equally practised to the perpetrators. Drug dealers and abusers should be done away with in each community because young people are involved in the ritual murder to get money for drugs. Therefore, there should be a campaign or workshop about drugs. A drug free community can hardly involve itself with ritual murder.

After all occurrences, some of the community members were arrested and released after paying bail. That happened after community members had barricaded roads, burnt tyres and setting alight the house and properties of one of the suspects.

Community blamed police for not arresting the suspects for further investigation because one of the escaped victims was ready to identify the person who picked him up from the playing sport. Community members had several meetings to come up with worthwhile decision that could assist community and those arrested. They demanded that at all community meetings, ritual murder should be in the agenda.

LITERATURE REVIEW

In 2020, three people were sentenced to life imprisonment for ritual murder. The accused killed a woman in Limpopo Province. They were found cutting the lips, breast and private parts while she was still alive. Amongst the perpetrators, there was a relative of the victim. One of the accused confirmed that the victim's legs were tied to a tree the whole night cutting body parts (Sunday World, 2020). Ritual killings and the misuse of human body parts for luck and fortune was believed to be a centuries old ritual that was practised among our communities throughout the province, the country and even the continent. The fact that it had been around, this did not however justify its continued practice. It is an abominable, cruel and violent act which all of us not only condemn, but actively work towards its total eradication. There is a need for establishing specialised police investigating unit in occult related crimes and the up-scalling of public awareness and sustainable education drive. The reports indicated that most of community members are reluctant to give evidence in courts of law against perpetrators because of fear (Moloto, 2006). For this study, community members should not for ritual murder to happen and then report to police station only, but community members should educate one another on the human rights in their community. They have to step up the mark to organise community education through awareness campaign so that each community members understand Human Rights and their impact in the life of an individual. Every individual has the right to live with dignity irrespective of gender, age, nationality and colour. Community Policing Forum should be established in each community support the police in the fight against ritual murder. In many cases, one or more of perpetrators appeared to be community members who could be joined by others from other communities. Community members must be workshopped on the reporting process to the police station. However, police should also participate in some of community education more especially those who belong to that particular community. The suggestion boxes should be introduced in each community for reporting ritual murder.

In Lesotho, the killing of witchcraft and ritual murder is still a problem even though there is a complete silence of these issues from different social sectors and more importantly from academic circles, mainly anthropologists, religious studies and educationists. It seemed as if only police are responsible for the arrest of witchcraft killers and ritual murder. Murders were initiated and predicted by traditional doctors who also prescribed the relevant qualities and characteristics of the victim. Therefore, ritual murder is motivated by belief which is religion and are initiated for prescriptions by traditional doctors who are also religious priests in African culture. For this reason, witchcraft is planned to be in school curriculum so that witchcraft can be taught and learnt as a moral code against unacceptable behaviour which every individual should avoid being called or labelled (Mokotso, 2015). For this study, the eradication of ritual murder is not the responsibility of the police only, but the responsibility of all community members irrespective of age and gender hence community education can play a significant role towards minimising the problem than individual education. The traditional doctors should be included in the community education as a community member whose contributions could assist the community.

In Jewish community, ritual murder is still practised for 1475 years ago. A two-year-old boy once disappeared, and community hunt managed to find the body of the boy floating on the water. Community struggled to find the perpetrators till six men were apprehended. They confirmed that they killed the boy to get Christian blood for use in the Jewish ceremonies of Passover (Kohl,2018). The Romans believe that in order to maintain favoured status they enjoy, they needed to perform ritual killings in violation of the established Roman law. Ritual murder often contained a loophole such as being prescribed by the gods. If the killing was kept away, they would be killed by gods. Then Roman technically avoided to engage in the barbaric practice of human sacrifice (Carver, Watson and Jr Curtiss, 2018). For this study, all community members irrespective of their religion, should fight against ritual murder. It is possible when all community members understand and respect human rights more especially the right to live by an individual. People should turn against their gods if they are motivated by these gods. However, community education promotes interactive processes that ultimately result group dynamic movements.

In Botswana, a schoolgirl of fourteen-year was killed in 1994. The murder was discussed in the community gathering where they concluded that the girl was brutally killed. The murderer took her private parts. It was confirmed that they cut her private part while she was still alive because it is assumed that the young girl's genetalia comprises an extremely potent medicine. They agreed that ritual murder increases towards election time when politicians feel a need of strengthening themselves. They make themselves invulnerable and lucky in attracting electoral support and they make other politicians flat and useless. Due to continuous community meeting and support, the body of the girl was found and two prosperous businessmen who were politicians were arrested. Unfortunately, police could not have enough evidence and they released. Shortly after that, four men who were both politician and businessmen were arrested ang amongst them, there was the victim's father. Community members felt provoked that their homes and properties were set alight. The father of the victim confirmed that he was amongst the murderers. If community members would not have united, the perpetrators would have not been arrested (Gulbrandsen,2002). For this study, such stubborn effort by the community members is a clear indication that unless community members come together and share decision-making processes, skills of dealing with such problem, good social order could hardly be achieved in each community. Community education can empower all community members irrespective of age and gender on strategies to report such cases and change that level of thinking of politicians, church leaders and businessmen.

CONCLUSION

An individual education is not enough for community-based problems, but community education can contribute significantly towards minimizing community-based problems including ritual murder which is threatening communities. Despite cultural and traditional beliefs that seem to promote ritual murder, community education can play a fundamental role in the modernisation of culture more especially that encourage the killing of human beings for body parts. There is a need of community development education so that people can understand the process of development without body parts of a person. If community members could respect Human Rights, interpersonal relationships can improve. People could therefore, live in peace and harmony. Children, old people, impaired people and mentally deranged people could feel protected as these are the vulnerable ones. Good social order would surface instead of public violence caused by public decision-making process. Community education could contribute magnificently to worthwhile decision-making process. Sharing resources in a particular community can also bring people together and build their relationships on trust and openness as an ultimate result of community education. Both the findings from the literature and participants confirmed that ritual murder is a serious community-based problem that needs to be addressed by the community concern. Children, old age people, impaired people, mentally deranged, albino are the most likely vulnerable victims of ritual murder. The perpetrators are likely to be the businessmen, traditional leaders, traditional health practitioners, church leaders and politician from a fastidious community for wealth, respect, and dignity. However, the strategies adopted by each community are likely to be evaluated after the implementation thereof. The study recommended community education through awareness campaign, workshops, and community projects for the changing of the mind-set of community members. The interpersonal relationship is also recommended for strengthen and sustaining a responsibly coherent community. Community education should be used as a tool for the modernization of culture and tradition more especially those that promote ritual murder. An analysis of newly established religion in a particular community was seriously considered.

REFERENCES

Carver, D. F., Watson, J., & Jr Curtiss, J. (2018). *Ritual Killings in Ancient Rome: Homicide and Roman Superiority. Corado*. Colorado State University Library.

De Beer, F., & Swanepoel, H. (2015). *Community Development and Beyond issues, structures and procedures*. Van Schaik Publishers.

De Jong, W. (2015). "Makhosi a via (Chiefs Commit Ritual Murder)" Why ritual murders in Southern Africa should be seen as meaningful violence. *Africa Fus.*, *28*(2), 9–26.

Dlamini, K. (2011). *Southern Africa: Breaking the Science on Ritual Killings*. SAGE Journal.

Etilyob, E., & Omiegbe, O. (2016). Religion,Culture and Discrimination against People with Disabilities in Nigeria. *African Journal of Disability*, *5*(1), 1–6.

Guldbrandsen, O. (2002). The Discourse of Ritual Murder, Popular Reaction to Political Leaders in Botswana. *Social Analysis*, *46*(3), 215–233.

Johannessen, M. R. (2020). *Handbook of Research on Politics in the Computer Age*. University of South-Eastern Norway.

Kohl, J. (2018). A Murder, a Mummy and a Bust: The newly Discovered Portrait of Simon of Trent at the Getting. *Getting Research Journal*, *10*, PP27–PP60. doi:10.1086/697383

Masoga, M. A., & Rugwiji, T. (2018). A Reflection on Ritual Murder in the Biblical text from an African Perspective. Scripture.Vol 117.Stellenbosch.

McConnel, C. (2002). *Community Learning and Development: The making of an Empowering Profession. Edinburgh Community Learning Scotland Merriam and Brocket (1997). The Profession and Practice of Adult Education*. Jossey-Bass Publishers.

Miller, C. (2008). The role of Adult Education in Community Development. Exploring the links. *International Journal of Lifelong Education*, *30*(4), 489–505.

Mokotso I.R (2015). A Sustainable educational response to the recent increased witch killing and ritual murder 'Liretlo' in Lesotho: Introducing Bosotho Traditional Religion in Lesotho School. *African Educational Research Journal, 3*(4), 209-220.

Moloto. (2006). *Ritual Killings Conference.* South African Government.

OECD. (2019). *Community Education and Training in South Africa: Getting Skills Right.* OECD Publisher.

Rannditsheni, A. E., Masoga, A., & Mavhandu-Mudzusi, A. H. (2016). Some Perspectives on the Impacts of Ritual Murders in Vhembe District of South Africa: An Interpretive Phenomenological Approach. *Journal of Social Sciences*, *48*(3), 239–245. doi:10.1080/09718923.2016.11893586

Scholtz, H. J., Philips, V. M., & Knobel, G. T. (1997). Muti or Ritual murder. National Library of Medicine Solisbury and Roberts (2012). An explanatory study on perceptions of factors influencing ritual murder. *htt://*vital.seals.ac.za:8080/vital/access/services/download/vital:40715/SOURCE *1.*

Stey, (2005). *Multi- murders form South Africa: a case report.* National Library of Medicine. National Centre for Biotechnology Information.

Wals, A. (2006). Action Research and Community-problem solving: Environmental education in an inner-city. *Journal Homepage.*, *17*, PP163–PP182.

Wikipedia. (2013). *Talk.* Community Education.

Chapter 8
Technology Integration in Mathematics to Promote Wellbeing of Learners During the Coronavirus Pandemic:
A Case Study in the Or Tambo Inland District

Thabisa T. Maqoqa
Walter Sisulu University, South Africa

ABSTRACT

The purpose of this chapter is to explore the effects of technology integration in mathematics teaching to promote wellbeing of learners during Covid-19. An interpretive approach together with face-to- face interviews were utilized to gather information from nine participants who teach grade ten mathematics from each of the three senior secondary schools in the OR Tambo Coastal District. The findings revealed that several teachers lacked the formal technology expertise required to embrace online learning successfully and found a dearth of learner connections while teaching online. It was also found out that there was a lack of access to technology. It is recommended that the department of basic education should ensure that all learners have the data card loaded with uncapped data for learning to run smoothly. It was advised that professional development programs be established to train teachers in the design, use, and application of ICT technologies for online teaching.

DOI: 10.4018/978-1-6684-6625-4.ch008

INTRODUCTION

Many facets of society were affected by the coronavirus pandemic, which forced nations and local communities to close offices, switch schools to online education, reduce in-person contact, postpone public events, and impose travel restrictions. Most of the world has experienced crises since 2020 because of COVID-19's spread. To ensure continuity in education when in-person learning was not possible, schools and colleges utilized digital technologies, such as Internet-connected PCs, laptops, and mobile phones. Globally, the amount of research on COVID-19's effects on schooling has increased dramatically. Researchers in mathematics education have investigated issues like necessary skills and curriculum development in regional contexts (Marav-Zavaleta, 2021; Aguilar & Castaneda, 2021), perceptions, uses, and barriers in technologically enhanced learning environments (Ylmaz, Gülbağcı Dede, Sears & Yıldız Nielsen, 2021), and parent-school communication (Gomez, 2021). Teachers, who make up one of the primary groups of educational actors, have had to adapt their daily routines while also figuring out how to keep the teaching process consistent and satisfy the expectations and goals of the students. Another significant topic in recent research is the ability of teachers to teach online in emergency situations. Technology use can enhance students' aptitudes in mathematics and scientific studies (Tan, Wijaya, Zou & Hermita, 2020). Therefore, the teacher must plan the usage of technology. Sometimes, teachers refrain from employing technology in the classroom for a variety of reasons (Tondeur, Scherer, Siddiq & Baran, 2020). Teachers refrain from using technology in the classroom for a variety of reasons, including a lack of time for lesson planning, a lack of technical expertise, a tendency to waste time on it, and a comfort level with the chalkboard as a teaching tool. This chapter seeks to explore technology integration in the teaching of mathematics to promote wellbeing of learners during coronavirus pandemic.

- What part did technology integration play in mathematics teaching in order to promote wellbeing of learners during the COVID-19 pandemic?
- What are the challenges of technology integration in mathematics teaching during the outbreak of COVID-19 pandemic?
- Which professional training is likely to improve technology integration in mathematics teaching?

The author also provides a brief background on the subject as it is described, the setting in which the issue is present, as well as the relevant literature and theoretical framework, before outlining their approach. The approach used to try to find answers to the research questions is further expanded upon in the proposal.

BACKGROUND

When the Ministry of Basic Education made the decision to close schools in response to the pandemic, teachers were forced to adjust and improvise. Prior to the pandemic, many teachers lacked the formal technological training necessary to effectively adopt online learning or to enable blended teaching and learning. The COVID-19 outbreak has had a significant impact on all human activities worldwide, leading to significant changes in human-related activities (Onyema, Eucheria, Obafemi, Sen, Atonye, Sharma & Alsayed, 2020). Due to the global pandemic and efforts to stop the virus' spread, university pedagogy has drastically changed across the globe. As a result, higher education institutions have moved away from in-person teaching and toward digital learning (Oyedotun, 2020). This was done to ensure that learning continued despite the challenges. As a result of the COVID-19 pandemic, travel has been restricted and schools have had to close. This has led to the remote delivery of education, notably at the preschool and primary levels, using a range of virtual learning settings and family pedagogical support (Hodgen, Taylor, Jacques, Tereshchenko, Kwok & Cockerill, 2020). The pandemic's impact on the transformation of distance education procedures compared to face-to-face teaching also generates mental health difficulties for learners, in addition to sudden shifts and the adoption of new virtual teaching and learning methods.

The COVID19 pandemic prevented normal teaching and learning activities (Wijaya, 2021; Murphy, 2020). No learners could attend classes; they had to study at home. The necessity for increased technological use in teaching and learning was brought on by this circumstance. Learning activities that were previously conducted informally in the classroom are now supported by meeting platforms, websites, or video tutorials. It is reported that many teachers were required to teach mathematics courses online in 2020 but had minimal training in how to do so (Hodges, Moore, Lockee, Trust & Bond, 2020).

It is of great importance to be able to understand from the perspective of teachers the coaptation of new teaching strategies that have allowed them to respond to the challenges of online and distance mathematics education (Goos, Beswick, 2021). The COVID-19 pandemic forced schools to adapt to fulfil their many functions, challenging teachers to rethink ways to support their teaching and their learners' learning. Countries attempted to fill the void left by school closures by offering a variety of distance learning solutions, including "hi-tech alternatives like real-time video classes conducted remotely to lower-tech options such as educational programming on radio and television" (UNESCO, 2020).

The novel human Covid-19 was first reported in Wuhan, China, in 2019 and subsequently spread globally to impact the lives of people around the globe. By November 2021, almost two years after COVID-19 was first identified, more than two hundred million confirmed cases and over 5 million lives were lost to the disease (Worldometer, 2021). The novel human coronavirus disease 2019 (COVID-19) was first reported in Wuhan, China, in 2019 and subsequently spread globally to impact the lives of people around the globe. This shift from the traditional face-to-face form of teaching to one born out of an immediate unforeseen necessity required educators to understand and frame what happened to teaching and learning during the COVID-19 pandemic with a different lens (Thompson & Copeland, 2020). Educational establishments across the world have been using online synchronous and asynchronous programs for decades (Arnesen, Hveem, Short, West, & Barbour, 2019). Before the pandemic approximately 2.7 million students were taking planned online classes (Barbour, 2019). While many teachers may be adept in the art of online teaching, prior to the pandemic school closures research reveal a general lack of awareness of the actual scope of online learning, (Siko & Barbour, 2022).

Based on the criteria of the World Population Review (2021), South Africa is considered a developing country. At the onset of COVID-19 in South Africa, the government was forced to enact a national lockdown, causing the closure of all educational establishments (Government of South Africa, 2020; World Bank, 2020). Primary and secondary school education sectors in South Africa are governed by the Department of Basic Education (DBE). Many schools governed by DBE had to close and provided no schooling at the start of COVID-19 as the African continent had numerous technological challenges, such as a lack of infrastructure, broadband, and data costs (Mhlanga & Moloi, 2020). As the pandemic continued, schools continued learning with ERT while navigating those infrastructure limitations. As the COVID-19 pandemic became longitudinal, governments, including South Africa, realized that learning must continue, and alternative strategies, including basic technologies, such as radio and television, were used (Mhlanga & Moloi, 2020). It is important to note that families in South Africa were challenged to ensure that learning continued along with ensuring their basic needs were met, (La Grange, 2021), such as running water (Ellis, 2020) and consistent electricity (Kambule, Yessoufou, K., Nwulu, N., & Mbohwa, 2019). This chapter adopts qualitative research with a case study to explore technology integration in three different secondary schools during the coronavirus pandemic.

THEORETICAL FRAMEWORK

The Technological Pedagogical Content Knowledge (TPACK) framework developed by Mishra and Koehler (Mishra & Koehler, 2008) provides assistance for this chapter. The combination of a teacher's technological, pedagogical, and content knowledge is referred to as "TPACK". Thus, according to Mishra (2019), TPACK is the fusion

Figure 1. Context chart

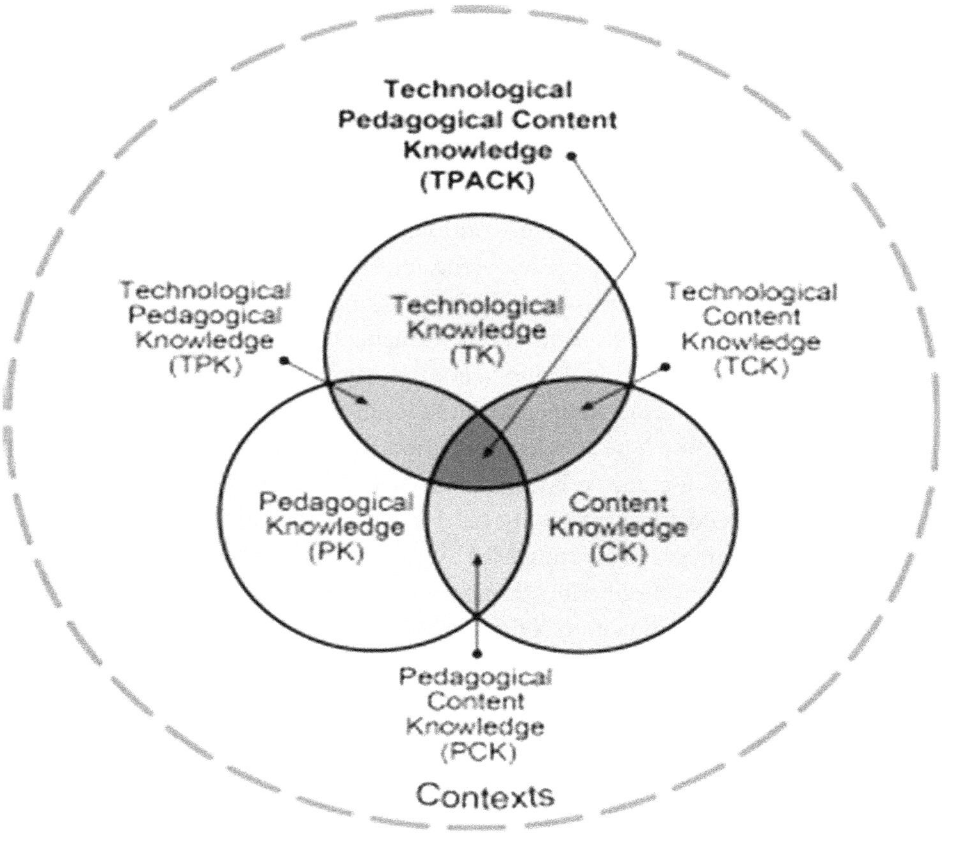

of an instructor's PK, CK, and technological expertise (TK). In this regard, TPACK is a sophisticated body of information influenced by a wide range of contextual factors, many of which are dynamic or undergoing rapid change, such as student socioeconomic backgrounds, school administration, curricula, and technology. The ability to combine two (TPK and TPK) or all three (TPACK) is crucial for teachers to possess. One needs a thorough understanding of the relationships among technology, content, and pedagogy to develop TPACK. Understanding how technology, content, and pedagogy are interconnected is essential for developing TPACK. Afterward, representations and processes must be made using that that understanding to create representations and procedures.

This theory is employed in the study because it is crucial for teachers to implement TPACK in the subject area (mathematics) in order for learning to be more successful.

As a result, in order to help teachers, teach TPACK, they must also create a design-based learner guide (Mishra & Koehler, 2008). For instance, when preparing to incorporate technology into a lesson, teachers should take into account the students' level of technology proficiency, the mathematical content required, and the most efficient methods for teaching both the technology and the mathematics (O'Neal, Gibson & Cotton, 2017). This need for assistance could be quite important, as according to Sipilä (2014), the choice of whether and how technology is included into teaching and learning rests on the teachers.

LITERATURE REVIEW

The Role of Technology Integration in Mathematics Teaching

The COVID-19 outbreak prevented the regular course of teaching and learning (Wijaya, 2021; Murphy, 2020). No learners were allowed to attend classes; they were required to study at home. This situation made it necessary to use technology more frequently in education and learning. Formerly informal classroom learning practices are now facilitated by meeting platforms, websites, or video lessons. According to reports, many teachers were expected to teach mathematics courses online in 2020, despite having no experience doing so (Hodges, Moore, Lockee, Trust & Bond, 2020).

A fresh COVID-19 instance was reported in Bangkok, Thailand, the first country outside of China, on January 13, 2020 (Intawong, Olson, & Chariyalertsak, 2021). Thailand now needs educational change more than ever as a result of the outbreak. To meet the needs for technological integration, blended learning (BL), which combines online and offline learning, was made available beginning in 2020. (SEAMEO Regional Centre for Higher Education and Development [SEAMEO RIHED], 2021). Thailand has since seen an increase in COVID-19 cases (Charoensuthipan, 2021). Learners were consequently forced to complete their homework at home.

The unexpected COVID-19 pandemic has compelled school teachers and learners to work and study totally from home, leading to the implementation of online teaching and learning even in rural schools contexts. The stakeholders (teachers and learners) have unavoidably experienced both advantages and disadvantages of using online education (Jiang et al., 2021; Tadesse & Muluye, 2020). According to their earlier research, the global COVID-19 pandemic has an impact on schools' learners continued health in the Asia Pacific area, including Thailand, because of difficulties with online learning.

In general, anxiety was identified as the biggest issue affecting learners, followed by sadness and stress (Jiang, Yan-Li, Pamanee, & Sriyanto, 2021). According to

Tadesse and Muluye (2020), the COVID-19 pandemic has impacted parents, teachers, learners, and schools in developing nations. Some underprivileged learners from schools or rural locations with little educational resources and ICT (Information and Communication Technology) infrastructure. Disadvantaged learners then lack the proper digital infrastructure needed to deliver remote teaching during online learning. The study's findings showed that learners' levels of stress, anxiety, and depression disorders were high while schools and universities were closed.

Challenges of Technology Integration in Mathematics During COVID-19

The COVID-19 pandemic greatly changed education, moving it from a traditional setting to one that was conducted online. As a result, the substantive situation highlights the significance of technology integration in education and calls for teachers to upgrade their competencies. The COVID-19 pandemic has, as is evident throughout the world, significantly disrupted every aspect of human life. Similar to how the closure of institutions from schools to universities and the move from traditional to online education presented numerous issues to the educational sector. (UN, 2020). According to numerous studies, using ICT in the classroom is now essential for satisfying learners' demands in the knowledge society (Martins, Branco, Gonçalves, Au-Yong-Oliveira, Oliveira, and Naranjo-Zolotov, 2019). Additionally, effective ICT integration can excite learners and maintain their motivation throughout the learning process (Hanafi, Said, Wahab & Samsuddin, 2017). Utilizing a mobile reality learning environment to increase learners' interest in taking ICT courses, which are thought to be the most important determinants of their academic achievement (Xu, Yuan & Liu, 2021). In a similar vein, the Pakistani government advises using ICT to improve educational outcomes because it helps teachers develop their pedagogical skills and encourages learners to engage in active learning [Pakistan Ministry of Education (MoE), 2018]. Additionally, systematizing an effective online educational program requires the proper integration of ICT. The effective use of ICT not only benefits learners' pleasure but also enables them to achieve their goals (Cervero, Castro-Lopez, AlvarezBlanco, Esteban & Bernardo, 2020). According to earlier studies, learners often perform better academically on digital platforms than on traditional ones. (Shehzadi, Nisar, Hussain, Basheer, Hameed & Chaudhry, 2020).

Professional Training Before and During COVID-19

During 2010–2020, research papers describing new literacies and teachers' professional development have been published (Tafazoli, 2021). Digital literacy is a necessary component of teachers' survival skills in the twenty-first century, and it must be considered while enhancing the capabilities of teachers, particularly mathematics teachers. To facilitate teachers gaining skills and abilities in online teaching, professional training is one of the major keys. Studies before and during the COVID-19 period (2010–2021) demonstrate perceptions of teachers' needs for professional training at each point in time.

More consideration was given to pedagogical concerns because teachers needed help setting up technology integration training programs (Llerena-Izquierdo & Ayala-Carabajo, 2021; Nguyen & Kieuthi, 2020). Compared to pre-COVID training programs, the importance of online teachers was emphasized more. The goal of training during the COVID-19 pandemic was to equip teachers to design, practice, and use ICT tools for online teaching and learning, as Llerena-Izquierdo and Ayala-Carabajo (2021) have eloquently shown. The findings of their study suggested that training programs might improve teachers' proficiency with ICT technologies and create new opportunities for simultaneous communication, which would help teachers start the new online school year off on the right foot. Information technology application in the classroom was listed as a required capability for teachers. It was intended that non-traditional educational approaches would improve students' learning experiences by incorporating digital literacies into teachers' professional development training.

Regardless of the time period (before or during COVID-19), there were numerous workshops regarding online teaching (Boonmoh & Khamprem, 2021; Khamprem & Boonmoh, 2019; Llerena-Izquierdo & Ayala-Carabajo, 2021; Nguyen & Kieuthi, 2020). However, the teachers' needs were not fully implemented into the training workshops in order to cover all the skillsets or abilities, according to the proposed models of Compton (2009), and Hampel and Stickler (2005). Furthermore, the training workshops were not adequately designed based on the teachers' needs as it did not provide teachers with the skill sets they required. Thus, this research aimed to seek ways to discover teachers' needs for their professional development according to the proposed models for online mathematics teaching. The implications of the research would be guidance for future teacher training regarding online language teachers' skills. Information technology application in the classroom was listed as a required capability for teachers. It was intended that non-traditional educational approaches would improve students' learning experiences by incorporating digital literacies into teachers' professional development training.

Regardless of the time period (before or during COVID-19), there were numerous workshops regarding online teaching (Boonmoh & Khamprem, 2021; Khamprem & Boonmoh, 2019; Llerena-Izquierdo & Ayala-Carabajo, 2021; Nguyen & Kieuthi, 2020). However, the teachers' needs were not fully implemented into the training workshops in order to cover all the skillsets or abilities, according to the proposed models of Compton (2009), and Hampel and Stickler (2005). Furthermore, the training workshops were not adequately designed based on the teachers' needs as it did not provide teachers with the skill sets they required.

METHODOLOGY

Research Paradigm

An interpretive method was utilized in this paper to gather information from nine participants, or three mathematics teachers of grade 10 from each of the nine schools in the OR Tambo Coastal District of the Eastern Cape. Based on people's beliefs, attitudes, and perceptions, the interpretive paradigm. Because the author wished to investigate the effects of technology integration in mathematics teaching during COVID-19, this paradigm was suited for the study. The interpretive paradigm, which differs from positivism in that it prioritizes the richness of the study context, enables participants to communicate their own sentiments, attitudes, and perceptions regarding how they deal with technology integration in teaching mathematics during COVID-19 (Alharahshah & Pius, 2020).

Research Method

The qualitative research method was explored as it relies on the collection of data using words and narratives in order to search for in-depth understanding of the technology integration in teaching mathematics during COVID-19 pandemic to promote wellbeing of learners (Maree, 2010).

Sample Technique

A purposeful sampling technique was employed. Purposeful sampling is widely used in qualitative research for the identification and selection of information-rich cases related to the phenomenon of interest (Palinkas, 2015). Perspectives in technology integration regarding, lack of adequate formal technological training, the level of technical knowledge of teachers, the years of experience, and the types of teaching strategies they use are discussed.

Population and Sampling

To Su (2018), population is the collection of objects, events or individuals having some common characteristics that the researcher is interested in studying. The study was conducted in one education district OR Tambo Inland in the Eastern Cape of

South Africa. The target population comprised all teachers of the three different schools. A sample of 9 participants will be drawn from a population of 25 grade 10 mathematics teachers in the OR Tambo Inland District.

Data Collection Instruments

Interviews will be the main source of data collection. Interviews are normally used to collect data from a small group of people (Kumar, 2018). Since the sample will be nine (9) participants, the instrument is deemed appropriate.

Data Analysis and Interpretation

Thematic analysis will be used using inductive reasoning which is likely to help me identify the multiple realities potentially present in the data (Maree, 2010). The above view is supported by Ngulube (2015) when saying that categories and patterns primarily emerge from the data, rather than being imposed on them prior to collection. Interviews will be transcribed, read over repeatedly, codes generated, and themes developed for analysis and interpretation.

Research Ethics

Permission will be sought from the Department of Education in line with ethical considerations. Furthermore, the ethical considerations including informed consent forms were given to participants to allow them to exercise their right to be part of the research or not (Hasan, Rana, Chowdhury, Dola & Rony (2021). Protection from harm implies that the settings and participants should not be identifiable in print. The other way of protecting the participants' right to privacy was through the promise of confidentiality.

Findings

Findings from the study are detailed into three emerging themes, including (1) technology integration in mathematics teaching and availability of access to technology, (2) benefits of technology integration that promote wellbeing of learners, (3) Professional training before and during COVID-19.

Technology Integration and Availability of Access to Technology

The first question concerned the employment of technology and internet accessibility in mathematics instruction. In response to one of their concerns, a teacher said, "I usually carry a cell phone everywhere, checking assignments sent by students to WhatsApp or Moodle. Therefore, I use Internet access more frequently via mobile phone." Another participant remarked, "I utilize the school's Wi-Fi.

I use a smartphone with personal data, a participant added. You could argue that because my internet connection has never been interrupted and is consistently stable, teaching is made easier for me, but the issue is that my students don't have cellphones. Since almost all teachers have smartphones as a communication tool, most of them utilize them to access the Internet.

According to the participant in the interview mentioned above, "This results in the completion of random assignments for pupils who do not understand. In order to prevent students' comprehension of the stuff I explain from declining during the COVID-19 pandemic, I need to get used to delivering learning materials using (learning videos).

"As long as I continue to lecture during the COVID-19 pandemic, learners retain only a small portion of the material. Due to the nature of online learning, it is challenging to ensure that all students grasp the material being taught, and some may not be diligent in applying what they have learned.

But according to another participant, "Working online, it is difficult to establish whether a learner is fully engaged and has sufficient understanding, a basic issue that has yet to be solved by technology."

"As long as I teach during the COVID-19 pandemic, learners absorb very little of the material familiar," claimed a different participant from another school.

"I have trouble explaining the information, especially because math is my area of study. I can't determine which students actually comprehend or which students are just pretending to grasp without direct offline engagement.

Benefits of Technology Integration That Promote Wellbeing of Learners

Participants were questioned regarding the advantages of technology integration that support learners' wellness. One participant replied, "I used computer algebra systems (CAS) like Mathematica during the pandemic, and I believe that this digital technology enhanced active learning approaches. Additionally, it allowed the students a chance to actively engage in the process of developing and solidifying their own knowledge". Another participant said: "Unfortunately, I did not try to employ any of this digital technologies in mathematical instruction before the coronavirus". However, the COVID-19 pandemic's unexpected and unprecedented shutdown of our country's school buildings made educators deal with the profession's most abrupt and rapid transformation in history". Another participant echoed this sentiment when she said: "I can state that COVID-19 is the gateway to digital learning in mathematics teaching; thus, I will never stop using digital technology in mathematical teaching, because digital technology brings mathematics education to life. To aid in the development of skills and understandings in our students, we can use films, animations, and other media into the learning process. Additionally, it may serve to inspire and motivate our students as they learn. Another participant echoed this sentiment when she said: "I can state that COVID-19 is the gateway to digital learning in mathematics teaching; thus, I will never stop using digital technology in mathematical teaching, because digital technology brings mathematics education to life.

Professional Training Before and During COVID-19

During interview on the issue of professional training, one participant responded, "I do attend professional training workshops that are organized but the problem they are for short of time." regarding professional training of technology integration during the COVID-19 pandemic. Another participant remarked, "I typically attend technology training, but it was only scheduled for a maximum of two days." He continued by saying it was challenging for him to claim to have taken part in digital trainings because these seminars were merely set up for them to register their marks.

Another participant has a similar complaint about the limited time, claiming that the department primarily concentrates on recording grades rather than on really teaching the subject.

A different participant observed: "There were small training workshops organized to develop teachers digitally before COVID-19."

Discussion of Findings

Globally, the COVID-19 pandemic has altered traditional educational practices and introduced digital teaching-learning. This change not only makes the nation's educational technology infrastructure more crucial, but it also makes it necessary for teachers to effectively integrate technology into their pedagogical practices in order to promote students' learning. Despite having no prior experience doing so, many teachers were apparently expected to teach mathematics courses online in 2020. (Hodges, Moore, Lockee, Trust & Bond, 2020). Even though teachers have access to technology, some of them encounter challenges, according to the study's findings. For instance, teachers and school officials in Kuwait have been unable to incorporate technology into their classrooms due to a lack of ICT training, teacher familiarity with technology, and a lack of technological resources. The MOE in Kuwait did not view educational technology as being crucial to the curriculum before the outbreak. According to Al-Harbi (2014), teachers lacked enough training in the use of ICT as a teaching tool. This study also demonstrates that online learning is less successful than in-person instruction because to the frequently erratic assignment collection schedule and connectivity concerns. Even while some teachers are now skilled at using technical tools, Internet connectivity still presents a difficulty, especially in locations where Internet networks are challenging owing to Internet bandwidth and geographic location. The constraints of the teachers' methods of subject presentation play a role in how well students understand the learning information. There will be fewer possibilities for students who don't understand the material to ask questions than there would be in face-to-face instruction. Undoubtedly, this situation causes students to become less interested in asking questions. This is quite difficult for practical lessons as well. Teachers are only permitted to watch practice movies that their pupils have provided. According to a number of studies, the use of ICT in the classroom is now essential for addressing students' demands in the knowledge society (Martins, Branco, Gonçalves, Au-Yong-Oliveira, 2019). According to comments made by instructors, there was little formal training provided to help teachers become more tech-savvy. In spite of their lack of experience, many teachers were reportedly expected to teach mathematics courses online in 2020. (Hodges, Moore, Lockee, Trust & Bond, 2020). Teachers' comments revealed that there was minimal organized training to help teachers become more tech-savvy. According to reports, many teachers were expected to teach mathematics courses online in 2020, despite having no experience doing so. (Hodges, Moore, Lockee, Trust & Bond, 2020).

CONCLUSION

It is clear from the results and debate above that some teachers have access to technology through their smartphones, while others have voiced frustration with internet restrictions. The majority of teachers reported that because other pupils didn't have smartphones, there wasn't enough time for internet access. Lack of computer skills, as well as a lack of education and exposure to technology, were the most often mentioned obstacles to technology integration. According to the participants' replies, COVID-19 is the starting point for digital learning in mathematics education. Teachers emphasized that they will never stop using digital technology in mathematics education since it makes the subject come alive. Accordingly, the study suggests that professional training should be employed in the professional development programs to develop teachers' for integrating technology efficiently by bridging the gap between

ICT knowledge and ICT practice even after COVID-19 pandemic. Accordingly, the report recommends using professional training in professional development programs to help instructors become more adept at integrating technology by bridging the knowledge and practice gaps in ICT, even after the COVID-19 pandemic.

Recommendations

This study's first recommendation is to increase teachers' access to technology by installing backup in load-shedding situations, allowing them to employ their newly learned computer skills to enhance present classroom practices. In the initial phase of implementation, fully equipped classrooms should be freely available for technology-based instruction. Additionally, the computer should already have the required learning software loaded, and students should each have access to the relevant lesson plans and worksheets as needed. Throughout the entire deployment period, a hybrid strategy that retains some conventional processes in place should be encouraged. Another important concept is the usage of e-assessment, which would match assessment procedures with instructional procedures. An electronic test can be administered at any time, with results being marked right away. The questions are computer-generated. Additionally, it is suggested that schools make sure that each student has a data card that is loaded with unlimited data in order to ensure that teaching and learning continue smoothly. In order to use ICT as a tool to enhance teaching and learning at the university level, I advise that frequent in-service training and capacity-building workshops on ICT literacy and its use for teaching and learning be conducted for these rural university lecturers. Teachers in this study claimed that they lacked the professional training.

REFERENCES

Aguilar, M. S., & Castaneda, A. (2021). What mathematical competencies does a citizen need to interpret Mexico's official information about the COVID-19 pandemic? *Educational Studies in Mathematics, 108*(1-2), 227–248. doi:10.100710649-021-10082-9 PMID:34934238

Al Harbi, H. E. M. (2014). *An examination of Saudi high school teachers' ICT knowledge and implementation* [Doctoral dissertation, Queensland University of Technology].

Alharahsheh, H. H., & Pius, A. (2020). A review of key paradigms: Positivism VS interpretivism. *Global Academic Journal of Humanities and Social Sciences, 2*(3), 39–43.

Arnesen, K. T., Hveem, J., Short, C. R., West, R. E., & Barbour, M. K. (2019). K-12 online learning journal articles: Trends from two decades of scholarship. *Distance Education, 40*(1), 32-53. https://doi. . 1080/ 01587 919. 2018. 15535 66. doi:org/10

Atmojo, A. E. P., & Nugroho, A. (2020). EFL classes must go online! Teaching activities and challenges during COVID-19 pandemic in Indonesia. *Register Journal, 13*(1), 49-76. https://journalregister.iainsalatiga.ac.id/index.php/register/article/view/4051

Bell, A. M. (2005). Behavioural differences between individuals and two populations of stickleback (Gasterosteus aculeatus). *Journal of Evolutionary Biology, 18*(2), 464–473. doi:10.1111/j.1420-9101.2004.00817.x PMID:15715852

Boonmoh, A., & Khamprem, K. (2021). Teachers' Rationale and Use of Technology: A Comparative Study Involving a Public Technical College and a Private High School. *Human Behavior. Development and Society*, *22*(1). https://so01.tci and thaijo.org/index.php/hbds/article/view/244938

Bozkurt, A., & Sharma, R. C. (2020). Emergency remote teaching in a time of global crisis due to Corona Virus pandemic. *Asian journal of distance education, 15*(1), i-vi.

Cervero, A., Castro-Lopez, A., Álvarez-Blanco, L., Esteban, M., & Bernardo, A. (2020). Evaluation of educational quality performance on virtual campuses using fuzzy inference systems. *PLoS One*, *15*(5), e0232802. doi:10.1371/journal.pone.0232802 PMID:32469875

Charoensuthipan, P. (2021, April 28). Third wave's unpalatable reality. *Bangkok Post*. https://www.bangkokpost.com/thailand/special-reports/2106859/third-waves-unpalatable-reality

Compton, L. K. L. (2009). Preparing language teachers to teach languages online: A look a t skills, roles, and responsibilities. *Computer Assisted Language Learning*, *22*(1), 73–79. https://www.tandfonline.com/doi/. doi:10.1080/09588220802613831

Ellis, E. (2020). COVID-19: Exposing a water crisis in the making. *Daily Maverick*. https:// www. Daily maver ick. co. za/ artic le/ 2020- 05- 14- COVID- 19- exposing-a-water- crisis- in- the- making/.

Gómez, N. L. (2021). La Educación Matemática en hogares venezolanos durante la pandemia. *Cuadernos de Investigación y Formación en Educación Matemática*, (20), 256–278.

Goos, M., & Beswick, K. (2021). *Learning and Development of Mathematics Teacher Educators*. Springer International Publishing.

Government of South Africa (2020). *Minister Angie Motshekga: Basic education sector recovery plans for the reopening of schools, following the Coronavirus COVID-19 lockdown adjustment of regulations.* Government of South Africa.

Hampel, R., & Stickler, U. (2005). New skills for new classrooms: Training tutors to teach languages online. *Computer Assisted Language Learning*, *18*(4), 311–326. doi:10.1080/09588220500335455

Hanafi, H. F., Said, C. S., Wahab, M. H., & Samsuddin, K. (2017, August). Improving students' motivation in learning ICT course with the use of a mobile augmented reality learning environment. In IOP Conference Series: Materials Science and Engineering (Vol. 226, No. 1, p. 012114). IOP Publishing. doi:10.1088/1757-899X/226/1/012114

Harisman, Y., Kusumah, Y. S., & Kusnandi, K. (2019, March). How teacher professionalism influences student behaviour in mathematical problem-solving process. In Journal of Physics: Conference Series (Vol. 1188, No. 1, p. 012080). IOP Publishing. doi:10.1088/1742-6596/1188/1/012080

Hasan, N., Rana, R. U., Chowdhury, S., Dola, A. J., & Rony, M. K. K. (2021). Ethical considerations in research. *Journal of Nursing Research, Patient Safety and Practise (JNRPSP) 2799-1210, 1*(01), 1-4. . doi:10.55529/jnrpsp11.1.4

Hermita, N., Ningsih, H. S., Alim, J. A., Alpusari, M., Putra, Z. H., & Wijaya, T. T. (2020). Developing Science Comics for Elementary School Students on Animal Diversity. *Solid State Technology*, *63*(1s), 2492–2500.

Hodgen, J., Taylor, B., Jacques, L., Tereshchenko, A., Kwok, R., & Cockerill, M. (2020). *Remote mathematics teaching during COVID-19: Intentions, practices and equity*. UCL. https://www.ucl.ac.uk/ioe/studentgroupingstudy

Hodges, C. B., Moore, S., Lockee, B. B., Trust, T., & Bond, M. A. (2020). *The difference between emergency remote teaching and online learning*. HDL. http://hdl.handle.net/10919/104648

Intawong, K., Olson, D., & Chariyalertsak, S. (2021). Application technology to fight the COVID-19 pandemic: Lessons learned in Thailand. *Biochemical and Biophysical Research Communications*, *534*, 830–836. doi:10.1016/j.bbrc.2020.10.097 PMID:33250175

Jiang, N., Yan-Li, S., Pamanee, K., & Sriyanto, J. (2021). Depression, anxiety, and stress during the COVID-19 pandemic: Comparison among higher education students in four countries in the Asia-Pacific region. [JPSS]. *Journal of Population and Social Studies*, *29*, 370–383. https://so03.tci-thaijo.org/index.php/jpss/article/view/244216. doi:10.25133/JPSSv292021.023

Kambule, N., Yessoufou, K., Nwulu, N., & Mbohwa, C. (2019). Exploring the driving factors of prepaid electricity meter rejection in the largest township of South Africa. *Energy Policy*, *124*, 199–205. doi:10.1016/j.enpol.2018.09.041

Khamprem, K., & Boonmoh, A. (2019). Teachers' stated needs and their actual use of technology. *Human Behavior. Development and Society*, *20*(4), 41–51. https://so01.tci-thaijo.org/index.php/hbds/article/view/193626

Kumar, R. (2018). Research methodology: A step-by-step guide for beginners. *Sage (Atlanta, Ga.)*.

Le Grange, L. (2021). Covid-19 pandemic and the prospects of education in South Africa. *Prospects*, *51*(1-3), 425–436. doi:10.100711125-020-09514-w PMID:33100404

Llerena-Izquierdo, J., & Ayala-Carabajo, R. (2021). University teacher training during the COVID-19 emergency: the role of online teaching-learning tools. In Information Technology and Systems: ICITS 2021, Volume 2 (pp. 90-99). Springer International Publishing. doi:10.1007/978-3-030-68418-1_10

Maraví Zavaleta, L. M. (2021). Emergent curriculum in basic education for the new normality in Peru: Orientations proposed from mathematics education. *Educational Studies in Mathematics*, *108*(1-2), 291–305. doi:10.100710649-021-10100-w PMID:34934241

Maree, K. (2010). *First steps in research* (Revised ed.). Van Schaik.

Mhlanga, D., & Moloi, T. (2020). COVID-19 and the digital transformation of education: What are we learning on 4IR in South Africa? *Education Sciences*, *10*(7), 180. doi:10.3390/educsci10070180

Mishra, P. (2019). Considering contextual knowledge: The TPACK diagram gets an upgrade. *Journal of Digital Learning in Teacher Education*, *35*(2), 76–78. doi:10.1080/21532974.2019.1588611

Mishra, P., & Koehler, M. J. (2008, March). Introducing technological pedagogical content knowledge. In *annual meeting of the American Educational Research Association* (*Vol. 1*, p. 16). AERA.

Murphy, M. P. (2020). COVID-19 and emergency eLearning: Consequences of the securitization of higher education for post-pandemic pedagogy. *Contemporary Security Policy*, *41*(3), 492–505. doi:10.1080/13523260.2020.1761749

Ngulube, P. (2015). Qualitative data analysis and interpretation: systematic search for meaning. *Addressing research challenges: making headway for developing researchers, 131*, 156. https://www.researchgate.net/publication/278961843

Nguyen, D. T., & Kieuthi, T. C. (2020). New trends in technology application in education and capacities of universities lecturers during the Covid-19 pandemic. [IJMPERD]. *International Journal of Mechanical and Production Engineering Research and Development, 10*(3), 1709–1714. https://www.researchgate.net/publication/343126027

O'Neal, L. J., Gibson, P., & Cotten, S. R. (2017). Elementary school teachers' beliefs about the role of technology in 21st-century teaching and learning. *Computers in the Schools, 34*(3), 192–206. doi:10.1080/07380569.2017.1347443

Onyema, E. M., Eucheria, N. C., Obafemi, F. A., Sen, S., Atonye, F. G., Sharma, A., & Alsayed, A. O. (2020). Impact of Coronavirus pandemic on education. *Journal of Education and Practice, 11*(13), 108–121. doi:10.7176/JEP/11-13-12

Oyedotun, T. D. (2020). Sudden change of pedagogy in education driven by COVID-19: Perspectives and evaluation from a developing country. *Research in Globalization, 2*, 100029. doi:10.1016/j.resglo.2020.100029

Pakistan Ministry of Education (MoE). (2018). National Education Policy 2018. services research, 42, 533-544. Islamabad: Government of Pakistan. doi:10.52223/JSSA20-010105-05

Palinkas, L. A., Horwitz, S. M., Green, C. A., Wisdom, J. P., Duan, N., & Hoagwood, K. (2015). Purposeful sampling for qualitative data collection and analysis in mixed method implementation research. *Administration and Policy in Mental Health, 42*(5), 533–544. https://link.springer.com/article/10.1007/s10488-013-0528-y. doi:10.100710488-013-0528-y PMID:24193818

SEAMEO Regional Centre for Higher Education and Development. (2021, September 26). *The 8th Meeting of the Working Group on Student Mobility and Quality Assurance of Higher Education among ASEAN Plus Three Countries (APT WG)*. SEAMEO RIHED. https://rihed.seameo.org/the-8th-meeting-of-aptwg/

Siko, J. P., & Barbour, M. K. (2022). Is it Any Wonder, I Reject You First: Pre-Pandemic Perceptions of K-12 Online Learning. *TechTrends, 66*(2), 301–309. doi:10.100711528-022-00709-w PMID:35229084

Sipilä, K. (2014). Educational use of information and communications technology: Teachers' perspective. *Technology, Pedagogy and Education, 23*(2), 225–241. doi:10.1080/1475939X.2013.813407

Soudien, C., Reddy, V., & Harvey, J. (2021). *The impact of COVID-19 on a fragile education system: The case of South Africa.* Springer. . doi:10.1007/978-3-030-81500-4

Su, N. (2018). Positivist qualitative methods. The Sage handbook of qualitative business and management research methods, 17-32.

Tadesse, S., & Muluye, W. (2020). The impact of COVID-19 pandemic on education system in developing countries: A review. *Open Journal of Social Sciences*, *8*(10), 159–170. doi:10.4236/jss.2020.810011

Tafazoli, D. (2021). CALL teachers' professional development amid the COVID-19 outbreak: A qualitative study. *Call-Ej, 22*(2), 4-13. https://www.researchgate.net/publication/350604667_

Tan, S., Wijaya, T. T., Zou, L., & Hermita, N. (2020, October). Proving the formula for the area of a circle using Hawgent dynamic mathematics software. In Journal of Physics: Conference Series, 1655(1), 012052. IOP Publishing. doi:10.1088/1742-6596/1655/1/012052

Thompson, K. M., & Copeland, C. (2020). Inclusive considerations for optimal online learning in times of disasters and crises. *Information and Learning Sciences*, *121*(7/8), 481–486. doi:10.1108/ILS-04-2020-0083

Thorn, W., & Vincent-Lancrin, S. (2022). Education in the time of COVID-19 in France, Ireland, the United Kingdom and the United States: The nature and impact of remote learning. *Primary and secondary education during COVID-19: Disruptions to educational opportunity during a pandemic*, 383-420. Springer. . doi:10.1007/978-3-030-81500-4

Tondeur, J., Scherer, R., Siddiq, F., & Baran, E. (2020). Enhancing pre-service teachers' technological pedagogical content knowledge (TPACK): A mixed-method study. *Educational Technology Research and Development*, *68*(1), 319–343. doi:10.100711423-019-09692-1

Trikoilis, D., & Papanastasiou, E. C. (2020). The potential of research for professional development in isolated settings during the COVID-19 crisis and beyond. *Journal of Technology and Teacher Education*, *28*(2), 295–300. https://www.learntechlib.org/primary/p/216071/

UN. (2020). *Education during COVID-19 and beyond.* UN. https://www.un.org/development/desa/dspd/wp-content/uploads/sites/22/ 2020/08/ sg_policy_brief_covid-19_and_education_august_2020.pdf

Wijaya, T. T. (2020). How chinese students learn mathematics during the coronavirus pandemic. . doi:10.46661/ijeri.4950

World Bank. (2020). *Rapid response briefing note: Remote learning and COVID-19 outbreak*. The World Bank.

Population Review. (2021). *Gini coefficient by country 2021*. UNESCO.

Xu, Z., Yuan, H., & Liu, Q. (2020). Student performance prediction based on blended learning. *IEEE Transactions on Education*, *64*(1), 66–73. doi:10.1109/TE.2020.3008751

Yılmaz, Z., Gülbağcı Dede, H., Sears, R., & Yıldız Nielsen, S. (2021). Are we all in this together? Mathematics teachers' perspectives on equity in remote instruction during pandemic. *Educational Studies in Mathematics*, *108*(1–2), 307–331. doi:10.100710649-021-10060-1 PMID:34934233

Yılmaz, Z., Gülbağcı Dede, H., Sears, R., & Yıldız Nielsen, S. (2021). Are we all in this together?: Mathematics teachers' perspectives on equity in remote instruction during pandemic. *Educational Studies in Mathematics*, *108*(1-2), 307–331. doi:10.100710649-021-10060-1 PMID:34934233

Chapter 9
Strategies for Motivating Learners to Complete the General Education and Training Certificate Level 1 in South Africa

Itumeleng I. Setlhodi
https://orcid.org/0000-0003-2644-9570
University of South Africa, South Africa

Motlagoiloe S. Moroe
University of South Africa, South Africa

ABSTRACT

The general education and training certificate: adult basic education and training provides learners with foundational learning through the acquisition of knowledge and skills needed for social and economic development and the promotion of justice and equality. However, national statistics show that the number of learners who enroll for the programme exceeds those who complete it. The qualitative study was conducted to explore strategies that can be used to motivate adult learners to complete the GETC: ABET. Interactive individual and focus interviews (=35) led to findings indicating that interventions used by teachers to encourage learners to complete their studies, and support given, minimise, or eliminate barriers against completing the programme. Thereupon, the Department of Higher Education and Training has an opportunity to strengthen the teachers' stratagems in ensuring that more learners complete the programme. Accordingly, this chapter proposes strategies found to be essential in this study, for consideration by community colleges.

DOI: 10.4018/978-1-6684-6625-4.ch009

INTRODUCTION

The White Paper on Post-School Education and Training (2013:5) states that education has potential to eradicate poverty and a way of ensuring there is equality of opportunities. Thus, it therefore implies that the socio-economic wellbeing of marginalised people can be redressed through education. Yeoh and Chu (2012:11) attest that underdevelopment and poverty can be expunged through literacy and education to bring about social changes. Furthermore, the White Paper states that education may not provide economic growth, but, without it, economic growth, social, and cultural development cannot be fulfilled. This perspective on education is closely aligned to the rationale for the GETC: ABET programme, as stated by the South African Qualifications Authority (SAQA). Namely, to prepare learners, by providing them with basic skills needed for social and economic development, as well as developing an appreciation for lifelong learning (South African Qualifications Authority n.d.).

In South Africa, adult basic education (ABE) was declared a constitutional right in 1996 and the responsibility to implement this was placed squarely on the government (McKay 2007:294). As a result, the development of the educational policy framework included a policy on adult education, the outcome of which was adult basic education and training (Beauzac 2010). Despite the successes of these policies, which aimed at improving participation in ABET programmes, not many learners, who enrol in ABET programmes, complete their basic education. It is against this background that the study sought to highlight strategies that can be used to motivate adult learners to complete the Adult Basic Education and Training Programme at NQF Level 1 and, consequently, overcome socio-economic problems.

Adult basic education and training (ABET) is essential for the development of human resource, particularly those that cannot access education in any other way. It also contributes to the economic development of people and for increasing people's life choices, thereby assuring the wellbeing. The 2030 Agenda for Sustainable Development (SD), as adopted by all United Nations member states in 2015, provides a shared blueprint for peace and prosperity for people and the planet, now and into the future (United Nations 2018). At the core of the SD goals is the need to home in the development of people and enhancement of livelihood. The Sustainable Development Goal (SDG) 4 calls on countries to ensure inclusive and equitable quality education and the promotion of lifelong learning for all; however, in order to achieve this goal, literacy and numeracy are indispensable (UNESCO 2017). Therefore, it should form the bedrock for basic education as well as the background to promoting the socio-economic wellbeing of marginalised individuals through development.

BACKGROUND

The changes taking place in society have made adult education an integral part of lifelong learning. According to UNESCO (2017), based on emancipatory, humanistic and democratic values, lifelong learning covers the integration of learning and living, covering learning activities for all ages, in all life contexts and through formal, non-formal and informal modalities. Lifelong learning is promoted for both an investment motive and a consumption motive. The investment motive equips learners with the competencies required in the workplace and the consumption motive assists in learners' personal development (Nafukho, Amutabi & Otunga 2005:150). However, there seems to be a lack of structured strategies in place to support completion of the GETC: ABET programme. Adult basic education and training is meant to offer a route that adults can take into general education, aimed at improving their quality of life (particularly for previously disadvantaged adults) and to promote lifelong learning. However, most adult learners, enrolled in the programme, do not complete their training, as indicated by the 2014 statistics on Post-School Education and Training in South Africa (Department of Higher Education and Training 2014:59). This suggests that livelihoods that would otherwise be improved through basic education are not supported, thereby compromising the likelihood to improve their socio-economic outlook.

LESSONS LEARNED

A formula-based approach was used to specifically support learners, whose education was not sponsored through the ABET Act (2000). This design was linked to an annual institutional plan to effect appropriate funding. Despite these efforts and the evident willingness to support adult learning in South Africa, certain factors compound the ability of adult learners to complete their learning programmes. These may range from personal, to social and psychological factors; hence, the need to investigate suitable strategies for adult learners to complete their qualifications. Table 1.1 presents the situation in South Africa between 2011-2014, which Moroe (2019) found did not change much in her study conducted after the period on the table.

A study conducted in the United States of America, by Gall (2013), reviewed effective motivational strategies that have the potential to increase retention and completion of ABET programmes. The study identified the following strategies as effective in realising increased learner retention and completion: allowing self-study options flexibility in scheduling; the ability by the facilitator to relate teaching to real life, while adhering to qualification requirements; offering counselling to address barriers; and determining goals. According to Gall (2013:68), allowing self-study

Table 1. Number of learners in public AET centres who registered, wrote, and completed the GETC-ABET NQF Level 1 qualification, from 2011 to 2014 (Department of Higher Education and Traininga: 2014)

Year	Number Registered	Number Wrote	Number completed	Completion rate (%)
2011	107 780	39 586	13 924	34.9
2012	109 883	55 735	23 325	41.8
2013	109 518	52 501	19 945	38.0
2014	133 363	102 534	38 592	37.6

options, flexibility, engagement and discussions of realistic expectations resulted in learning increasing from 13%, in 2007, to 44%, in 2008. It was also found that, when learning was related to real life, such as relating learning content to current events through the use of newspapers, websites and magazines, students reported that such activities instilled a sense of academic achievement (Gall 2013:69).

A study conducted by Sogunro (2015) indicated that the top five motivating factors in adult learning were the quality of education, quality of curriculum, relevance and pragmatism, an interactive classroom environment and progressive assessment (Sogunro 2015:27). Research by Byrne, O'Grady and Roche (2016), which comprised various case studies on strategies for motivating learners in adult education in Ireland, found that establishing good relationships and creating a stimulating environment, from the onset, helped learners overcome previous bad schooling experiences through reflection. Other effective strategies to motivate adult learners included understanding that learners had different learning styles and that they needed to be accommodated. In addition, there needs to be a focus on learners' goals. According to the findings, most learners, who were reluctant to attend classes, but had to, because non-attendance would lead to the withdrawal or reduction of social welfare payments, changed their attitude and began to actively engage in the learning process when tutors implemented the strategies mentioned above (Byrne et al. 2016:64). Thus, it can be said that adult learning programmes should be structured in such a manner that they help learners to participate in their learning and, therefore, motivate them to learn (Knowles, Holton & Swanson 2013).

The challenge to retain adult students is explained by Wonacott (2001) and Petty and Thomas (2014:474), who mention that participation and persistence by adults in educational activities is a complex phenomenon, which is dependent on situational factors such as work, family and finances; dispositional factors relating to expectations and past educational experiences; and institutional factors such as red tape and scheduling of classes. These factors are also mentioned by Wahlgren and Mariager-Anderson (2017:20), who group it into internal and external factors, where a learner's financial situation would be an external factor that might lead to him/her dropping out of a programme; while internal factors include the student's ability, aptitude and level of engagement, study conditions and teacher performance. All these factors play a role in relation to dropout rates in educational programmes, because they can act as barriers to participation and completion of programmes. On the other hand, effective strategies can motivate learners to overcome barriers and complete the programme.

The statistics on Post-School Education and Training in South Africa, for 2014, indicated that, although there was an increase in the registration of learners on the GETC: ABET NQF Level 1, the number of learners, who wrote examinations and completed the programme was lower than the registrations; almost half of the learners, who register for the qualification, do not write the examinations (Department of Higher Education and Training 2014). There is evidence that ABET can improve the lives of those who write and successfully complete the programme. For example, one learner indicated that, by completing the ABET programme, he not only received an education, but started a soccer team at the rehabilitation centre he had been admitted to. The learner indicated that the ABET centre he attended had encouraged him to engage with the community in order to gain an understanding of himself. According to the learner, the ABET facilitators and psychologists encouraged him to go back to school and finish his schooling (We-Can=Change-Our-World, 2011). Although the strategies used are not set out, the facilitators seemed to have played an active role in ensuring that the learner remained in the programme.

Quan-Baffour (2011) posits that stringent measures should be devised, at an institutional level, to enable adult learners to direct their own learning and finish their qualification. This requires properly structured adult education programmes. These programmes should be geared at addressing adult learners' needs and be well thought out (Gboku and Lekoko 2007).

THEORETICAL FRAMEWORK

The theoretical framework used for this study is transformative learning. Key to transformative learning is that the process of learning involves change, which is central to how we see ourselves and the world we live in (Merriam, Caffarella & Baumgartner 2007:130). According to Mezirow (1997:5), transformative learning is the process of carrying out change in a frame of reference, which he defines as "structures of assumptions through which we understand our experiences". In this context, change that can be brought about through acquiring the ABET: GETC. The aforementioned frames of reference restrict our expectations, cognition and perceptions, and often lead to a rejection of any ideas that do not fit into this frame of reference. Transformative learning is said to have taken place when the adult learner moves towards an inclusive and self-reflective frame of reference. This means that the adult learner has a mindset shift and is able to assimilate new experiences into their existing frame of reference to create a new flexible experience. There are adult learners, who have had bad educational experiences in the past (Clapper 2010:8) and these experiences can become assumptions through which learning is seen. A transformative learning environment can be a strategy to address or shift a negative perception of learning to a positive experience. One of the perspectives or approaches to transformative learning is to analyse experiences in order to achieve liberation from psychological repression or social and political oppression, which learners may have experienced in the past. This approach to transformative learning is commonly associated with the work of Freire (Tennant 2006:122). According to Merriam, Caffarella and Baumgartner (2007:140), Freire's approach stems from a context of poverty, illiteracy and oppression, and the larger framework of radical social change. Such is the context within which the majority of learners, who do not complete their ABET: GETC, find themselves. The result of this scenario defeats the very intent of improving the wellbeing of these individuals, majority of whom are marginalised. What is needed is "conscientisation" and empowerment in order for these learners to understand that their view of the world is shaped by social and historical forces (Tennant 2006:122). Hence the essence of transformative learning that can turn around their dire socio-economic situation. Transformative learning, according to this approach, means the adult learner is aware of the social and historical oppression that has shaped their experiences and is able to reflect on these experiences in order to bring social change and justice.

Based on the legacy of apartheid in South Africa, which left the majority of South Africans illiterate and poor, and despite the post-apartheid government's commitment and efforts to increase literacy levels, progress is not as expected, due to high dropout rates. It is against this background that transformative learning was deemed an ideal theoretical framework for this study. If learners can be empowered and conscientised to understand the benefits of completing the programme, their motivation levels may increase, effectively responding to the SDG 4 and increase the prospects of changing lives. If a transformative learning approach is adopted as a strategy, adult learners might develop an awareness of how historical and social oppression have shaped their experiences regarding education and thus be able to reflect by making a shift that could help them complete the ABET: GETC programme and enable them overcome the problems afflicting them.

RESEARCH PROBLEM

Self-reported satisfaction, better health, a healthy inclination to question those in political power and greater prospects of employment are associated with improved literacy rates (Gustafsson, Van der Berg, Shepherd and Burger 2010:39). Illiteracy prevents adults from contributing and participating in wider activities in society (Machobane 2010:6). The challenge is that adult learners are not motivated to complete the GETC: ABET, because at present, there are no strategies in place in South Africa to support completion of the ABET programme. The following research question and sub-questions were explored:

Question: How can completion strategies be developed to support and motivate the accomplishment of the GETC: ABET qualification by adult learners in a South African context?

a. How can adult learners be supported to recognise the value and benefit of completing a GETC: ABET qualification?
b. What are the motivating factors to acquire learning by adult learners enrolled in the GETC: ABET?
c. What are the contributing factors to non-completion of the GETC: ABET qualification by adult learners?

RESEARCH DESIGN AND METHODOLOGY

Data was collected from a community education and training college, in the Mangaung district, Free State, Republic of South Africa, using a three-pronged approach, thereby triangulating (discussed below) the qualitative data collection (Creswell, 2014). To gain an understanding of the attitudes, behaviours and the context of the study, whose objective was to identify suitable strategies that adult learners require to be supported and motivated to complete their GETC: ABET qualification; three focus groups of 10 learners each (first year group, learners with two or more years in the programme and learners who have either completed or could not complete the programme), three lecturers and two managers were interviewed individually. Hence a total number of 35 people participated in the study.

Interactive interviews were conducted with both focus groups and individuals. Interactive interviews enable deeper engagement and free flow of responses and interactions. This interview approach capitalised on the interactions between the researcher and the respondents towards obtaining insight and allowing deeper interaction into the phenomenon under study (Brotherson 1994:103). First, questions were introduced to the group, one by one, in order to facilitate interaction within the group and, as participants responded, the researcher probed to encourage flow in discussions (Dilshad and Latif 2013:195). Second, the study also included observations and the aspects observed were adult learners' understanding and perceptions, the teachers' interactions with the adult learners, and the values at play in each case, as guided by an observation grid. Informal conversations between the facilitators and learners also provided useful information that was included in the data collection process. Third, document analysis, comprising 2011 to 2014, and 2015 to 2017 data on completion rates was used to study the existing documents of adult learners' enrolment rate and completion rate for the two sets of the period of three years. The learners, who participated, were those that had classes during the day and agreed to participate in the study. The teachers and managers, who participated, were those who had the most experience in teaching, based on the assumption that they understood the value of the qualification for the learners, might have devised ways to support the learners during the programme to enable completion, and were willing to participate.

The three modes of collecting data enabled triangulation, which enabled balance in the responses, information gathered from analysed documents (Johnson and Christensen, 2017). These data collection steps also aligned with the ethical expectations and consequently formed part of the credibility and trustworthiness (Johnson and Christensen, 2017; McMillan and Schumacher, 2014).

Ethical Considerations

The World Health Organisation (2018) states that adherence to ethical principles is important in order to protect the dignity, rights and welfare of participants when conducting scientific research. In adhering to the ethical principles, an ethical clearance certificate was applied for from the College of Education, at the University South Africa's Ethical Clearance Committee (Reference number: 2018/02/14/33092575/11/MC). Permission to conduct the research was requested from the College and a copy of the permission letter was shared with the participants at the centre.

Consent was also acquired from the participants (managers, teachers and learners), whereby forms were prepared and distributed among the participants to complete and give consent. Information about the study was given to participants, so they can make an informed decision about participating in the research before giving consent. Confidentiality for participants was ensured by consolidating responses, and numbers were used to identify participants (from M1 for managers, T1 for teachers, and L1 for learners) (Creswell, 2014).

Validity and Reliability

This study employed three methods for data collection to ensure validity and reliability. This three-pronged approach is termed triangulation, which means a process whereby different measures of the same phenomenon are captured for validation (Kennedy 2009).

Data Analysis

The constant comparative method was used to analyse the data. In this method, data is not grouped into predefined categories, but categories are derived from the data through inductive reasoning (QDA Training 2012). According to Mathison (2005:2), this type of analysis enables the investigator to build an understanding of the phenomenon under investigation through the lives, words, relations and actions of the participants' lived experiences. The data collected from the interviews and observations in the form of notes was grouped into managers, lectures, and learner responses, as part of organising the data.

Once the data was organised, it was read through, keeping the research objectives in mind. The purpose of reading through the data was to obtain a general idea of the participants' responses and behaviour from the interviews and observations, as this would give an indication whether the objectives of the study would be met. In order to begin with the coding process, responses on similar questions from both the teachers and learners were organised into similar topics, to determine their underlying meaning, and the topics then became the themes for analysis. Document analysis was used to compare the registration rate and completion rate of learners over three years. This was used as a basis to determine the reasons why learners do not complete the programme.

The themes that emerged from this analysis were as follows: employment opportunities, the importance of education, socio-economic issues and support mechanisms to complete the qualification.

FINDINGS AND DISCUSSIONS

This section discusses the themes, based on the objectives and aim of the study as indicated below:

a. Describe factors contributing to the non-completion of the GETC: ABET by adult learners.

b. Identify ways to support learners so that they can recognise the value of the GETC: ABET.
c. Detect factors that have motivated adult learners to enrol in the GETC: ABET with the view to identify suitable strategies for finishing the ABET programme.
d. Explore strategies that can be used to motivate adult learners to complete the GETC: ABET.

Factors Contributing to the Non-Completion of the GETC: ABET by Adult Learners

The study found that learners dropped out mainly because of economic and social reasons. The learners and the teachers revealed that, when learners obtain employment, most of which is seasonal, they drop out of school and, when they want to return, they are not able to catch up. Wonacott (2001) concurs that participation and persistence by adults in educational activities is a complex phenomenon, which is dependent on situational factors such as work, family and finances; dispositional factors relating to expectations and past educational experiences as well as institutional factors such as red tape and scheduling of classes. Other reasons for dropping out include drug use, pregnancy, lack of sanitary towels, lack of money for learning materials and sexual harassment by male teachers of female students. Some of the learners' responses regarding non-completion were:

"Some are offered employment and they choose that over attending classes." L4.

"We do not receive stationery and textbooks and have to provide for ourselves. So, sometimes money is a problem, especially when we have to make copies." L21

Managers and teachers responses on factors contributing to non-completion were:

"Learners from poor family backgrounds drop out when they find employment." T1

"Learners drop out when they find employment. Employment is seasonal and sometimes by the time the work ends, they cannot catch up." M2

In trying to assist the learners, some of the teachers indicated that, when possible, they provide food to struggling students and sanitary pads to female learners, while other teachers make an effort to go to the houses of the learners to determine the reasons for non-attendance. This was also observed during the researcher's visit at the centre, Such acts of compassion demonstrate ubuntu, and may strengthen adult learners' willingness to take responsibility for their learning and to initiate measures to ensure that they complete their qualification (Setlhodi, 2019). In a study conducted by the British Columbia Teachers' Federation (2016), on finding possible solutions to non-attendance related to poverty, teachers indicated that some of the strategies they use include being supportive, providing counselling to and meeting with the family, listening, caring and being understanding about challenges, without judgement (acts of ubuntu). These factors are similar to those mentioned by the managers and teachers during the interviews.

Ways to Support Learners: Encouraging Recognition of GETC: ABET Value

The findings indicate that most of the managers and teachers interacted with at the centre see ABET as an enabler towards lifelong learning, while most of the learners see ABET as a doorway to employment opportunities. A few of the learners did, however, recognise the foundation ABET laid for lifelong learning. Considering the aims of ABET, as defined, there are no evident strategies used by the teachers or the institution under study to assist the learners to recognise the value of ABET in its entirety. This means that the focus is only on employment and continuing education, which can help them change their circumstances and gain greater control of their lives. Hence, if these learners do not see a connection between attending an adult education programme and an improvement of life, enrolment is unlikely because priority is on addressing personal challenges (Dhlamini and Heeralal, 2014)

There is scant evidence that the management, teachers and the Department of Education challenged the learners to see the bigger picture, in terms of the transformative learning theory, by helping the learners to critically reflect on their current frames of reference, or that learners are made aware of the social structures that have bound them. According to Mezirow (1997: 5), transformative learning is the process of carrying out change in a frame of reference, which he defines as "structures of assumptions through which we understand our experiences." These frames of reference restrict our expectations, cognition and perceptions, and often lead to a rejection of any ideas that do not fit into this frame of reference at any given time. One teacher lamented,

"Often learners think about immediate solutions and fail to see the broader picture. This is unfortunate because even when advised to soldier on as their situation can change when they acquire basic skills from the ABET programme, they fail to see things beyond their current situation" T2

The learners, therefore, do not see that they are being empowered, not only to participate in the economy, but that the qualification gives them skills, attributes and knowledge to participate in society and politics, and to start questioning unfavourable social structures, which might have led them to where they are and enable them to change their current situation permanently whilst improving their wellbeing. Another interesting perspective from the teachers is that obtaining the qualification will assist learners to enrol at technical vocational education and training (TVET) colleges and also to enrol for Grade 12, which will help them obtain the National Senior Certificate that is a requirement to study at a university or any higher education institution of their choice.

The teachers see an opportunity for lifelong learning; however, of the learners interviewed, only 10% agreed with the teachers, while the other 90% were focused on completing and getting employment. This could be attributed to the high levels of poverty in the area (as indicated by the reasons why learners drop out) and employment being prioritised more than education, whereas the teachers, based on the experience of age, realise the long-term benefits of lifelong learning. This contradiction is evidenced by Rothes and Goncalves (2014), whose study indicated that unemployed participants and those with low-level qualifications enrol in vocational courses for extrinsic reasons, compared to those with higher qualifications. This is further supported by a study conducted by Dæhlen and Ure (2009), who found that low skilled adults enrol in programmes for job-related factors, because they understand that education can help them get out of a vulnerable situation.

There is a need to motivate learners to realise the value of self-upliftment through development of skills and or committing to lifelong learning with intent to continue improving, developing to change their socio-economic situations and well-being. Baloyi (2014:613) concurs by stating that ABET is the general conceptual foundation towards lifelong learning and development, comprising knowledge, skills and attributes required for social, economic and political participation and transformation applicable to a range of contexts. To that end, it is essential to motivate learners finish their GETC: ABET qualification.

Some Factors That Have Motivated Adult Learners to Enroll In the GETC: ABET

The importance of education was the emergent theme from the questions relating to the reasons for enrolment. It was found that, regardless of the reasons why learners enrolled, they all realised that to achieve the goals they have set for themselves, they will need a certain level of education. One teacher mentioned:

"Some of the entry-level employment opportunities in the area require GETC: ABET." T2

Other learners were forced by their parents to enrol in the programme because they were failing in mainstream schools, while others, who dropped out, saw their peers advancing and decided to enrol. The learners said that they enrolled to enable themselves to find employment, achieve their goals, to study further, or to set a good example for their siblings. From the findings, it appears that the factors that motivate the learners to enrol relate to them experiencing a disorienting dilemma, as explained by the transformative learning theory. They realise that, in order to achieve either extrinsically or intrinsically motivated goals, or both, they need to enrol in the programme.

According to Merriam et al. (2007:63), a study conducted on reasons for participation in adult education indicated that most adult learners could point out a life event, in the past, present or future - such as marriage, at childbirth, retirement or job changes - as developmental tasks that prompted learning. Developmental tasks indicate that adulthood is not a period of stability, where previously learnt skills, attitudes and values can be applied at work, in the family, or civic life. Instead, the various responsibilities that adults need to meet throughout their lives are inevitable and fluid, and people need to be adaptable to cope with these responsibilities as they arise (Tennant 2006:36). Hence learners enrol to this programme because of some of these reasons. One manager commented,

"Our learners come from dire situations and most of them see enrolment to this programme as the way out of their current socio-economic situation. So, for them, acquiring the ABET certificate will spur them and open opportunities to further education and acquire skills that can earn them employment"

The study by Rothes and Goncalves (2014) also indicated that unemployed participants and those with low-level qualifications enrol in vocational courses for extrinsic reasons, compared to those with higher qualifications. This is further supported by a study conducted by Dæhlen and Ure (2009), which found that low skilled adults enrol in programmes for job-related factors because they understand that education can help them get out of a vulnerable situation. It can also be argued that although job-related factors are extrinsic, the results of employment can change the learners' social standing and current situation, which means that extrinsic reasons can help achieve intrinsic ambitions, especially when the learners' age group is taken into consideration. The learners in this study are young and an assumption is made that they want to achieve goals and boost their self-esteem and compare well with their peers.

Other factors mentioned by participants were,

- Learners end up realising the importance of education, especially when they see their peers advancing in life and therefore wish to also change their change their lives and that of their families.
- Learners fall pregnant and are not able to attend mainstream school, some are excluded from school due to age, and others are expelled due other issues such as gangsterism.

- Most learners realise that in order to get decent work, certain levels of qualifications are required, so they enrol to obtain a matric certificate.
- Some learners are forced to enrol by their parents after they were excluded from mainstream schools for various reasons.
- To debunk opions formed about them for various reasons by society and to appease their parents as well as be role models to their siblings.

The average completion rate at the centre where the study was conducted, over a period of three years, was 56%. In general, the number of learners that enrol, is much higher than those who complete the qualification. However, the centre's completion rate was above the national completion rate of 37.3% over the same period. There is an indication that various approaches are used by the teachers to motivate the adult learners to complete the programme, though these are not formalised. The interventions that teachers have undertaken out of their own free will in encouraging learners complete their studies as well as support and offer help to minimise or eliminate barriers to completion where practically possible.

To address situational and dispositional barriers, such as a lack of food and sanitary towels, the teachers indicated that they try to provide food and sanitary towels, whenever possible, while other situational barriers were addressed through counselling by qualified teachers. The teachers also played a leading role, whereby they often encouraged learners to approach them with any challenges they were facing. Some of the teachers mentioned that they have faced similar challenges to those of the learners, such as dropping out of school, and they could identify with what the learners were going through. Hence, they related their experiences when learners faced challenges, thereby urging them to assume leadership in directing their own learning by pacing themselves to attain desired learning outcomes.

Moreover, the teachers said that career guidance, excursions and extra classes were offered as a way to encourage completion, which the learners confirmed. The sentiment from both groups was that more excursions and career guidance events were needed, as these helped learners to make career choices, based on their chosen learning areas. The teachers also used the learners' reasons for enrolling in the programme as a strategy to assist, motivate, and encourage other learners. Magy (2010)' study found that adult learners were motivated to learn when what they study was related to their individual goals and needs. So, when teachers keep the end goal in mind, learners are encouraged to stay the course and complete their qualification. Hence the need to have working strategies that can be employed to motivate, enable and encourage completion.

Proposed Strategies to Motivate Adult Learners Complete the GETC: ABET

The following strategies, found to be essential in this study, are proposed for consideration by community colleges:

- Providing counselling services at colleges to assist learners with challenges that could influence completion. Community colleges are part of the post-school education sector and like most institutions in the post-school sector, counselling services could assist with completion and career choices.
- Community colleges should be actively involved in the community. They are to determine the needs, but not only educational needs, of the community so as to assist in creating awareness of other services in the public sector that can assist in high poverty areas. This will ensure that learners are aware of what is available to them.
- Induction before enrolment is another strategy that can be used to ensure that learners are aware of what the programme entails, and what challenges they could possibly face during the programme. This will ensure that learners are prepared for the demands of the programme.
- During training, learners can be linked to mentors who will support and guide them throughout their learning. Having an agreement with a mentor could strengthen adult learners' chances of completing their education.
- The values of commitment, initiative, reflection, and responsibility should be cardinal tenets underpinning the mentorship agreement and ought to be based on the understanding that adult learners know the value of education and therefore want to fulfil their desire to learn.
- General acts of ubuntu, such as offering voluntary extra classes for learners to grasp content and therefore stand a chance to succeed in their studies should be encouraged, particularly from graduates who may currently be unemployed, where practically possible, should be encouraged to motivate adult learners towards completing their qualification.

CONCLUSION

This study focused on exploring strategies for motivating learners to complete the general education and training certificate qualification. Completion of this qualification could enable learners a better chance at improving their socio-economic situation and wellbeing. Based on the findings above, it can be concluded that the teachers have their own formular to motivate the learners to complete the GETC:

ABET. However, these are individual teachers' ways and tactics that they believed worked and were not formalised strategies that the community college implement to ensure learners' completion of the programme.

The individual approaches by teachers have helped mitigate the risk of non-completion by identifying the reasons for enrolment and for dropping out, and they use those to motivate the learners to complete their qualification. There was no evidence that the value of ABET in its entirety was used as a strategy to assist the learners to complete the programme. Only the aspects relating to lifelong learning and participation in the economy were recognised by both the teachers and the learners as the value of ABET. Consequently, this chapter presents strategies for completion based on the successful approaches used by teachers, which earned the centre a completion rate much higher than that of the national completion percentage.

Based on the findings and conclusion of this study on strategies to motivate adult learners to complete the GETC: ABET NQF 1, the following recommendations were made:

- All the aspects of the value of the GETC: ABET should be shared with the learners to make them realise that education is not only important to gain employment or to study further, but it also equips them with skills and attitudes that can make them agents of change within their communities.
- There should be a policy to eliminate sexual harassment, guided by the Department of Higher Education and Training, to curb the sexual harassment of learners and encourage them to report these incidents. According to research conducted by Joubert, Van Wyk and Rothmann (2011), into the effectiveness of sexual harassment policies in higher education institutions, it was found that such Policies on sexual harassment exist, but the implementation thereof seem to be lacking. This means that teachers must be trained on the contents of the policy and examples of sexual harassment should be provided. Disciplinary measures should be taken against those found guilty of harassing learners. Learners should equally be trained about their rights and processes to follow when they are violated.
- Community learning centres, as fairly newly established institutions managed by the Department of Higher Education and Training, should consider flexible teaching periods and online tuition sessions to accommodate learners who find employment, while enrolled in the programme.
- The introduction of learnerships, skills programmes and apprenticeships to the centre ought to be considered as they would encourage attendance because an immediate skill would be learnt and thus position learners for possible employment or self-employment.

- The Department of Higher Education should consider establishing portals for community centre students to have access to support services that provide guidance and assistance related to the problems they encounter, similar to those at higher education institutions. These could be centralised per region or district, or accessed online, particularly by learners who are employed.
- It is recommended that the Department of Higher Education and Training consider the strategies mentioned in this study and use them to regulate how learners in community centres can be supported.
- The values underpinning adult learners' intention to learn could be used as the basis for learners to commit to their education and desire to achieve learning outcomes.

REFERENCES

Baloyi, G. P. (2014). The Role of the Adult Basic Education and Training in Addressing Human Rights in Rural Communities in South Africa. *Mediterranean Journal of Social Sciences*, *5*(2), 613–617.

Beauzac, C. B. (2010). *The Relationship between Adult Basic Education and Training (ABET) literacy programme and women's lives in Semi-urban context, in Cape Peninsula*. [Master's thesis. Western Cape: University of the Western Cape].

British Columbia Teachers' Federation. (2016). *Poverty and School Attendance: Barriers and possible solutions*. BCTF. https://www.bctf.ca/uploadedFiles/Public/SocialJustice/Issues/Poverty/Research/BCTF%20Poverty%20and%20Education%20Survey--Chapter%205.pdf

Brotherson, M. J. (1994). Interactive Focus Group Interviewing: A Qualitative Research Method in Early Intervention. *Topics in Early Childhood Special Education*, *14*(1), 101–118. doi:10.1177/027112149401400110

Byrne, T., O'Grady, M., & Roche, E. (2016). *Meeting the challenge: Strategies for motivating learners in adult education in Ireland*. National Adult Literacy Agency. https://www.nala.ie/sites/default/files/.../meeting_the_challenge_web_version.pdf

Clapper, T. C. (2010). Beyond Knowles: What those conducting simulation need to know about adult learning theory. *Clinical Simulation in Nursing*, *6*(6), e7–e14. doi:10.1016/j.ecns.2009.07.003

Creswell, J. W. (2014). Research design: Qualitative, Quantitative and Mixed Method Approaches. Sage Publications.

Dæhlen, M., & Ure, O. B. (2009). Low-skilled adults in formal continuing education: Does their motivation differ from other learners? *International Journal of Lifelong Education, 28*(5), 661–674.

Dhlamini, J. P., & Heeralal, P. J. H. (2014). Factors and Circumstances Leading to Adults Dropping Out from Community Colleges. *Journal of Educational and Social Research, [Online] 4*(3), 449-458. https://www.mcser.org/journal/index.php/jesr/article/view/2747/2712

Gall, R. (2013). Effective Motivational Strategies in Adult Basic Education Programs. *PAACE Journal of Lifelong Learning, 22*, 63–79. https://www.iup.edu/WorkArea/DownloadAsset.aspx?id=162681

Gboku, M., & Lekoko, R. N. (2007). *Developing Programmes for Adult Learners in Africa.* UNESCO Institute for Lifelong Learning: Feldbrunnenstr. 8.

Gustafsson, M., Van Der Berg, S., Sheperd, D., & Burger, C. (2010). *The costs of illiteracy in South Africa.* University of Stellenbosch's Department of Economics Working Paper 14/10. https://www.ekon.sun.ac.za/wpapers/2010/wp142010/wp-14 2010.pdf

Johnson, R. B., & Christensen, L. B. (2017). *Education Research: qualitative and mixed approaches* (6th ed.). SAGE.

Joubert, P., Van Wyk, C. & Rothmann, S. (2011). The effectiveness of sexual harassment policies and procedures at higher education institutions in South Africa. *SA Journal of Human Resource Management/SA Tydskrif vir Menslikehulpbronbestuur, 9*(1). doi:10.4102/sajhrm.v9i1.310

Kennedy, P. (2009) *How to combine multiple research options: Practical Triangulation* Johnny Hollard. https://johnnyholland.org/2009/08/20/practical-triangulation

Knowles, M., Holton, E. F., & Swanson, R. A. (2013). *The adult learner: The definitive classic in adult education and human resource development.* Routledge Taylor & Francis.

Machobane, A. M. (2010). *Strategies for Facilitating Learning in Adult Basic Education and Training.* [Dissertation, University of Pretoria]. http://hdl.handle.net/2263/27925

Magy, R. (2010). *Learner Goal Setting.* Pearson Longman. http://www.pearsonlongman.com/ae/emac/newsletters/RMagy_Monograph.pdf. [Accessed 5 October 2018].

Mathison, S. (2005). *Encyclopedia of evaluation.* Sage Publications, Inc. doi:10.4135/9781412950558

McKay, V. (2007). Adult Basic Education and Training in South Africa. In: *Review of Adult Learning and Literacy, 7.* NSCALL. http://www.ncsall.net/fileadmin/resources/ann_rev/rall_v7_ch9.pdf

McMillan, J., & Schumacher, S. (2014). *Research in Education: Evidence-Based Inquiry* (7th ed.). Pearson.

Merriam, S. B., Caffarella, R. S., & Baumgartner, L. M. (2007). *Learning in Adulthood: A Comprehensive Guide* (3rd ed.). Jossey-Bass.

Mezirow, J. (1997). Transformative learning: Theory to practice. *New Directions for Adult and Continuing Education, 1997*(74), 5–12. doi:10.1002/ace.7401

Moroe, M. S. (2019). Strategies to motivate adult learners to complete the NQF 1 [Unpublished master's thesis, Academic. University of South Africa, Pretoria, South Africa].

Nafukho, F., Amutabi, M., & Otunga, R. (2005). *Foundations of Adult Education in Africa* [ebook]. UNESCO Institute for Education. https://unesdoc.unesco.org/images/0014/001413/141340E.pdf

Petty, T., & Thomas, C. C. (2014). Approaches to a successful adult education programme. *College Student Journal*, 473–480.

QDA Training Ltd. (2012). *Defining the Constant Comparison Method.* QDA Training. https://qdatraining.com/defining-the-constant-comparison-method/

Quan-Baffour, K.P. (2011). *Education for development: Adult basic education as a tool for socio-economic transformation.* Unpublished Inaugural lecture.

Rothes, A., Lemos, M. S., & Goncalves, T. (2014). Motives and beliefs of learners enrolled in adult education. *Procedia: Social and Behavioral Sciences, 112*, 939–948. http://www.sciencedirect.com/science/article/pii/S1877042814012695?via%3Dihub. doi:10.1016/j.sbspro.2014.01.1252

Setlhodi, I. I. (2019). Ubuntu Leadership: An African Panacea for Improving School Performance, *Africa. Education Review, 16*(2), 126–142. doi:10.1080/18146627.2018.1464885

Sogunro, O. (2015). Motivating Factors for Adult Learners in Higher Education. *International Journal of Higher Education, 4*(1), 22–37. https://www.sciedu.ca/journal/index.php/ijhe/article/view/5874

South African Qualifications Authority (SAQA). (n.d). *General Education and Training Certificate: Adult Basic Education and Training*. SAQA. https://regqs.saqa.org.za/viewQualification.php?id=71751.

Tennant, M. (2006). *Psychology and Adult Learning* (3rd ed.). Routledge.

United National Educational, Scientific and Cultural Organisation. (2017). *Literacy and numeracy from a lifelong learning perspective.* UNESCO. https://unesdoc.unesco.org/images/0024/002470/247094E.pdf

United Nations. (2018). *Sustainable Development Goals Knowledge Platform.* UN. https://sustainabledevelopment.un.org/?menu=1300

Wahlgren, B. & Mariager-Anderson, K. (2017). Improving Completion Rates in Adult Education through Social Responsibility. *Adult Learning*, *28*(1), 20-26. . doi:10.1177/1045159516634078

World Health Organisation. (2018). *Ethics and Health.* WHO. https://www.who.int/ethics/research/en

Yeoh, E. K. K., & Chu, K. M. (2012). Literacy, education and economic development in contemporary China. *SSRN*, *2*(1&2), 11–30. doi:10.2139srn.2207559

Chapter 10
Marginalisation of Older Adults in the Digitalisation Drive in Ghana:
Exploring the Potential of Adult Learning and Education

Ellen Abakah
https://orcid.org/0000-0003-0362-2908
University of Ghana, Legon, Ghana

Kofi Konadu Berko
University of Ghana, Legon, Ghana

ABSTRACT

The past decade has witnessed an overwhelming digital wave, with the Internet and associated information communication technologies (ICT) permeating every facet of life. This has had governments implement digitalisation agendas to provide their services online. However, although globally, the number of Internet and ICT users have increased tremendously, there continues to persist a digital divide in access and use of these ICT and related technologies. One such divide is generational, prevailing among younger and older adults. This chapter examines such a divide within the Ghanaian context. The chapter analyses Ghana's digitalising attempts and the positioning of adult learning and education in bridging the digital inequalities affecting older adults in Ghana. The chapter argues that the continual marginalisation of adults in the digitalised space could create a new form of social exclusion. However, adult learning and education can be harnessed as a nexus in bridging such a generational gap and must be considered within Ghana's broader digitalisation policy frameworks.

DOI: 10.4018/978-1-6684-6625-4.ch010

INTRODUCTION

The rapid changes in today's 21st-century societies have increased the impetus for the demand for learning among all and sundry. The ongoing technological changes, the emerging global economy, and the recent Covid-19 repercussions have made digitalisation of societies more pronounced, warranting continuous learning for ease in technology usage. One of the critical characteristics of these digitalised societies is the diffusion and use of information and communication technologies (ICT) for everyday interaction. Hence today, ICT and its associated technologies have become an essential part of life, affecting education, economies, governance, employment, and our daily life activities such as shopping, banking transactions, leisure time life, communication, and interaction with others (Polat, 2012; Wildemeersch & Jütte, 2017).

While the upsurge in digital technologies is becoming more pervasive, it opens a new space for learning by acquiring corresponding digital literacies to be functional in usage. Digital literacy refers to a person's ability to understand and use ICT in multiple formats, mainly through the Internet (Gilster, 1997). Globally, Internet and ICT users are rising. In 2021, Internet users increased by 17% since 2019 to about 63% (4.9 billion people) (ITU, 2022). In the same year, there were about 54% of people in EU countries aged 16 to 74 with basic digital literacy skills, with the highest found in the Netherlands and Finland (79%) and Ireland (70%) (European Commission-Eurostats, 2022). Despite the overwhelming increase in the adoption and use of ICTs, the digital divide is still prevalent and remains a concern for both developed and developing countries. There is a recognition of a "second digital divide" that identifies inequalities among some social groups regarding their adoption and use of ICT (Howard et al., 2010; Ono & Zavodny, 2007). These social groups lag behind in technology adoption and use, not because they cannot afford the tools but because they need the necessary skills to use digital devices for varied tasks (Chen & Persson, 2002).

One such group is the older adults, persons above 60 years. Even though the number of older adults adopting technology is growing, there is still a grey divide, or generational gap, that disadvantage them (Friemel, 2016). Internationally, 23% of adults are digitally illiterate (US Department of Education, 2018). For older adults above 60, evidence suggests their lower engagement with digital technologies because of their digital illiteracy (Friemel, 2016; Hale et al., 2010; Schreurs et al., 2017). Older adults lack direct and easy access to digital technologies (Hunsaker & Hargittai, 2018) and risk facing exclusion from the digital world and their meaningful participation in 21st-century society and the global economy. Once this marginalisation persists, a newer form of social exclusion is likely to be created; thus, urgent redress is needed.

In Ghana, there has been an increasing commitment on the part of successive governments to prioritise ICT for social and economic transformation. Governments have prioritised investment and provided the legal and institutional framework to guide citizens' access, usage, and participation in a digitalised economy (Kpessa-Whyte & Dzisah, 2022). This has led to the initiation and implementation of various digitalisation efforts in recent years, notably in the following areas: port and harbour systems, National Health Insurance payments, water and electricity, the financial sector, mobile money interoperability (MMI), and the implementation of digital addressing systems (Ayakwah et al., 2021; Frimpong et al., 2022). There is also the Ghana biometric card, government services portal and sim card registration, and some services rolled out on digitalised platforms. In fact, the climax of Ghana's digitalisation agenda is the creation of the Ministry of Communication and Digitalisation (Effa et al., 2020; Owusu et al., 2022).

However, for all these new digitalisation tools to work, there is a need for adult learning and education to help Ghanaians, especially older adults, to learn to be functional with the digital technologies and navigate their lives in the emerged digitalised space (Ayakwah et al., 2021). This chapter argues for digital inclusion for both younger and older adults and advocates a harnessing of adult learning and education's potential in supporting older adults' digital skills acquisition to participate meaningfully in digitalised societies. There is a need to ensure that adults are not disadvantaged and that everyone can take advantage of the wide range of well-being benefits technology offers. The chapter thus examines Ghana's digitalisation efforts and discusses the role of adult learning and education in ensuring digital inclusion for all citizens. Adult education promotes lifelong learning; hence, its role cannot be disputed, especially in equipping older adults with the knowledge and skills to use ICT meaningfully. The chapter addresses the following questions: Is adult learning and education considered in Ghana's digital transformation agenda? How are older adults navigating lives in the digital environment in Ghana? How can we support older adults in acquiring digital literacies to function in response to the proliferation of e-services in Ghana?

A LOOK AT GHANA'S DIGITALISATION AGENDA

Digitalisation is the 'new normal' and remains a policy buzzword, with countries implementing varied digitalisation agendas to drive changes in service provision and participatory governments. Digitalisation started as a means of scanning and preserving official documents using modern technology; however, with time, digitalisation has expanded to include the use of ICTs in a variety of activities, such as service delivery and new forms of interaction between and among governments, citizens, and businesses (Kpessa-Whyte & Dzisah, 2022). Today, digitalization is defined by the Internet, web-based innovations, and ICT-related technologies such as computers, laptops, tablets, and smartphones that rely on telecommunication infrastructure for communication and information service delivery (Heeks, 2001).

In Africa, countries are presently making giant strides in implementing various digitalisation agendas (Kariba, 2020). Although described as an 'untapped' region, the continent is leapfrogging development in the digitalisation agenda by setting up various start-ups and creating international tech hubs (Chelenz & Schopp, 2018). For instance, Egypt has committed to enhancing telecommunications and digital infrastructure and automating several core government platforms in promoting the digitalisation agenda by launching the Digital Egypt platform that allows citizens to access about 103 government services (World bank, 2021; El Din, 2022). Kenya is currently implementing eCitizen- Gateway to All Government services that allows Kenyans to access immigration services, business registration services and other services offered by the government, which were previously only available in person (Kwanya, 2018). Similarly, South Africa has also made efforts at digitalization with the government's introduction of the Integrated ICT Policy Framework to assist national digitalisation across the country (Duncan, 2015).

To remain competitive in the global market, Ghana's government is embarking on a digitalization transformation agenda with World Bank support of $200 million (Ghanaian Times, 2020). Many projects have sprung from this agenda, including the recently launched e-transform Ghana project, which aims to "create an enabling environment for digital inclusion and innovation; streamline governance and delivery of public services; and facilitate smallholder engagement in data-driven digital agriculture" (The Ghanaian Times, 2020). There have also been initiatives that have served as a model. E-governance, for example, entails the implementation of digital governance policies such as the issuance of the digital national identification card, e-justice system, e-property addressing system, mobile money interoperability system, paperless port system, Ghana Post GPS, e-smart driver's license, electronic renewal of the National Health Insurance Card, e-Immigration system, e-Cabinet system, e-Parliament, e-procurement (Demuyakor, 2020). There is also mobile-enabled digital transformation where beyond connectivity, mobile phones facilitate access to other core services, including financial services (e.g., Mobile money), health care access (mobile technology for community health (MOTECH), water and energy efficiency through the Internet of things (IoT) (Hatt et al.,2017).

These increasing provisions of digital services are laudable. Ghana is considered one of the African countries with many public e-services (United Nations E-Government Survey, 2018). This means there must be an accompanying digital literacy to reap these digital services' benefits. Generally, Ghanaians are very optimistic about the flagship of e-services in promoting efficient service provisions, reducing corruption and increasing productivity (Demuyakor, 2021; Kpessa-Whyte & Dzisah, 2022). However, the digitalisation of essential services is characterised by an inclusion deficit as some citizens are unable to participate in the use of digitalised services (Kpessa-Whyte & Dzisah, 2022) due to infrastructural challenges such as the unavailability of internet services and the lack of digital knowledge and skills to do so.

Meanwhile, the growing digital services in Ghana imply that all persons are compelled to patronise regardless of their digital literacy levels. With the prevailing digital divide (in access and use) across genders, regions, and generations, one wonders how all citizens could reap the utility of these services. According to the ICT household survey report (2020), the digital literacy level of Ghanaians is only 39.71%, with a gender digital divide of 45.2% male and 34.6% female. The Ghana Living Standard Survey (GLSS) report (2020) confirms these lower statistics by affirming that only one-fifth (21.1%) of Ghana's population has acquired ICT skills, with a marked difference between urban dwellers (30.5%) and rural dwellers (10.5%). Among generations, there is equally a gap between younger and older Ghanaians in digital literacy (Dovie, 2019).

How do we foster digital inclusivity among all citizenry to live a meaningful life in the digitalised space? To reap the benefits that digitalisation proffers, digital literacy is an essential prerequisite. Digital literacy is the "ability to access, manage, understand, integrate, communicate, evaluate, and create information safely and appropriately through digital technologies for employment, decent jobs, and entrepreneurship. It includes competencies that are variously referred to as computer literacy, ICT literacy, information literacy and media literacy" (Law et al., 2018, p.6). With the varied digitalisation technologies, acquiring digital skills is essential for older adults, as their adoption may benefit their lives (Schreurs et al., 2017).

Older adults in Ghana are excluded and marginalised in the digital space due to their high illiteracy and digital illiteracy. Adult literacy is a 'prerequisite for developing personal, social, economic and political empowerment' (UNESCO, 2010, p.38). However, only 3.8% of the adult population aged 15 years and older in Ghana had ever attended a literacy course, with female participation slightly higher than male participation (Ghana Statistical Service (GSS) 2014). Meanwhile, Agenda 2030 of the SDGs, emphasising goal 9, recognises the need to develop knowledge societies where everyone has opportunities to learn and engage with others, which starkly highlights the need for access to Information and Communication Technologies (ICTs). States are mandated to build resilient infrastructure, promote inclusive and sustainable industrialization and foster innovation. With about eight years to reach the target, Ghana can be seen lagging in achieving this target as a cross-section of its population still needs access to computers or the Internet to be digitally functional. Ghana is challenged in ensuring ICT inclusivity for all as the need to bridge the digital divide continues to be a major concern to the government.

Nevertheless, digital opportunities have been created for the marginalised, the elderly, and people in rural, remote, and underserved areas under the Universal Telecommunications/ICT Fund Management. Under the Universal Telecommunications/ICT funds management, now the Ghana Investment Fund for Electronic Communications (GIFEC), flagship initiatives aiming to bridge the existing digital divide among the Ghanaian populace have been implemented. Established in 2004, GIFEC facilitates the implementation of universal access to electronic communication and the provision of internet points of presence in underserved and unserved communities. The GIFEC facilitates capacity-building programs and promotes ICT inclusion in the unserved and underserved communities, the deployment of ICT equipment to educational, vocational and other training institutions (Ohemeng & Ofosu-Adarkwah, 2014). Presently, GIFEC-implemented projects include the School Connectivity Project (SCP), providing educational institutions with fully furnished and equipped ICT laboratories with accessories and Internet access and the provision of laptops to basic schools; the Community Information Centres (CIC) with the provision of fully furnished and equipped to provide community internet access, low-cost ICT training and also to serve as community information resource centres, security connectivity (GIFEC, n.d).

The government's digitalisation initiatives seem to favour segments of the population already conversant with technology usage, that is, the digital natives and not the older generation of digital immigrants. The digitalisation agenda was a means to ensure that the unreached segment of the population could be reached, including having the elderly and senior citizens participate more comfortably in the delivery and acquisition of services. However, even though the government has made some effort at inclusive digitalisation, especially through the GIFEC initiatives, more attention should be given to the older generation. There have also yet to be attempts or programs targeting adults' learning regarding their digital needs and literacy. This is particularly disconcerting in that the full participation of adults in the digitalisation drive hinges on the digital literacy competence of the adult population. Such competence could translate into greater acceptance of and participation in the drive.

ADULT LEARNING AND EDUCATION PROVISION IN GHANA

The right to education, irrespective of gender, age, race, ability, or disability, is at the centre of the United Nations which Ghana is a member. Adult learning and education (ALE) underlies the goal 4 target of the SDGs, which seeks to 'ensure inclusive and equitable quality education and promote lifelong learning opportunities for all' (Webb et al.,2017). Under this goal, the following targets are related directly to adult education and learning.

1. Ensure equal access for all women and men to affordable and quality technical, vocational, and tertiary education, including university.
2. Increase the number of youth and adults with relevant skills, including technical and vocational skills, for employment, decent jobs, and entrepreneurship.
3. Eliminate gender disparities in education and ensure equal access to all levels of education and vocational training for the vulnerable, including persons with disabilities, indigenous peoples, and children in vulnerable situations.
4. Ensure that all youth and a substantial proportion of adults, both men and women, achieve literacy and numeracy.

In Ghana, the Education Act 2008 recognises education as basic free and compulsory for all citizens. Various initiatives have been introduced toward the realisation of this goal, including the Free Compulsory Universal Basic Education (FCUBE), School feeding program, and Free Senior High School Initiative (Akyeampong, 2009; Goldsmith et al., 2019; Mohammed & Kuyini, 2021). However, the same level of attention has yet to be given to adult learning and education. In the 1992 constitution of Ghana, Article 25 Section 1c says that "Higher *Education shall be made equally accessible to all, based on capacity by every appropriate means (p.20).*" Section 1d adds, "*Functional literacy shall be encouraged or intensified as far as possible (p.20)*" whereas Article 38 1 quotes that "*the state shall provide educational facilities at all levels and in all the regions of Ghana, and shall to the greatest extent feasible, make those facilities available to all citizens (p.30).*" The Ministry of Education, Science and Sports (2008) also notes that sections 3b and 3c of article 38 guarantees *"Free adult literacy, vocational training as well as rehabilitation and resettlement of disabled people (p.30)"* and finally, *"Lifelong learning (p.30)."*

Despite these constitutional provisions highlighting ALE, in practice, ALE is yet to gain the recognition and importance it deserves, especially as a tool to enhance adult literacy that can foster the realisation of other SDGs. Consequently, adult illiteracy continues to be a concern. The 2021 GSS report reveals that about 1.2 million more illiterate adults (15 years and older) were added to the population from 4.3 million in the previous Population and Housing Census to 5.5 million in 2021. The primary foundation of a learning society is ALE (UNESCO, 2015); hence, ALE is a 'greenfield' to be explored for equipping adults with the essential digital skills to participate fully in the emerging digital economy. ALE presents a more significant opportunity for improving access by adults to a variety of learning opportunities and promoting equity and inclusion.

ALE activities vary widely, including providing literacy and basic skills, continuing training and professional development, active citizenship, community, popular or liberal education, and ICT training (UNESCO, 2015). In Ghana, the most famous provision of ALE has been the functional literacy programs by the Non-formal Education Division, now the Complementary Education Agency (CEA). In 2020, the Non-Formal Education division responsible for literacy education was re-established as the Complementary Education Agency. The agency is responsible for the following: providing basic functional literacy, occupation skills for trade groups, policy creation and guidelines on complementary education, curricula and instructional material development, monitoring and the creation of opportunities for continuous learning for citizens that expands to young adults and out of school youth (Complementary Education Agency Act, 2020). As an institution for the promotion of ALE, the agency is challenged with many obstacles that affect its mandates. The non-formal sector receives the least budgetary support from the government, as recorded in the Education Strategic Plan 2018-2030 (MOE, 2019), and this raises the question of whether they can assist in achieving improved opportunities for non-literate youth and adults to have free access to meaningful quality education and training as noted in education Strategic plan 2018 to 2030.

Another challenge is the absence of an ALE policy framework to systematise the provision of adult learning across all learning settings, whether formal, non-formal or informal. There is also a lack of clarity of ALE in educational policy documents, especially regarding the provision of adult literacy (Tagoe & Abakah, 2023). Adult literacy has moved beyond the acquisition of functional skills to "a continuum of learning and proficiency levels which allows citizens to engage in lifelong learning and participate fully in the community, workplace and wider society" (UNESCO, 2015a, para. 4). The acquisition of basic literacy skills or foundational skills include a larger set of skills, such as digital skills, media literacy, information literacy, scientific literacy, financial literacy, citizenship literacy as well as job-specific skills (UNESCO, 2019). However, the provision of adult literacy by the non-formal division in Ghana is silent on introducing digital skills to adult learners (Tagoe & Abakah, 2023).

METHODOLOGY

This chapter draws on relevant national policy documents relating to ICT and digitalisation in documentary analysis. Documentary analysis involves the systematic procedure for reviewing or evaluating printed and electronic documents (Bowen, 2009). Documents reviewed for the chapter include ICT for Accelerated Development (ICT4AD) policy (2003), the National broadband policy and other digitalisation initiative documents and from digital websites. In addition, qualitative interviews were relied upon as a data source. In-depth interviews were conducted with ten persons involving five faculty members from the Department of Adult Education and Human Resource Studies, University of Ghana and five older adults for their views on how adult education can be harnessed to foster digital inclusion and how older adults are navigating lives in the digitalised space in Ghana respectively. Data from the interviews were transcribed and analysed using Braun and Clarke's (2006, 2012) thematic analysis approach.

GHANA'S ICT AND DIGITALISATION POLICY FRAMEWORK

Globally, countries worldwide are embracing digitalisation as a strategic move to boost economic development and progress. Thus, policies are aimed at maximizing the potential of digitalisation in transforming their economies. It is argued that digitalised countries reap 20% more economic benefits than less digitalised countries, especially in productivity, job creation, and improved business and living standards of their citizenry (Sabbagh et al., 2012).

In Ghana, serious digitalisation efforts began in the early 2000s (Adu & Dube, 2016), following a series of ICT-related reforms that began in the 1980s. However, the arrival of the Internet in June 2003 incensed interest in the need for an ICT policy to transform and address the country's challenges (Kpessah-Whyte & Dzissah, 2022). This led to "The Ghana ICT for Accelerated Development (ICT4D) Policy". The ICT4D policy was adopted to address Ghana's development challenges, including the following: (a) limited human resource capacity, as evidenced by a lack of professional, technical, and managerial manpower; (b) inadequate scientific research base and Research and Development (R&D) capacity; (c) social and economic pressures of a youthful population, as well as the challenges of transforming a youthful population into a development asset; (d) a low job creation capacity dominated by an under-performing agricultural sector with a weak and under-developed industrial and services sector; (e) heavy national debt burden characterized by a high per capita ratio and a high debt servicing ratio; (f) an underdeveloped and under-performing private sector with a disproportionate informal sector; (g) a high proportion of the population with no educational attainment; a high school dropout rate and limited access to higher education by the vast majority of the population, particularly girls and women; (h) a narrow export base dominated by traditional exports; and (i) poor and limited communication and telecommunication infrastructure (Government of Ghana, 2003, p. 6-7).

The ICT4D policy establishes priorities and strategies to "transform Ghana into an information-rich knowledge-based society and economy through the development, deployment, and exploitation of ICTs within the economy and society" (Government of Ghana, 2003, p. 1). The policy's strategic focus has been on ICTs in Education - particularly formalised institutions, facilitating government and service delivery, facilitating private sector development, modernization of agriculture, health, human resource management, infrastructure, research and development, law and order, and ICT development in communities. Its goal is to ensure that technology is effectively mainstreamed in the performance and delivery of public services to improve service quality and governance processes, economic management, and state-society relations.

The ICT4D policy paved the way for other legislations and policies to improve the operational environment as implementation was broadened to include digitalisation (Kpessa-Whyte & Dzisah, 2022). The National Broadband Policy and Implementation Strategy was later developed to facilitate the deployment of ICT knowledge systems and digital technologies in public and private institutions. According to the Ministry of Communication (2012), the goal of the national broadband policy is to provide "an IT architectural and infrastructural networks and their propellants that will provide a superhighway for the effective and efficient transmission of voice, data, video, and internet services to impact on the transformativity of the country" (p.7).

Over the past years, the current government's vision to harness digitalisation as a catalyst for transforming the country has had many more initiatives to be implemented under Ghana's Digital Transformation Agenda in the areas of healthcare, education, energy resources, human resources, public safety, civic participation, government's engagement with the citizenry and information dissemination (Ministry of Communication, 2012). For instance, in addition to the e-transform Ghana project under the digitalisation agenda, the World Bank is supporting a new Ghana Digital Acceleration Project to "advance the whole-of-government digital transformation agenda to accelerate the adoption of digital technologies and innovation by key productive sectors, such as agriculture, to foster an economy-wide digital transformation" (World Bank, 2022). This project will increase access to mobile and broadband services in rural areas and foster digital inclusion for women, persons with disabilities and rural communities (World Bank, 2022).

Despite the commendable nature of these initiatives and efforts, there are significant inequality issues that must be addressed by digital inclusion policies in order to reap the full benefits of digitalisation. There are socio-economic inequalities, such as rural-urban differences, a lack of digital infrastructure in some parts of the country, limited access to the Internet and the cost of digital tools, low educational backgrounds, issues of gender inclusion, and low participation of older citizens in the digitalization drive, all of which serve as roadblocks to implementation. It has also been discovered that digitalization processes are not integrated or synchronized with the institutions and services that operate them (Kpessa-Whyte & Dzisah,

2022). Therefore, despite numerous services and data collection points, there is less coordination.

Furthermore, many government work activities (or jobs) are still paper-based, bureaucratic, and simply a repetition of work processes. Most digitalised services incorporate technology into traditional service provision practices and operations (Kpessa-Whyte & Dzisah, 2022). As a result, digitalisation has not significantly altered the structures and processes of new and existing government services to citizens. A digitalised economy would result in more efficient resource use, fewer repetitive tasks performed by different people, and fewer errors generated by paper-based activities.

IS THERE A CONSIDERATION OF ADULTS' LEARNING AND EDUCATION?

Indeed, Ghana's digitalisation agenda is a step in the right direction. It provides a good channel for addressing Ghana's developmental challenges and allows the citizenry to easily access efficient services and systems. However, there is an overlook of an element of ALE in policies and initiative attempts to foster inclusivity among younger and older adults.

There is much evidence that older adults are the least technologically savvy, so a gap exists in their use of digital technologies. Older adults often find it difficult to use digital devices like smartphones and often lack the basic digital literacy required to use multimedia interactive devices with touchscreen technology (Blazic & Blazic, 2020). Therefore, there is the need to develop targeted strategies to fully empower them to embrace the digitalisation drive through adult learning initiatives. Currently, much focus on digital inclusion efforts targets developing the skills and capacities of the youthful workforce and population to the detriment of the older adult population. Some mention is made of the implementation of ICT-based community initiatives, telecentre projects, and tele education as inclusion mechanisms. However, most inclusion policies are yet to show measurable and calculated ways of reaching the older adult population.

NAVIGATING LIFE IN THE DIGITAL SPACE AS AN OLDER ADULT IN GHANA

In Ghana, the rate of internet users has grown exponentially from 2.31 million in 2012 to 17 million in 2022 (Marfo, 2022). However, statistics on older adults' internet use and digital engagement are unclear, as researchers are yet to explore this grey area. The national household survey on ICT reveals that 75.8% of adults aged 60-64 own mobile phones, compared to 53.8% of older adults above 70 years. It was further revealed that these phones were not smartphones (GSS & NMA, 2020) and could not access the Internet or other multimedia functions via their phones. A recent survey by Kpessa-Whyte and Dzisah (2022) also revealed that most non-internet users (about 81.3%) are the elderly between ages 60 and above.

Given the importance of internet services to access and use of digitalised services, having most of the older adults not using internet services raises critical questions about their possible exclusion and the possibility of accessing other digital initiatives and services introduced by the government of Ghana. Generally, there is a broader acceptance of the recent proliferation of e-services, especially in curbing corruption and facilitating easy access to services. While some older adults have, for example, fully embraced the idea of digitisation by signing on to the Ghana card and synchronizing their cards with their bank accounts, making online transactions like payment of utility bills, many more do not even wish to use it due to its complexity. There is also limited information among older adults on the various digital services and tools to navigate life as knowledge about available services and potential benefits is minimal.

Interestingly, some level of apathy exists among older adults about their possible exclusion from the digitalised space. Ageist stereotypes (McDonough, 2017), the difficulty in keeping up with technological updates and the fact that they did not have an urgent need for digital services and tools in a way affected older adults' motivation and zeal to adopt and use digitalised technologies and services. Nevertheless, older adults relied on assistance from younger ones to mediate their learning and use of digital tools; hence, they needed to be more informed about their inability to access and use digital services. Compared to younger adults, older adults are challenged by knowledge gaps, access barriers and difficulties in their adoption and use of these new technologies, thereby limiting their opportunities in the increasingly digitalised world (Anderson & Perrin, 2017; Francis et al., 2019; Merriam & Baumgartner, 2020; Quan-Haase et al., 2018). To enjoy full participation in the digitalised space older adults require digital competencies, technological access, and skills to function effectively. Thus, as Ghanaian society is increasingly becoming digitalised, older adults need to be empowered and resourced through training to participate fully and extract any benefits from these technologies, lest a new social exclusion be created as adults remain at the periphery of the digitalised society.

Older Adults and Digital Use

There is disaggregated data on older adults' access to and use of the Internet and other digital technologies in Ghana. The ICT household survey fails to address the heterogeneity of the adult population and their peculiar digital needs and uses. Adults are heterogenous and, for that matter, have different digital needs with differences in their Internet use and other digital tools. Older adults are most likely to use their mobile phones and tablets to access the Internet instead of laptops or desktop computers (Bianchi, 2021), and use the Internet for informational and entertainment purposes, shopping and banking, communication, access to health-related services, and civic services (Choi & DiNitto, 2013; van Deursen & Helsper,2015; Nimrod, 2018; Rochat,2021).

The most common digital tool among older adults in Ghana is the smartphone, however, its uses vary across literate and illiterate adults, thereby reiterating the significance of digital or ICT knowledge in the adoption and use of digital tools. Smartphones are used among literate adults for information and communication purposes, but adults lacked basic digital literacy to use other multimedia and interactive functions with touch screen technology on their phones (Blazic & Blazic, 2020). Regarding access and use of e-services, a need for it became a predictive factor for older adults' use or patronage. That is, aside from their limited digital literacies, adults also reported they did not have a need to access any of the government's e-services or other digital tools. Older adults are generally not explorative with digital tools, and hence, once they do not find a need, they may not adopt or use a particular tool or service. The importance of need was much more profound for older adults with little or no educational background. Such adults relied on external persons when accessing any of the e-services and would instead prefer the human interface in their dealings and transactions. Hence, their preferred digital tool was simple mobile phones that could allow them to make and receive calls. However, Bianchi (2021) argues that when older adults learn and are directed with the necessary assistance, they can thrive in navigating their lives in the digitalised space. This makes adult learning and education imperative to foster older adults' learning and meaningful function in accessing and utilising various e-services introduced in the country.

Clearly, the older adult population in Ghana is under utilising the benefits of digitalisation, and one of the major reasons is the lack of basic digital literacy. Elsewhere, the use of the Internet and associated technologies among older adults have been found to have positive health implications. For instance, computer use among older adults improves their cognition and executive control functions (Tan & Lachman, 2010) and lowers the risk of dementia (Almeida et al., 2012). It also promotes healthy behaviours and lifestyles, including physical activity, consumption of healthy foods, less smoking, and more adherence to health screening (Xavier et al., 2014). Older adults use internet resources to promote their health (Czaja et al., 2013), as they are more likely to participate in health check-ups than older adults who do not, leading to improved well-being (Nakagoni et al., 2022). Internet use among older adults has also been observed to foster social connectedness that alleviates loneliness in old age (Cotton et al., 2013; Khalaika & Vitman-Schorr, 2018) and improves the mental health of the aged (Sum et al., 2008; Amoah et al., 2022).

The Internet and other digital technologies act as an intermediary allowing older adults to initiate and maintain contact with their social relationships, improving loneliness and wellness (Yu et al., 2021). Interestingly, only a few older adults are extracting any of these benefits from the Internet and its associated technologies in Ghana. The high illiteracy rate among the aged implies a lack of digital literacy essential to operate many of the e-services introduced and using digital technologies for personal benefits. There is a need for a policy framework targeting older adult inclusion in the overall digitalisation framework that pays attention to older adults' learning regarding their digital needs and literacies. In this regard, the non-formal education or the CEA should be resourced to add on digital literacy of the adult population as part of their mandate to implement learning episodes alongside the provision of the various e-services in Ghana.

Factors Affecting Older Adults' Access and Use of Digital Technologies

Research abounds to ascertain that older adults' use of digital technologies is affected significantly by age, educational attainment, socio-economic circumstances, and place of residence. As older adults grow (more than 75), they have difficulties using the Internet compared to those who are much younger (less than 75) (Klimova et al., 2018; Veer et al.,2018) due to a decline in physical and mental health.

The educational level impacts older adults' Internet use and other digital technologies. Internet use requires a certain amount of education and digital literacy, thus older adults who use the Internet for a variety of tasks have a higher level of education than those who used the Internet for minor tasks or not at all (Elliot et al., 2014; Seifert,2020)—likewise, the place where an older adult stay may impact internet use. Older adults in urban areas are more likely to use the Internet and associated technologies due to the high level of internet penetration in those cities and towns compared to older adults in rural areas with low internet penetration or no internet penetration at all (CINIC, 2020; Zhang & Wang, 2020). Other factors also enlisted to impact older adults' adoption and use of the Internet and related technologies are having children, social capital, marital status, and employment history (Czaja et al., 2013; van Deursen & Helsper, 2015; Arief et al., 2018; Neves et al., 2018), lack of instructions and guidance, lack of knowledge and confidence, health-related challenges, cost, and resistance (Vaportzis et al., 2017; Bianchi,2021).

These challenges resonate with older adults within the Ghanaian context. In addition, to the above factors is the older adults' motivation to use and adopt digital technologies and services. For adults, motivation and engagements are intricately related. Adults' motivation comes with a need for adoption and use, especially with the government's e-services. Thus, to the extent that they did not need particular services, older adults were shunned from its use. Other factors that affect Ghana's digitalisation of essential services include lack of internet access, cost of internet devices and data, income levels and rural–urban inequalities (Kpessa-Whyte & Dzisah, 2022).

HARNESSING THE POTENTIAL OF ADULT LEARNING AND EDUCATION

Today digital transformation opens entire new spaces of education and learning with knowledge and information widely accessible through the Internet. There is a need to engage older adults with the opportunities of digitalisation fully. This underscores the need and criticality of adult learning and education. How can we support older adults in acquiring digital literacies to function in response to the proliferation of e-services in Ghana?

In Ghana, the Non-formal education division (now the CEA) is an institutionalised agency responsible for providing adult learning activities. Adult learning and education is a core component of lifelong learning comprising all forms of education and learning that aim to ensure that all adults participate in their societies and the world of work (UNESCO, 2015). There is a greater potential for ALE in Ghana's digital transformation agenda because ALE provides a variety of learning pathways and flexible learning opportunities, including second chance programs to make up for the lack of initial schooling for people who have never been to school, early school leavers and dropouts (UNESCO, 2015).

First, public education through the popular media could equip older adults with the requisite digital literacies that could help them become functional in an era of growing e-services in Ghana. The Presidential special initiative on distance education could be re-introduced with older adults as the target. Further, initiatives can be made to develop multimedia literacy programs and instructional curricula for older adults to integrate technology into their basic literacy skills training.

Adult educators with gerontology backgrounds should develop training models and facilitate a training that takes cognizance of the physiology and psychology of older adults in a technology society. Adult educators can set up community forums where older adults can express their sentiments regarding technology use. These could serve as reliable data for developing models for building capacity in using technology for older adults. Training programs, workshops, sensitization seminars, and community durbars are mediums adult educators could use to improve older adults' awareness and digital literacy skills.

Additionally, human resource development activities by employers within organisations could be an essential tool through which adult learning and education may be harnessed to promote digital literacy among older adults. These encompass training and development, career and organisational development activities, using different strategies to introduce, facilitate and enhance digital skills among older adult staff. The core aim of building human resources in organisations is to improve productivity. Several studies show that having digital skills staff impacts their performance (Markhaichuk & Panshin, 2022; George et al., 2022) Thus, adult educators in the form of human resource managers must endeavour to design and implement digital training programs using strategies like 'buddy system'-where older adults are paired with younger adults, job rotation, job enrichment, reverse coaching, and mentoring. Older adults will improve their digital literacy and translate this knowledge and skills into other facets of their lives.

Research may be another avenue to support digital literacy among older adults, mainly because there needs to be more data on older adults' use and appreciation of digitalised tools and services. Data collected through studies could highlight patterns, trends, links, lifestyle contrast and similarities among older adults which is crucial in guiding policy framing, development of 'older-adult friendly' technology and general digitalisation efforts (Duh et al, 2010). These simple, functional but not moderately sophisticated digital tools would encourage digital literacy among older adults.

Many illiterate older adults work as entrepreneurs or in the technical and vocational industries. Highlighting the importance of digital literacy to the success of their business might be one way to support older adults to become digitally literate to better adjust to the digitalised Ghana. Educating adults through this lens linking digital literacy to business and profit may influence older adults who are still in the world of work or retired to leverage these services to make a profit and monitor and track their financial investments.

Due to declining health or wish to stay healthy, older adults might frequent hospitals. Noting the massive impact of digital skills on older adult health (Zelinski,2009,) medical and education personnel could note the importance of digital tools like phone games, smart sensors, and devices and apply it in the treatment of medical conditions such as stroke, speech problems, sight-related problems and trauma. Additionally, older adults can use these skills to book appointments and receive updates on treatment plans or emails of medical records.

CONCLUSION

Ghana's digital transformation agenda focuses mainly on younger adults who are more digitally literate, leaving older adults who cannot efficiently use these digital technologies behind. Digital illiteracy, a problem born from the significant illiteracy rate among older adults, makes it near impossible for older adults to thrive in the ongoing digitalisation drive in Ghana. This raises concerns as this illiteracy further deepens existing forms of inequality between younger and older adults in health, age, education, and socio-economic circumstance. Notably, the digitalization agenda's positive impacts on older adults' lives have been documented and well-established. This creates an urgency in the need to bridge the gap between younger and older adults in digital literacy and help older adults to 'catch up.' The study highlights how adult learning and education can be utilised to bridge the chasm between older and young adults and halt the growing digital divide. Various policies support adult learning and education in Ghana and can be harnessed to create more digitally literate older adults. State organisations like the Complementary Education Agency (CEA) promoting functional adult literacy, which affects digital literacy, extensive public education, collection and analysis of data on older adults, development of training models that rely on implementation by well-equipped adult educators, invest in organisational human resource development and health education may be the remedy to the digital divide problem. Through these, ALE will act as a link helping older adults be on par with younger adults in their use of digital technologies and improve their quality of life.

RECOMMENDATIONS

- ICT and digitalisation policies must include a framework on adult learning and education emphasising adult education as a key ingredient in the digital transformation drive in the country. In this regard, efforts at digital inclusion should include the digital literacy of older citizens.
- The CEA as the major provider of ALE in Ghana, should be mandated to provide adult digital literacies and must be resourced fully to undertake such a mandate. CEA must liaise with the government in providing digital services to older adults, especially in urban centres and district capitals across the country.
- Government should ensure greater internet penetration and regulate the cost of digital devices and access to the Internet. More information on e-services must be made available in local news outlets and other informational mediums.

- Organisations must invest in regular training and retraining of staff, including those headed towards retirement, so they continue to apply their digital skills even after leaving the workforce.
- Social organisations and amenities like schools, hospitals, and churches, where digitalised technology has been introduced in operations, should offer education to older adult customers and well-trained customer service personnel to encourage digital literacy among adults.
- Digitalise technology designers should consider older adults and design simple and easy to understand systems that older adults can use effectively.
- Younger adults should act as helpers and facilitators by assisting older adults around them.

REFERENCES

Adu, K. K., Dube, L., & Adjei, E. (2016). Digital preservation: The conduit through which open data, electronic government and the right to information are implemented. *Library Hi Tech*, *34*(4), 733–747. doi:10.1108/LHT-07-2016-0078

Akyeampong, K. (2009). Revisiting free compulsory universal basic education (FCUBE) in Ghana. *Comparative Education*, *45*(2), 175–195. doi:10.1080/03050060902920534

Almeida, O. P., Yeap, B. B., Alfonso, H., Hankey, G. J., Flicker, L., & Norman, P. E. (2012). Older men who use computers have lower risk of dementia.

Amoah, P. A., Osei-Tutu, A., & Adjei, S. B. (2022). Socio-economic and technological aspects of mental health of older persons: The role of strong and weak ties in Ghana. *Ageing and Society*, 1–23. doi:10.1017/S0144686X21001859

Anderson, M., & Perrin, A. (2017). *Technology use among seniors*. Pew Research Center for Internet & Technology.

Arief, M., Rissanen, S., & Saranto, K. (2018). Influence of previous work experience and education on Internet use of people in their 60s and 70s. *Journal of Innovation in Health Informatics*, *25*(3), 132–141. PMID:30398457

Ayakwah, A., Damoah, I. S., & Osabutey, E. L. (2021). Digitalization in Africa: The Case of Public Programs in Ghana. In *Business in Africa in the Era of Digital Technology* (pp. 7–25). Springer. doi:10.1007/978-3-030-70538-1_2

Bianchi, C. (2021). Exploring how internet services can enhance elderly well-being. *Journal of Services Marketing*, *35*(5), 585–603. doi:10.1108/JSM-05-2020-0177

Blažič, B. J., & Blažič, A. J. (2020). Overcoming the digital divide with a modern approach to learning digital skills for the elderly adults. *Education and Information Technologies*, *25*(1), 259–279. doi:10.100710639-019-09961-9

Bowen, G. A. (2009). Document analysis as a qualitative research method. *Qualitative Research Journal*, *9*(2), 27–40. doi:10.3316/QRJ0902027

Braun, V., & Clarke, V. (2006). Using thematic analysis in psychology. *Qualitative Research in Psychology*, *3*(2), 77–101. doi:10.1191/1478088706qp063oa

Braun, V., & Clarke, V. (2012). *Thematic analysis*. American Psychological Association. doi:10.1037/13620-004

Chen, Y., & Persson, A. (2002). Internet use among young and older adults: Relation to psychological wellbeing. *Educational Gerontology*, *28*(9), 731–744. doi:10.1080/036012702900999921

China Internet Network Information Center (CINIC). (2022). *Statistical report on internet development in China.* CINIC.

Choi, N. G., & DiNitto, D. M. (2013). Internet use among older adults: Association with health needs, psychological capital, and social capital. *Journal of Medical Internet Research*, *15*(5), e2333. doi:10.2196/jmir.2333 PMID:23681083

Cotten, S. R., Anderson, W. A., & McCullough, B. M. (2013). Impact of internet use on loneliness and contact with others among older adults: Cross-sectional analysis. *Journal of Medical Internet Research*, *15*(2), e2306. doi:10.2196/jmir.2306 PMID:23448864

Czaja, S. J., Sharit, J., Lee, C. C., Nair, S. N., Hernández, M. A., Arana, N., & Fu, S. H. (2013). Factors influencing use of an e-health website in a community sample of older adults. *Journal of the American Medical Informatics Association : JAMIA*, *20*(2), 277–284. doi:10.1136/amiajnl-2012-000876 PMID:22802269

De Veer, A. J., Peeters, J. M., Brabers, A. E., Schellevis, F. G., Rademakers, J. J., & Francke, A. L. (2015). Determinants of the intention to use e-Health by community dwelling older people. *BMC Health Services Research*, *15*(1), 1–9. doi:10.118612913-015-0765-8 PMID:25889884

Demuyakor, J. (2020). Ghana go digital Agenda: The impact of zipline drone technology on digital emergency health delivery in Ghana. *Humanities (Washington)*, *8*(1), 242–253. doi:10.34293ijash.v8i1.3301

Demuyakor, J. (2021). Ghana's Digitization Initiatives: A Survey of Citizens Perceptions on the Benefits and Challenges to the Utilization of Digital Governance Services. *International Journal of Publication and Social Studies*, *6*(1), 42–55. doi:10.18488/journal.135.2021.61.42.55

Demuyakor, J. (2021). Ghana's Digitization Initiatives: A Survey of Citizens Perceptions on the Benefits and Challenges to the Utilization of Digital Governance Services. *International Journal of Publication and Social Studies*, *6*(1), 42–55. doi:10.18488/journal.135.2021.61.42.55

Dovie, D. A. (2019). The status of older adult care in contemporary Ghana: A profile of some emerging issues. *Frontiers in Sociology*, *4*, 25. doi:10.3389/fsoc.2019.00025 PMID:33869350

Duh, H. B. L., Do, E. Y. L., Billinghurst, M., Quek, F., & Chen, V. H. H. (2010). Senior-friendly technologies: Interaction design for senior users. In CHI' 10 Extended Abstracts on Human Factors in Computing Systems (pp. 4513-4516).

Duncan, J. (2015). Debating ICT policy first principles for the Global South: The case of South Africa. *Communication*, *41*(1), 1–21.

Effah, J., Owusu-Oware, E., & Boateng, R. (2020). Biometric identification for socio-economic development in Ghana. *Information Systems Management*, *37*(2), 136–149. doi:10.1080/10580530.2020.1732528

El-Din, M. A. (2022) Egypt is one of the largest growing countries in digitisation in the Middle East: Micro Focus International. *Daily News Egypt*. https://dailynewsegypt.com/2022/06/21/egypt-is-one-of-the-largest-growing-countries-in-digitisation-in-middle-east-micro-focus-international/

Elliot, A. J., Mooney, C. J., Douthit, K. Z., & Lynch, M. F. (2014). Predictors of older adults' technology use and its relationship to depressive symptoms and well-being. *The Journals of Gerontology. Series B, Psychological Sciences and Social Sciences*, *69*(5), 667–677. doi:10.1093/geronb/gbt109 PMID:24304556

Francis, J., Rikard, R. V., Cotten, S. R., & Kadylak, T. (2019). Does ICT use matter? How information and communication technology use affects perceived mattering among a predominantly female sample of older adults residing in retirement communities. *Information Communication and Society*, *22*(9), 1281–1294. doi:10.1080/1369118X.2017.1417459

Friemel, T. N. (2016). The digital divide has grown old: Determinants of a digital divide among seniors. *New Media & Society*, *18*(2), 313–331. doi:10.1177/1461444814538648

Frimpong, L. K., Mensah, S. L., Okyere, S. A., Abunyewah, M., Diko, S. K., Enning, S. B., & Attigah, J. M. (2022). Digitalisation for whom: the determinants of residents' use of the digital property address system in Accra, Ghana. *Smart and Sustainable Built Environment.*

Gegenfurtner, A., Schmidt-Hertha, B., & Lewis, P. (2020). Digital technologies in training and adult education. *International Journal of Training and Development, 24*(1), 1–4. doi:10.1111/ijtd.12172

George, T. M., Okwu, E., & Ogunbodede, K. F. (2022). *Digital Literacy and Job Performance of Librarians in Rivers State University Libraries.* Library Philosophy & Practice.

Ghana Statistical Service (GSS), Ghana Health Service (GHS), and ICF International. (2015). *Ghana Demographic and Health Survey 2014.* GSS, GHS, and ICF International.

Ghanaian Times. (2022) World Bank provides $200m to accelerate Ghana's digital transformation agenda. *Ghanaian Times.* www.ghanaiantimes.com.gh/world-bank-provides-200m-to-accelerate-ghanas-digital-transformation-agenda/

GIFEC. (n.d) *Cyberlabs Programme.* GIFEC. https://gifec.gov.gh/project/cyberlaboratory programme/

Gilster, P. (1997). *Digital literacy.* Wiley Computer Publications.

Goldsmith, P., Andrade, J., Cornelius, M., Asigbee, M., Atim, P., & Tamimie, C. (2019). National school lunch nutrition and cost profile: A case study of the Ghana school feeding programme. *Food and Nutrition Bulletin, 40*(1), 41–55. doi:10.1177/0379572119825960 PMID:30734574

Hale, T. M., Cotten, S. R., Drentea, P., & Goldner, M. (2010). Rural-urban differences in general and health-related internet use. *The American Behavioral Scientist, 53*(9), 1304–1325. doi:10.1177/0002764210361685

Hatt, T., James, H., & Arese Lucini, B. (2017). *Country overview: Ghana. Driving mobile-enabled digital transformation.* GSMA.

Heeks, R. (2001). *Understanding e-governance for development.Institute for Development Policy and Management Household Survey on ICT (2020).Household Survey on ICT Abridged Report.* National Communications Authority and Ghana Statistical Service.

Howard, P., Busch, L., & Sheets, P. (2010). Comparing digital divides: Internet access and social inequality in Canada and the United States. *Canadian Journal of Communication, 35*(1), 109–128. doi:10.22230/cjc.2010v35n1a2192

Hunsaker, A., & Hargittai, E. (2018). A review of Internet use among older adults. *New Media & Society, 20*(10), 3937–3954. doi:10.1177/1461444818787348

ITU. (2021). *Measuring digital development Facts and figures 2021*. ITU.

Kariba, F. (2020). *The Burgeoning Africa Youth Population: Potential or Challenge?* Cities Alliance. https://www.citiesalliance.org/newsroom/news/cities-alliance-news/%C2%A0burgeoning-africa-youth-population-potential-or-challenge%C2%A0

Khalaila, R., & Vitman-Schorr, A. (2018). Internet use, social networks, loneliness, and quality of life among adults aged 50 and older: Mediating and moderating effects. *Quality of Life Research: An International Journal of Quality of Life Aspects of Treatment, Care and Rehabilitation, 27*(2), 479–489. doi:10.100711136-017-1749-4 PMID:29210015

Klímová, B., Poulová, P., Šimonová, I., Pražák, P., & Cierniak-Emerych, A. (2018). *Internet use by the older adults in the Czech Republic*.

Kpessa-Whyte, M., & Dzisah, J. S. (2022). *Digitalisation of Basic Services in Ghana: State of Policies in Action and Lesson for Progress*. INCLUDE.

Marfo, E. A. (2022). *Ghanaian Internet Users Spend Five Hours Daily on Mobile Phones-CSA*. GNA. https://gna.org.gh/2022/09/ghanaian-internet-users-

Markhaichuk, M., & Panshin, I. (2022). The Impact of Digital Literacy on Labor Productivity in the Context of the Educational Environment Transformation. *Eurasian Journal of Educational Research (EJER)*, (97).

McDonough, C. C. (2016). The effect of ageism on the digital divide among older adults. *HSOA Journal of Gerontology & Geriatric Medicine*, 2(008), 1–7. doi:10.24966/GGM-8662/100008

Merriam, S. B., & Baumgartner, L. M. (2020). *Learning in adulthood: A comprehensive guide*. John Wiley & Sons.

Ministry of Communication. (2012). *National Broadband Policy and Implementation Strategy*. Government of Ghana.

Ministry of Education. (2019b). Education strategic plan (2018-2030). Ghana. MoE.

Mohammed, A. K., & Kuyini, A. B. (2021). An evaluation of the free senior high school policy in Ghana. *Cambridge Journal of Education*, *51*(2), 143–172. doi:10.1080/0305764X.2020.1789066

Nakagomi, A., Shiba, K., Kawachi, I., Ide, K., Nagamine, Y., Kondo, N., Hanazato, M., & Kondo, K. (2022). Internet use and subsequent health and well-being in older adults: An outcome-wide analysis. *Computers in Human Behavior*, *130*, 107156. doi:10.1016/j.chb.2021.107156

Neves, B. B., Waycott, J., & Malta, S. (2018). Old and afraid of new communication technologies? Reconceptualising and contesting the 'age-based digital divide'. *Journal of Sociology (Melbourne, Vic.)*, *54*(2), 236–248. doi:10.1177/1440783318766119

Ng, W. (2012). Can we teach digital natives' digital literacy? *Computers & Education*, *59*(3), 1065–1078. doi:10.1016/j.compedu.2012.04.016

Nimrod, G. (2018). Technophobia among older Internet users. *Educational Gerontology*, *44*(2-3), 148–162. doi:10.1080/03601277.2018.1428145

Ofosu-Adarkwa, K. (2012). National Broadband Policy and Implementation Strategy. *Ministry of Communications, Republic of Ghana.*

Ohemeng, F. L. K., & Ofosu-Adarkwa, K. (2014). Overcoming the digital divide in developing countries: An examination of Ghana's strategies to promote universal access to information communication technologies (ICTs). *Journal of Developing Societies*, *30*(3), 297–322. doi:10.1177/0169796X14536970

Ono, H., & Zavodny, M. (2007). Digital inequality: A five country comparison using microdata. *Social Science Research*, *36*(3), 1135–1155. doi:10.1016/j.ssresearch.2006.09.001

Owusu, A., Akpe-Doe, C. E., & Taana, I. H. (2022). Assessing the Effectiveness of E-Government Services in Ghana: A Case of the Registrar General's Department. [IJEGR]. *International Journal of Electronic Government Research*, *18*(1), 1–23. doi:10.4018/IJEGR.289827

Polat, R. K. (2012). Digital exclusion in Turkey: A policy perspective. *Government Information Quarterly*, *29*(4), 589–596. doi:10.1016/j.giq.2012.03.002

Quan-Haase, A., Williams, C., Kicevski, M., Elueze, I., & Wellman, B. (2018). Dividing the grey divide: Deconstructing myths about older adults' online activities, skills, and attitudes. *The American Behavioral Scientist*, *62*(9), 1207–1228. doi:10.1177/0002764218777572

Republic of Ghana. (1992). *1992 constitution of the Republic of Ghana*. Ghana Publishing Corporation.

Republic of Ghana (2003b). *The Ghana ICT for accelerated development (ICT4D) policy*. Republic of Ghana.

Republic of Ghana. (2008). *Education Act (Act 778)*. Accra, Ghana: Republic of Ghana.

Rochat, L., Wilkosc-Debczynska, M., Zajac-Lamparska, L., Rothen, S., Andryszak, P., Gaspoz, J., Colombo, L., Khazaal, Y., & Achab, S. (2021). Internet use and problematic use in seniors: A comparative study in Switzerland and Poland. *Frontiers in Psychiatry*, *12*, 609190. doi:10.3389/fpsyt.2021.609190 PMID:34177634

Schelenz, L., & Schopp, K. (2018). Digitalization in Africa: Interdisciplinary perspectives on technology, development, and justice. *International Journal of Digital Society*, *9*(4), 1412–1420. doi:10.20533/ijds.2040.2570.2018.0175

Schreurs, K., Quan-Haase, A., & Martin, K. (2017). Problematizing the Digital Literacy Paradox in the Context of Older Adults' ICT Use: Aging, Media Discourse, and Self-Determination. *Canadian Journal of Communication*, *42*(2), 359–377. doi:10.22230/cjc.2017v42n2a3130

Seifert, A. (2020). The digital exclusion of older adults during the COVID-19 pandemic. *Journal of Gerontological Social Work*, *63*(6-7), 674–676. doi:10.1080/01634372.2020.1764687 PMID:32401181

Siemens, J. (2005). Connectivism: A learning theory for the digital age. *International Journal of Instructional Technology and Distance Learning*, *2*(1). http://www.itdl.org/spend-five-hours-daily-on-mobile-phones-csa/

Sum, S., Mathews, R. M., Hughes, I., & Campbell, A. (2008). Internet use and loneliness in older adults. *Cyberpsychology & Behavior*, *11*(2), 208–211. doi:10.1089/cpb.2007.0010 PMID:18422415

Tagoe, M. A., & Abakah, E. (2023). Analysis of Ghana's adult learning and education policy environment and governance framework: Towards meeting the goal of lifelong learning for all. In M. Milana, Palle Rasmussen, & M. Bussi (Eds.), Research Handbook on Adult Education Policy. Edward (In Press)

Tsugawa, S. (2022). Bridging the Digital Divide: Distance music learning among older adult musicians. *International Journal of Music Education*, 02557614221091888.

Tun, P. A., & Lachman, M. E. (2010). The association between computer use and cognition across adulthood: Use it so you won't lose it? *Psychology and Aging*, *25*(3), 560–568. doi:10.1037/a0019543 PMID:20677884

UNESCO. (2010). *Reaching the marginalized. EFA Global Monitoring Report*. UNESCO.

UNESCO. (2015). *Recommendation on Adult Learning and Education*. UNESCO and UIL Publication.

UNESCO Institute for Lifelong Learning (UIL). (2010). *Belém framework for action*. UNESCO.

UNHCR. (2023). Older Persons. *UNHCR Emergency Handbook*. UNHCR. https:/ /emergency.unhcr.org/entry/43935/older-persons#:~:text=An%20older%20 person%20is%20defined,or%20age%2Drelated%20health%20conditions

United Nations E-Government Survey (2018) *Gearing E-Government To Support Transformation Towards Sustainable And Resilient Societies*. United Nations Department of Economic and Social Affairs (UNDESA).

Van Deursen, A. J., & Helsper, E. J. (2015). The third-level digital divide: Who benefits most from being online? In *Communication and information technologies annual* (Vol. 10, pp. 29–52). Emerald Group Publishing Limited. doi:10.1108/S2050-206020150000010002

Van Laar, E., Van Deursen, A. J., Van Dijk, J. A., & De Haan, J. (2017). The relation between 21st-century skills and digital skills: A systematic literature review. *Computers in Human Behavior*, *72*, 577–588. doi:10.1016/j.chb.2017.03.010

Vaportzis, E., Giatsi Clausen, M., & Gow, A. J. (2017). Older adults' perceptions of technology and barriers to interacting with tablet computers: A focus group study. *Frontiers in Psychology*, *8*, 1687. doi:10.3389/fpsyg.2017.01687 PMID:29071004

Webb, S., Holford, J., Hodge, S., Milana, M., & Waller, R. (2017). Lifelong learning for quality education: Exploring the neglected aspect of sustainable development goal 4. *International Journal of Lifelong Education*, *36*(5), 509–511. doi:10.1080/02601370.2017.1398489

Wildemeersch, D., & Jütte, W. (2017). Digital the new normal-multiple challenges for the education and learning of adults. *European journal for Research on the Education and Learning of Adults*, *8*(1), 7-20.

World Bank. (2021). *Egypt Economic Monitor, December 2021: The Far-Reaching Impact of Government Digitalization*. World Bank.

Worldbank. (2022). *World Bank Provides $200 Million to Accelerate Ghana's Digital Transformation Agenda for Better Jobs*. World Bank. https://www.worldbank.org/en/news/press-release/2022/04/28/afw-world-bank-provides-200-million-to-accelerate-ghana-digital-transformation-agenda-for-better-jobs

Xavier, A. J., d'Orsi, E., de Oliveira, C. M., Orrell, M., Demakakos, P., Biddulph, J. P., & Marmot, M. G. (2014). English Longitudinal Study of Aging: Can Internet/E-mail use reduce cognitive decline? *Journals of Gerontology Series A. The Journals of Gerontology. Series A, Biological Sciences and Medical Sciences*, *69*(9), 1117–1121. doi:10.1093/gerona/glu105 PMID:25116923

Yu, K., Wu, S., & Chi, I. (2021). Internet use and loneliness of older adults over time: The mediating effect of social contact. *The Journals of Gerontology. Series B, Psychological Sciences and Social Sciences*, *76*(3), 541–550. doi:10.1093/geronb/gbaa004 PMID:31942629

Zelinski, E. M., & Reyes, R. (2009). Cognitive benefits of computer games for older adults. *Gerontechnology: international journal on the fundamental aspects of technology to serve the ageing society, 8*(4), 220.

Zhang, C., & Wang, Y. (2022). A study on internet use and well-being among Chinese older adults: based on CGSS (2012-2018) five-wave mixed interface survey data. *Europe PMC.*

Compilation of References

Ackoff, R. L. (1999, June/July). A Lifetime of Systems Thinking. *The Systems Thinker, 10*(5).

Adu, K. K., Dube, L., & Adjei, E. (2016). Digital preservation: The conduit through which open data, electronic government and the right to information are implemented. *Library Hi Tech, 34*(4), 733–747. doi:10.1108/LHT-07-2016-0078

Aguilar, M. S., & Castaneda, A. (2021). What mathematical competencies does a citizen need to interpret Mexico's official information about the COVID-19 pandemic? *Educational Studies in Mathematics, 108*(1-2), 227–248. doi:10.100710649-021-10082-9 PMID:34934238

Aitchison, J. (2003). Brak! - Vision, mirage and reality in the post apartheid globalisation of South African adult education and training. *Journal of Education*, (31), 47–74.

Aitchison, J. (2003). Struggle and compromise: A history of South African adult education from 1960 to 2001. *Journal of Education*, (29), 125–178.

Aitchison, J., & McKay, V. (2021). A historical remembrance of Paulo Freire in South Africa: A tale of two activists. *Australian Journal of Adult Learning, 61*(3), 334–354.

Akyeampong, K. (2009). Revisiting free compulsory universal basic education (FCUBE) in Ghana. *Comparative Education, 45*(2), 175–195. doi:10.1080/03050060902920534

Al Harbi, H. E. M. (2014). *An examination of Saudi high school teachers' ICT knowledge and implementation* [Doctoral dissertation, Queensland University of Technology].

Alharahsheh, H. H., & Pius, A. (2020). A review of key paradigms: Positivism VS interpretivism. *Global Academic Journal of Humanities and Social Sciences, 2*(3), 39–43.

Allison, J., Gorringe, S., & Lacey, J. (2006). *Building learning communities: Partnerships, social capital and VET performance*. NCVER.

Almeida, O. P., Yeap, B. B., Alfonso, H., Hankey, G. J., Flicker, L., & Norman, P. E. (2012). Older men who use computers have lower risk of dementia.

American Association of Community Colleges (AACC). 2012. *Reclaiming the American dream: Community colleges and the nation's future (21st century report).* Washington, DC: AACC. Retrieved from https://www.aacc.nche.edu/aboutcc/21stcenturyreport/index.html (accessed 20 September 2018).

Amoah, P. A., Osei-Tutu, A., & Adjei, S. B. (2022). Socio-economic and technological aspects of mental health of older persons: The role of strong and weak ties in Ghana. *Ageing and Society*, 1–23. doi:10.1017/S0144686X21001859

Anderson, M., & Perrin, A. (2017). *Technology use among seniors*. Pew Research Center for Internet & Technology.

Arafat, M. A. N. (2016). *The rise of the local economy in South Africa: The five pillars of networking enterprise*. SesLocal.

Arief, M., Rissanen, S., & Saranto, K. (2018). Influence of previous work experience and education on Internet use of people in their 60s and 70s. *Journal of Innovation in Health Informatics*, *25*(3), 132–141. PMID:30398457

Arinto, P. B. (2013). A framework for developing competencies in open and distance learning. *International Review of Research in Open and Distance Learning*, *4*(1), 167–185. doi:10.19173/irrodl.v14i1.1393

Arnesen, K. T., Hveem, J., Short, C. R., West, R. E., & Barbour, M. K. (2019). K-12 online learning journal articles: Trends from two decades of scholarship. *Distance Education, 40*(1), 32-53. https://doi. . 1080/ 01587 919. 2018. 15535 66. doi:org/10

Aronowitz, S. (2012). *Paulo Freire's radical democratic humanism: The fetish of method* (Vol. 422). Counterpoints.

Atmojo, A. E. P., & Nugroho, A. (2020). EFL classes must go online! Teaching activities and challenges during COVID-19 pandemic in Indonesia. *Register Journal, 13*(1), 49-76. https://journalregister.iainsalatiga.ac.id/index.php/register/article/view/4051

Ayakwah, A., Damoah, I. S., & Osabutey, E. L. (2021). Digitalization in Africa: The Case of Public Programs in Ghana. In *Business in Africa in the Era of Digital Technology* (pp. 7–25). Springer. doi:10.1007/978-3-030-70538-1_2

Baatjes, I., & Mathe, K. (2004). Adult education and social change in South Africa (1993-2004). *Changing class: Education and social change inpost-apartheid South Africa*, 393-420. HSRC Press.

Baatjes, I., Kgobe, M., & Sotuku, N. (2012). *Report of the CLING Project*. CLING.

Baatjes, B. (2016). *Umhlaba omutsha uyafufusa. Reflections on community participation in education: The Community Literacy and Numeracy Group (CLING)*. Education Policy Consortium.

Balogun, T., & Kalusopa, T. (2021). A framework for digital preservation of Indigenous Knowledge System (IKS) in repositories in South Africa. *Records Management Journal*, *31*(2), 177–195. doi:10.1108/RMJ-12-2020-0042

Baloyi, G. (2014). Learner support in open distance and e-learning for adult students using technologies. *Journal of Communication*, *5*(2), 127–133. doi:10.1080/0976691X.2014.11884832

Baloyi, G. P. (2014). The Role of the Adult Basic Education and Training in Addressing Human Rights in Rural Communities in South Africa. *Mediterranean Journal of Social Sciences*, *5*(2), 613–617.

Baro, E. E., Obaro, G. O., & Aduba, D. E. (2019). An Assessment of digital literacy skills and knowledge-based competencies among librarians working in university libraries in Africa. *Digital Library Perspectives*, *35*(3/4), 172–192. doi:10.1108/DLP-04-2019-0013

Barthes, R., & Duisit, L. (1975). An introduction to the structural analysis of narrative. *New Literary History*, *6*(2), 237–272. doi:10.2307/468419

Bartlett, L. (2005). Dialogue, knowledge, and teacher-student relations: Freirean pedagogy in theory and practice. *Comparative Education Review*, *49*(3), 344–364. doi:10.1086/430261

Bates, T. 2014. "Why learner support is an important component in the design of teaching and learning." Online Learning and Distance Education Resources. Retrieved from https://www.tonybates.ca/2014/08/26/why-learner-support-is-an-important-component-in-the-design-of-teaching-and-learning/ (accessed 30 October 2018).

Beauzac, C. B. (2010). *The Relationship between Adult Basic Education and Training (ABET) literacy programme and women's lives in Semi-urban context, in Cape Peninsula*. [Master's thesis. Western Cape: University of the Western Cape].

Beel, E. D., Wallace, D. C., Webster, G., Nguyen, H., Tait, E., Macleod, M., & Mellish, C. (2017). Cultural resilience: The production of rural community heritage, digital archives, and the role of volunteers. *Journal of Rural Studies*, *54*, 459–468. doi:10.1016/j.jrurstud.2015.05.002

Bell, A. M. (2005). Behavioural differences between individuals and two populations of stickleback (Gasterosteus aculeatus). *Journal of Evolutionary Biology*, *18*(2), 464–473. doi:10.1111/j.1420-9101.2004.00817.x PMID:15715852

Bezuidenhout, A. (2018). Analysing the importance-competence gap of distance educators with the increased utilisation of online learning strategies in a developing world context. *International Review of Research in Open and Distance Learning*, *19*(3), 263–281. doi:10.19173/irrodl.v19i3.3585

Bhebhe, S (2021). Proposed independent organizational structure for memory institutions in Zimbabwe and South Africa. *Collection and Curation*.

Bianchi, C. (2021). Exploring how internet services can enhance elderly well-being. *Journal of Services Marketing*, *35*(5), 585–603. doi:10.1108/JSM-05-2020-0177

Billett, S., Ovens, C., Clemans, A., & Seddon, T. (2007). Collaborative working and contested practices: Forming, developing and sustaining social partnerships in education. *Journal of Education Policy*, *22*(6), 637–656. doi:10.1080/02680930701625288

Bishop, E. (2014). Critical Literacy:Bringing Theory to Praxis. *Journal of Curriculum Theorizing*, *30*(1), 51–63. doi:10.4324/9781315635385

Blažič, B. J., & Blažič, A. J. (2020). Overcoming the digital divide with a modern approach to learning digital skills for the elderly adults. *Education and Information Technologies*, *25*(1), 259–279. doi:10.100710639-019-09961-9

Boddy-Evans, A. 2017. "Julius Kambarage Nyerere – Father of Tanzania and initiator of *ujamaa*." Retrieved from https://www.thoughtco.com/julius-kambarage-nyerere- 43589istory & Culture (accessed 17 March 2017).

Boonmoh, A., & Khamprem, K. (2021). Teachers' Rationale and Use of Technology: A Comparative Study Involving a Public Technical College and a Private High School. *Human Behavior. Development and Society*, *22*(1). https://so01.tci and thaijo.org/index.php/hbds/article/view/244938

Botha, L. (2011). Mixing methods as a process towards indigenous methodologies. *International Journal of Social Research Methodology*, *31*(4), 3–325. doi:10.1080/13645579.2010.516644

Bourdieu, P. (1992). *The Logic of Practice*. Stanford University Press.

Bow, C. (2019). Diverse Socio-technical aspects of a digital archive of Aboriginal languages. *Archives and Manuscripts*, *47*(1), 94–112.

Bowen, G. A. (2009). Document analysis as a qualitative research method. *Qualitative Research Journal*, *9*(2), 27–40. doi:10.3316/QRJ0902027

Bozkurt, A., & Sharma, R. C. (2020). Emergency remote teaching in a time of global crisis due to Corona Virus pandemic. *Asian journal of distance education, 15*(1), i-vi.

Braun, V., & Clarke, V. (2006). Using Thematic Analysis in Psychology. *Qualitative Research in Psychology*, *3*(2), 77–10. doi:10.1191/1478088706qp063oa

Braun, V., & Clarke, V. (2012). *Thematic analysis*. American Psychological Association. doi:10.1037/13620-004

Briggs, A. R., Morrison, M., & Coleman, M. (2012). *Research methods in educational leadership and management*. Sage Publications. doi:10.4135/9781473957695

British Columbia Teachers' Federation. (2016). *Poverty and School Attendance: Barriers and possible solutions.* BCTF. https://www.bctf.ca/uploadedFiles/Public/SocialJustice/Issues/Poverty/Research/BCTF%20Poverty%20and%20Education%20Survey--Chapter%205.pdf

Brookfield, S. (2017). Teaching for critical thinking. In V. C. X. Wang (Ed.), *Adult education and vocational training in the digital age* (pp. 1–17). IGI Global. doi:10.4018/978-1-5225-0929-5.ch001

Brotherson, M. J. (1994). Interactive Focus Group Interviewing: A Qualitative Research Method in Early Intervention. *Topics in Early Childhood Special Education*, *14*(1), 101–118. doi:10.1177/027112149401400110

Burke, M. (2021) Collaboration with language Community Members to Enrich Ethnographic Descriptions in a language Archive. *Proceedings of the Ist International workshop on Digital Language Archives*. HDL. http://hd1.handle.net/2142/111706

Byrne, T., O'Grady, M., & Roche, E. (2016). *Meeting the challenge: Strategies for motivating learners in adult education in Ireland*. National Adult Literacy Agency. https://www.nala.ie/sites/default/files/.../meeting_the_challenge_web_version.pdf

Carver, D. F., Watson, J., & Jr Curtiss, J. (2018). *Ritual Killings in Ancient Rome: Homicide and Roman Superiority. Corado*. Colorado State University Library.

Casey, C., & Delaney, H. (2022). The effort of partnership: Capacity development and moral capital in partnership for mutual gains. *Economic and Industrial Democracy*, *43*(1), 52–71. doi:10.1177/0143831X19883007

Casey, C., Fiedler, A., & Fath, B. (2016). The European Company (SE): Power and participation in the multinational corporation. *European Journal of Industrial Relations*, *22*(1), 73–90. doi:10.1177/0959680115593653

Centre for Education Rights and Transformation (CERT). (2010). *Annual Report, 2010*. CERT.

Cervero, A., Castro-Lopez, A., Álvarez-Blanco, L., Esteban, M., & Bernardo, A. (2020). Evaluation of educational quality performance on virtual campuses using fuzzy inference systems. *PLoS One*, *15*(5), e0232802. doi:10.1371/journal.pone.0232802 PMID:32469875

Chang, V., & Gütl, C. (2007). E-Learning Ecosystem (ELES) – A Holistic Approach for the Development of more Effective Learning Environment for Small-to-Medium Sized Enterprises (SMEs). In Proc. Inaugural IEEE International Digital EcoSystems Technologies Conference (IEEE-DEST 2007), Cairns, Australia.

Charoensuthipan, P. (2021, April 28). Third wave's unpalatable reality. *Bangkok Post*. https://www.bangkokpost.com/thailand/special-reports/2106859/third-waves-unpalatable-reality

Chaskin, R. J. (2001). Building Community Capacity: A Definitional Framework and Case Studies from a Comprehensive Community Initiative. *Urban Affairs Review*, *36*(3), 291–323. doi:10.1177/10780870122184876

Chen, L., Chen, H., & Wang, H. (2009). Distance education in China: The current state of e-learning. *Campus-Wide Information Systems*, *26*(2), 82–89. doi:10.1108/10650740910946792

Chen, Y., & Persson, A. (2002). Internet use among young and older adults: Relation to psychological wellbeing. *Educational Gerontology*, *28*(9), 731–744. doi:10.1080/03601270290099921

Chen, Z., & Hardy, S. B. (2023). Snapshot of the present, glimpse into the future: Impact of COVID-19 on higher education and adult training. *International Journal of Mobile Learning and Organisation*, *17*(1/2), 76–92. doi:10.1504/IJMLO.2023.128350

Chen, Z., Pavlova, M., & Ramos, C. (2021). A systematic approach to adult educators' professional development in Singapore: Challenges and future developments. *International Journal of Lifelong Education, 40*(5-6), 455–470. doi:10.1080/02601370.2021.1978006

Chen, Z., & Ramos, C. (2022). Work satisfaction of adult educators in Singapore: An empirical analysis. *Journal of Vocational Education and Training*, 1–25. doi:10.1080/13636820.2022.2049624

Cheu-jey, L. (2011). Myths about Critical Literacy: What Teachers Need to Unlearn. *Journal of Language & Literacy Education, 7*(1), 95–102.

Chilcott, A. (2019). Towards protocols for describing racially offensive language in UK public archives. *Archival Science, 19*(4), 359–376. doi:10.100710502-019-09314-y

China Internet Network Information Center (CINIC). (2022). *Statistical report on internet development in China.* CINIC.

Choi, N. G., & DiNitto, D. M. (2013). Internet use among older adults: Association with health needs, psychological capital, and social capital. *Journal of Medical Internet Research, 15*(5), e2333. doi:10.2196/jmir.2333 PMID:23681083

Clapper, T. C. (2010). Beyond Knowles: What those conducting simulation need to know about adult learning theory. *Clinical Simulation in Nursing, 6*(6), e7–e14. doi:10.1016/j.ecns.2009.07.003

CLING Project. (n.d.) *CLING Findings and Methodology*. CLING.

CLING. (n.d.). *Community Literacy and Numeracy Group (CLING) Policy Brief.* Draft.

Compton, L. K. L. (2009). Preparing language teachers to teach languages online: A look a t skills, roles, and responsibilities. *Computer Assisted Language Learning, 22*(1), 73–79. https://www.tandfonline.com/doi/. doi:10.1080/09588220802613831

Conquergood, D. (1991). Rethinking ethnography: Towards a critical cultural politics. *Communication Monographs, 58*(2), 179–194. doi:10.1080/03637759109376222

Cook-Sather, A., & Luz, A. (2015). Greater engagement in and responsibility for learning: What happens when students cross the threshold of student-faculty partnership. *Higher Education Research & Development, 34*(6), 1097–1109. doi:10.1080/07294360.2014.911263

Cotten, S. R., Anderson, W. A., & McCullough, B. M. (2013). Impact of internet use on loneliness and contact with others among older adults: Cross-sectional analysis. *Journal of Medical Internet Research, 15*(2), e2306. doi:10.2196/jmir.2306 PMID:23448864

Creswell, J. W. (2014). Research design: Qualitative, Quantitative and Mixed Method Approaches. Sage Publications.

Čubajevaitě, M. (2015). Transformative adult learning in new social movement – a case study from South Africa. *International Journal of Area Studies, 10*(2), 139–171. doi:10.1515/ijas-2015-0007

Czaja, S. J., Sharit, J., Lee, C. C., Nair, S. N., Hernández, M. A., Arana, N., & Fu, S. H. (2013). Factors influencing use of an e-health website in a community sample of older adults. *Journal of the American Medical Informatics Association : JAMIA*, *20*(2), 277–284. doi:10.1136/amiajnl-2012-000876 PMID:22802269

Dæhlen, M., & Ure, O. B. (2009). Low-skilled adults in formal continuing education: Does their motivation differ from other learners? *International Journal of Lifelong Education*, *28*(5), 661–674.

Danglot, B., Vera-Perez, O., Yu, Z., Zaidman, A., Monperrus, M., & Baudry, B. (2019). A snowballing literature study on test amplification. *Journal of Systems and Software*, *157*, 110398. doi:10.1016/j.jss.2019.110398

Darder, A. (2018). *The student guide to Freire's 'Pedagogy of the Oppressed.* Bloomsbury Academic.

Das, T. K. (2018). *Managing Trust in Strategic Alliances*. Information Age Publishing.

Davis, A. D. (2015). A conceptual model of systems thinking leadership in community colleges, 333-353. Springer.

De Beer, F., & Swanepoel, H. (2015). *Community Development and Beyond issues, structures and procedures*. Van Schaik Publishers.

De Cooman, R., Stynen, D., Van den Broeck, A., Sels, L., & De Witte, H. (2013). How job characteristics relate to need satisfaction and autonomous motivation: Implications for work effort. *Journal of Applied Social Psychology*, *43*(6), 1342–1352. doi:10.1111/jasp.12143

De Jong, W. (2015). "Makhosi a via (Chiefs Commit Ritual Murder)" Why ritual murders in Southern Africa should be seen as meaningful violence. *Africa Fus.*, *28*(2), 9–26.

De Vaal-Senekal, P., De Kock, C., & Putter, M. (2018). Challenges in the Archives of the Afrikaans Language Museum, Paarl, Western Cape, South Africa: A case Study. *Atlanti*, *28*(1), 195–205. doi:10.33700/2670-451X.28.1.195-205(2018)

De Veer, A. J., Peeters, J. M., Brabers, A. E., Schellevis, F. G., Rademakers, J. J., & Francke, A. L. (2015). Determinants of the intention to use e-Health by community dwelling older people. *BMC Health Services Research*, *15*(1), 1–9. doi:10.118612913-015-0765-8 PMID:25889884

Demuyakor, J. (2020). Ghana go digital Agenda: The impact of zipline drone technology on digital emergency health delivery in Ghana. *Humanities (Washington)*, *8*(1), 242–253. doi:10.34293ijash.v8i1.3301

Demuyakor, J. (2021). Ghana's Digitization Initiatives: A Survey of Citizens Perceptions on the Benefits and Challenges to the Utilization of Digital Governance Services. *International Journal of Publication and Social Studies*, *6*(1), 42–55. doi:10.18488/journal.135.2021.61.42.55

Desjardins, R. (2017). *Political economy of adult learning systems. Comparative study of strategies, policies and constraints*. Bloomsbury. doi:10.5040/9781474273671

Desjardins, R., & Ioannidou, A. (2020). The political economy of adult learning systems—Some institutional features that promote adult learning participation. *ZfW*, *43*(2), 143–168. doi:10.100740955-020-00159-y

DHET. (2016). *National policy for the monitoring and evaluation of Community Education and Training Colleges. Government Gazette No.39867*. DHET.

DHET. (2019). *The Community Education and Training College System: National Plan for the implementation of the White Paper for Post-School Education and Training System*. Pretoria: DHET.

Dhlamini, J. P., & Heeralal, P. J. H. (2014). Factors and Circumstances Leading to Adults Dropping Out from Community Colleges. *Journal of Educational and Social Research, [Online] 4*(3), 449-458. https://www.mcser.org/journal/index.php/jesr/article/view/2747/2712

Dittmar, L & Entin, J (2016). Introduction: Archives and Radical Education. *Radical Teacher. A Socialist, Feminist, and Anti- racist Journal on the Theory and Practice of Teaching, 105*, 1 – 6.

Dlamini, K. (2011). *Southern Africa: Breaking the Science on Ritual Killings*. SAGE Journal.

Dovie, D. A. (2019). The status of older adult care in contemporary Ghana: A profile of some emerging issues. *Frontiers in Sociology*, *4*, 25. doi:10.3389/fsoc.2019.00025 PMID:33869350

Drawson, A. S., Toombs, E., & Mushquash, C. J. (2017). Indigenous research methods: A systematic review. *International Indigenous Policy Journal*, *8*(2). Advance online publication. doi:10.18584/iipj.2017.8.2.5

Duh, H. B. L., Do, E. Y. L., Billinghurst, M., Quek, F., & Chen, V. H. H. (2010). Senior-friendly technologies: Interaction design for senior users. In CHI' 10 Extended Abstracts on Human Factors in Computing Systems (pp. 4513-4516).

Duncan, J. (2015). Debating ICT policy first principles for the Global South: The case of South Africa. *Communication*, *41*(1), 1–21.

Effah, J., Owusu-Oware, E., & Boateng, R. (2020). Biometric identification for socio-economic development in Ghana. *Information Systems Management*, *37*(2), 136–149. doi:10.1080/10580530.2020.1732528

El-Din, M. A. (2022) Egypt is one of the largest growing countries in digitisation in the Middle East: Micro Focus International. *Daily News Egypt*. https://dailynewsegypt.com/2022/06/21/egypt-is-one-of-the-largest-growing-countries-in-digitisation-in-middle-east-micro-focus-international/

Elliot, A. J., Mooney, C. J., Douthit, K. Z., & Lynch, M. F. (2014). Predictors of older adults' technology use and its relationship to depressive symptoms and well-being. *The Journals of Gerontology. Series B, Psychological Sciences and Social Sciences*, *69*(5), 667–677. doi:10.1093/geronb/gbt109 PMID:24304556

Ellis, E. (2020). COVID-19: Exposing a water crisis in the making. *Daily Maverick*. https:// www. Daily maver ick. co. za/ artic le/ 2020- 05- 14- COVID- 19- exposing-a- water- crisis- in-the- making/.

Ellis, C. (2007). Telling secrets, revealing lives: Relational ethics in research with intimate others. *Qualitative Inquiry*, *13*(1), 3–29. doi:10.1177/1077800406294947

Ellis, C., Adams, T. E., & Bochner, A. P. (2011). Autoethnography: An overview. *Historical Social Research (Köln)*, *36*(4), 273–290.

Essays, U. K. November 2013. "Labov's model of narrative analysis." Retrieved from https://www.ukessays.com/essays/english-language/labovs-model-narrative-analysis-2563.php?vref=1 (accessed 13 September 2018).

Etilyob, E., & Omiegbe, O. (2016). Religion,Culture and Discrimination against People with Disabilities in Nigeria. *African Journal of Disability*, *5*(1), 1–6.

Fabunmi, A. B. (2007). The roles of librarians in Copyright Protection in Nigeria. *International Journal of African & African American Studies*, *V1*(1), 84–93.

Ferrier, F., Dumbrell, T., & Burke, G. (2008). *Vocational education and training providers in competitive training markets*. NCVER.

Foley, G. (1999). *Learning in social action*. Zed.

Francis, J., Rikard, R. V., Cotten, S. R., & Kadylak, T. (2019). Does ICT use matter? How information and communication technology use affects perceived mattering among a predominantly female sample of older adults residing in retirement communities. *Information Communication and Society*, *22*(9), 1281–1294. doi:10.1080/1369118X.2017.1417459

Freire, A. M. A., & Macedo, D. (1998). The Paulo Freire reader. New York, NY: Continuum.

Freire, P. (1970). *Pedagogy of the Oppressed. New York, NY: Continuum. Freire, P. (1994). Pedagogy of Hope: Reliving the Pedagogy of the Oppressed*. Continuum.

Freire, P. (1998). Cultural Action for Freedom Paulo Freire. *Harvard Educational Review*, *68*(4), 1–12. http://www.thinkingtogether.org/rcream/archive/110/culturalaction.pdf. doi:10.17763/haer.68.4.656ku47213445042

Freire, P. (2013). *Education for critical consciousness*. Bloomsbury.

Freire, P., & Freire, A. M. A. (2004). *EPZ pedagogy of hope: Reliving pedagogy of the oppressed*. A&C Black.

Friemel, T. N. (2016). The digital divide has grown old: Determinants of a digital divide among seniors. *New Media & Society*, *18*(2), 313–331. doi:10.1177/1461444814538648

Frimpong, L. K., Mensah, S. L., Okyere, S. A., Abunyewah, M., Diko, S. K., Enning, S. B., & Attigah, J. M. (2022). Digitalisation for whom: the determinants of residents' use of the digital property address system in Accra, Ghana. *Smart and Sustainable Built Environment*.

Gall, R. (2013). Effective Motivational Strategies in Adult Basic Education Programs. *PAACE Journal of Lifelong Learning*, *22*, 63–79. https://www.iup.edu/WorkArea/DownloadAsset.aspx?id=162681

Gannon, S. 2017. "Education, cultures, and ethnicities: Research and assessment methods." *Oxford Research Encyclopedia: Education*. Doi: . doi:10.1093/acrefore/9780190264093.013.71

Garaba, F. (2014). Preparing collections for digitization: The case of religious archives in Pietermaritzburg, Kwazulu – Natal, South Africa. *Verbum et Ecclesia 35*(1). http://dx.doi.org// ve.v35i1.1319. doi:10.4102

Gardiner, M. (2010). *CLING project activities*. CEPD. http//www.cepd.org.za/files/ CLING_activities_May2010.pdf

Gardiner, M. (n.d.). *Making the best of local experience: Perspectives on community education and training centers*. CEPD. http//www.cepd.org.za/files/

Garrett, N. (2011). An e-portfolio design supporting ownership, social learning, and ease of use. *Journal of Educational Technology & Society*, *14*(1), 187–202.

Gboku, M., & Lekoko, R. N. (2007). *Developing Programmes for Adult Learners in Africa*. UNESCO Institute for Lifelong Learning: Feldbrunnenstr. 8.

Gboku, M. L., & Modise, O. M. (1999). Literacy work and the Freirean approach to literacy teaching: Lessons from the Botswana Literacy Pilot Project. *Australian Journal of Adult and Community Education*, *39*(3), 162–171.

Geary, J., & Trif, A. (2011). Workplace partnership and the balance of advantage: A critical case analysis. *British Journal of Industrial Relations*, *49*, s44–s69. doi:10.1111/j.1467-8543.2010.00827.x

Gegenfurtner, A., Schmidt-Hertha, B., & Lewis, P. (2020). Digital technologies in training and adult education. *International Journal of Training and Development*, *24*(1), 1–4. doi:10.1111/ijtd.12172

George, T. M., Okwu, E., & Ogunbodede, K. F. (2022). *Digital Literacy and Job Performance of Librarians in Rivers State University Libraries*. Library Philosophy & Practice.

Ghana Statistical Service (GSS), Ghana Health Service (GHS), and ICF International. (2015). *Ghana Demographic and Health Survey 2014*. GSS, GHS, and ICF International.

Ghanaian Times. (2022) World Bank provides $200m to accelerate Ghana's digital transformation agenda. *Ghanaian Times*. www.ghanaiantimes.com.gh/world-bank-provides-200m-to-accelerate-ghanas-digital-transformation-agenda/

Giddens, A. (1991). *Modernity and Self-identity*. Stanford University Press.

GIFEC. (n.d) *Cyberlabs Programme*. GIFEC. https://gifec.gov.gh/project/cyberlaboratory programme/

Gilliland, A., & McKemmish, S. (2014). The Role of Participatory Archives in Furthering Human Rights, Reconciliation, and Recovery. *Atlanti: Review for Modern Archival Theory and Practice*, *24*, 74–88.

Gilster, P. (1997). *Digital literacy*. Wiley Computer Publications.

Glass, R. D. (2001). On Paulo Freire's philosophy of praxis and the foundations of liberation education. *Educational Researcher*, *30*(2), 15–25. doi:10.3102/0013189X030002015

Goldsmith, P., Andrade, J., Cornelius, M., Asigbee, M., Atim, P., & Tamimie, C. (2019). National school lunch nutrition and cost profile: A case study of the Ghana school feeding programme. *Food and Nutrition Bulletin*, *40*(1), 41–55. doi:10.1177/0379572119825960 PMID:30734574

Gómez, N. L. (2021). La Educación Matemática en hogares venezolanos durante la pandemia. *Cuadernos de Investigación y Formación en Educación Matemática*, (20), 256–278.

Goos, M., & Beswick, K. (2021). *Learning and Development of Mathematics Teacher Educators*. Springer International Publishing.

Government of South Africa (2020). *Minister Angie Motshekga: Basic education sector recovery plans for the reopening of schools, following the Coronavirus COVID-19 lockdown adjustment of regulations*. Government of South Africa.

Grundy, S. (2006). *Curriculum: product or praxis?* Routledge.

Gueguen, G., Boucher, P., & Torres, V. (2006). *Between cooperation and competition: The benefits of collective strategies within business ecosystems—The example of the software industry*. Gaelgueguen. www.gaelgueguen.fr/wp-content/uploads/GueguenPellegrinTorres.pdf

Guldbrandsen, O. (2002). The Discourse of Ritual Murder, Popular Reaction to Political Leaders in Botswana. *Social Analysis*, *46*(3), 215–233.

Gustafsson, M., Van Der Berg, S., Sheperd, D., & Burger, C. (2010). *The costs of illiteracy in South Africa*. University of Stellenbosch's Department of Economics Working Paper 14/10. https://www.ekon.sun.ac.za/wpapers/2010/wp142010/wp-14 2010.pdf

Hale, T. M., Cotten, S. R., Drentea, P., & Goldner, M. (2010). Rural-urban differences in general and health-related internet use. *The American Behavioral Scientist*, *53*(9), 1304–1325. doi:10.1177/0002764210361685

Hammersley, M., & Atkinson, P. (2007). *Ethnography Principles in practice* (3rd ed.). Routledge.

Hampel, R., & Stickler, U. (2005). New skills for new classrooms: Training tutors to teach languages online. *Computer Assisted Language Learning*, *18*(4), 311–326. doi:10.1080/09588220500335455

Hanafi, H. F., Said, C. S., Wahab, M. H., & Samsuddin, K. (2017, August). Improving students' motivation in learning ICT course with the use of a mobile augmented reality learning environment. In IOP Conference Series: Materials Science and Engineering (Vol. 226, No. 1, p. 012114). IOP Publishing. doi:10.1088/1757-899X/226/1/012114

Harisman, Y., Kusumah, Y. S., & Kusnandi, K. (2019, March). How teacher professionalism influences student behaviour in mathematical problem-solving process. In Journal of Physics: Conference Series (Vol. 1188, No. 1, p. 012080). IOP Publishing. doi:10.1088/1742-6596/1188/1/012080

Harley, A., & Langdon, J. (2018). Ethics and power in visual research methods. In R. Iphofen & M. Tolich (Eds.), *The SAGE Handbook of qualitative research ethics*. SAGE. doi:10.4135/9781526435446.n13

Harris, P. J., Campbell Casey, S. A., Westbury, T., & Florida-James, G. (2016). Assessing the link between stress and retention and the existence of barriers to support service use within HE. *Journal of Further and Higher Education*, *40*(6), 824–845. doi:10.1080/0309877X.2015.1014316

Hasan, N., Rana, R. U., Chowdhury, S., Dola, A. J., & Rony, M. K. K. (2021). Ethical considerations in research. *Journal of Nursing Research, Patient Safety and Practise (JNRPSP) 2799-1210, 1*(01), 1-4. . doi:10.55529/jnrpsp11.1.4

Hatt, T., James, H., & Arese Lucini, B. (2017). *Country overview: Ghana. Driving mobile-enabled digital transformation.* GSMA.

Heeks, R. (2001). *Understanding e-governance for development.Institute for Development Policy and Management Household Survey on ICT (2020).Household Survey on ICT Abridged Report.* National Communications Authority and Ghana Statistical Service.

Hermita, N., Ningsih, H. S., Alim, J. A., Alpusari, M., Putra, Z. H., & Wijaya, T. T. (2020). Developing Science Comics for Elementary School Students on Animal Diversity. *Solid State Technology*, *63*(1s), 2492–2500.

Hindal, S., & Wyller, H. E. (2004). The Norwegian Archive, Library and Museum Authority – Our role in a society based on knowledge and culture. *Library Review*, *53*(4), 207–212. doi:10.1108/00242530410531820

Hoag, C. N. (2009). *Social justice struggles in Freedom Park: Linking advocacy, research and community organizing* [Unpublished Masters paper, SIT Graduate Institute in Brattleboro, Vermont, USA].

Hodgen, J., Taylor, B., Jacques, L., Tereshchenko, A., Kwok, R., & Cockerill, M. (2020). *Remote mathematics teaching during COVID-19: Intentions, practices and equity*. UCL. https://www.ucl.ac.uk/ioe/studentgroupingstudy

Hodges, C. B., Moore, S., Lockee, B. B., Trust, T., & Bond, M. A. (2020). *The difference between emergency remote teaching and online learning*. HDL. http://hdl.handle.net/10919/104648

Holton, G. (2012). Language archives: They're not just for linguists anymore. *Language & Conservation Special Publication*, *3*, 105–110.

Horton, M., & Freire, P. (1990). *We make the road by walking: Conversations on education and social change* (B. Bell, J. Gaventa, & J. Peters, Eds.). Temple University Press.

Howard, P., Busch, L., & Sheets, P. (2010). Comparing digital divides: Internet access and social inequality in Canada and the United States. *Canadian Journal of Communication*, *35*(1), 109–128. doi:10.22230/cjc.2010v35n1a2192

Hunsaker, A., & Hargittai, E. (2018). A review of Internet use among older adults. *New Media & Society*, *20*(10), 3937–3954. doi:10.1177/1461444818787348

IATA. (2021*). The impact of COVID-19 on aviation*. IATA.

Intawong, K., Olson, D., & Chariyalertsak, S. (2021). Application technology to fight the COVID-19 pandemic: Lessons learned in Thailand. *Biochemical and Biophysical Research Communications*, *534*, 830–836. doi:10.1016/j.bbrc.2020.10.097 PMID:33250175

ITU. (2021). *Measuring digital development Facts and figures 2021*. ITU.

Janks, H. (2012). The importance of critical literacy. *English Teaching*, *11*(1), 150–163.

Janks, H. (2013). Critical literacy in teaching and research1. *Education Inquiry*, *4*(2), 225–242. doi:10.3402/edui.v4i2.22071

Jiang, N., Yan-Li, S., Pamanee, K., & Sriyanto, J. (2021). Depression, anxiety, and stress during the COVID-19 pandemic: Comparison among higher education students in four countries in the Asia-Pacific region. [JPSS]. *Journal of Population and Social Studies*, *29*, 370–383. https://so03.tci-thaijo.org/index.php/jpss/article/view/244216. doi:10.25133/JPSSv292021.023

Jimerson, R. C. (2007). Archives for all: Professional Responsibility and Social Justice. *The American Archivist*, *70*(2), 252–281. doi:10.17723/aarc.70.2.5n20760751v643m7

Johannessen, M. R. (2020). *Handbook of Research on Politics in the Computer Age*. University of South-Eastern Norway.

Johnson, R. B., & Christensen, L. B. (2017). *Education Research: qualitative and mixed approaches* (6th ed.). SAGE.

Jones, M., & O'Neill, C. (2014). Identity, records and archival evidence: Exploring the needs of Forgotten Australians and Former Child Migrants. *Archives and Records (Abingdon, England)*, *35*(2), 110–125. doi:10.1080/23257962.2014.951032

Joubert, P., Van Wyk, C. & Rothmann, S. (2011). The effectiveness of sexual harassment policies and procedures at higher education institutions in South Africa. *SA Journal of Human Resource Management/SA Tydskrif vir Menslikehulpbronbestuur, 9*(1). doi:10.4102/sajhrm.v9i1.310

Jowallah, R. (2014). An investigation into the management of online teaching and learning spaces: A case study involving graduate research students. *International Review of Research in Open and Distance Learning*, *15*(4), 186–199. doi:10.19173/irrodl.v15i4.1585

Kambule, N., Yessoufou, K., Nwulu, N., & Mbohwa, C. (2019). Exploring the driving factors of prepaid electricity meter rejection in the largest township of South Africa. *Energy Policy*, *124*, 199–205. doi:10.1016/j.enpol.2018.09.041

Kariba, F. (2020). *The Burgeoning Africa Youth Population: Potential or Challenge?* Cities Alliance. https://www.citiesalliance.org/newsroom/news/cities-alliance-news/%C2%A0burgeoning-africa-youth-population-potential-or-challenge%C2%A0

Kaufman, R., & Guerra-Lopez, I. (2013). *Needs assessment for organizational success.* ASTD Press.

Kennedy, P. (2009) *How to combine multiple research options: Practical Triangulation* Johnny Hollard. https://johnnyholland.org/2009/08/20/practical-triangulation

Kerka, S. (1997). Popular education: Adult education for social change. *ERIC Digest No. 185.*

Khalaila, R., & Vitman-Schorr, A. (2018). Internet use, social networks, loneliness, and quality of life among adults aged 50 and older: Mediating and moderating effects. *Quality of Life Research: An International Journal of Quality of Life Aspects of Treatment, Care and Rehabilitation, 27*(2), 479–489. doi:10.100711136-017-1749-4 PMID:29210015

Khamprem, K., & Boonmoh, A. (2019). Teachers' stated needs and their actual use of technology. *Human Behavior. Development and Society, 20*(4), 41–51. https://so01.tci-thaijo.org/index.php/hbds/article/view/193626

Khoza, R. J. (2011). *Attuned leadership: African humanism as compass.* Penguin Books.

Kilpatrick, S., & Guenther, J. (2003). Successful VET partnerships in Australia. *International Journal of Training Research, 1*(1), 23–43. doi:10.5172/ijtr.1.1.23

Kilpatrick, S., Johns, S., & Mulford, B. (2010). Social Capital, Educational Institutions and Leadership. In P. Peterson, E. Baker, & B. McGaw (Eds.), *International Encyclopedia of Education* (3rd ed., pp. 113–119). Elsevier. doi:10.1016/B978-0-08-044894-7.00426-7

Klímová, B., Poulová, P., Šimonová, I., Pražák, P., & Cierniak-Emerych, A. (2018). *Internet use by the older adults in the Czech Republic.*

Knowles, M., Holton, E. F., & Swanson, R. A. (2013). *The adult learner: The definitive classic in adult education and human resource development.* Routledge Taylor & Francis.

Kochan, T. A., & Riordan, C. A. (2016). Employment relations and growing income inequality: Causes and potential options for its reversal. *The Journal of Industrial Relations, 58*(3), 419–440. doi:10.1177/0022185616634337

Kohl, J. (2018). A Murder, a Mummy and a Bust: The newly Discovered Portrait of Simon of Trent at the Getting. *Getting Research Journal, 10*, PP27–PP60. doi:10.1086/697383

Kovach, M. (2009). *Indigenous methodologies: Characteristics, conversations, and contexts.* University of Toronto Press.

Kpessa-Whyte, M., & Dzisah, J. S. (2022). *Digitalisation of Basic Services in Ghana: State of Policies in Action and Lesson for Progress.* INCLUDE.

Kumar, A. (2008). Development education and dialogical learning in the 21st century. *International Journal of Development Education and Global Learning*, *1*(1), 37–48. doi:10.18546/IJDEGL.01.1.04

Kumar, R. (2018). Research methodology: A step-by-step guide for beginners. *Sage (Atlanta, Ga.)*.

Larty, J., & Hamilton, E. (2011). Structural approaches to narrative analysis in entrepreneurship research: Exemplars from two researchers. *International Small Business Journal*, *29*(3), 220–237. doi:10.1177/0266242611401796

Le Grange, L. (2021). Covid-19 pandemic and the prospects of education in South Africa. *Prospects*, *51*(1-3), 425–436. doi:10.100711125-020-09514-w PMID:33100404

Letseka, M. (2012). In defence of *ubuntu*. *Studies in Philosophy and Education*, *31*(1), 47–60. doi:10.100711217-011-9267-2

Letseka, M., & Pitsoe, V. (2014). The challenges and prospects of access to higher education at Unisa. *Studies in Higher Education*, *39*(10), 1942–1954. doi:10.1080/03075079.2013.823933

Linchtenstein, D. R., Netemeyer, R. G., & Burton, S. 1991. "Using a theoretical perspective to examine the psychological construct of coupon proneness", in NA- Advances in Consumer Research Volume 18 (eds), Holman, R.H. and Solomon, M.R. Provo, UT: Associatin for Consumer Research, 501-508.

Llerena-Izquierdo, J., & Ayala-Carabajo, R. (2021). University teacher training during the COVID-19 emergency: the role of online teaching-learning tools. In Information Technology and Systems: ICITS 2021, Volume 2 (pp. 90-99). Springer International Publishing. doi:10.1007/978-3-030-68418-1_10

Machobane, A. M. (2010). *Strategies for Facilitating Learning in Adult Basic Education and Training*. [Dissertation, University of Pretoria]. http://hdl.handle.net/2263/27925

Magy, R. (2010). *Learner Goal Setting*. Pearson Longman. http://www.pearsonlongman.com/ae/emac/newsletters/RMagy_Monograph.pdf. [Accessed 5 October 2018].

Makhanya, M. S. (2011). Speaking at the launch of the Unisa Charter on Transformation. University of South Africa., Retrieved from https://www.unisa.ac.za/static/corporate_web/Content/About/Executive%20management/Unisa%20Principal%20and%20Vice-Chancellor/documents/PROF_MAKHANYA_CharterLaunchAddress.pdf, Retrieved August 30, 2018, from.

Maraví Zavaleta, L. M. (2021). Emergent curriculum in basic education for the new normality in Peru: Orientations proposed from mathematics education. *Educational Studies in Mathematics*, *108*(1-2), 291–305. doi:10.100710649-021-10100-w PMID:34934241

Maree, K. (2010). *First steps in research* (Revised ed.). Van Schaik.

Marfo, E. A. (2022). *Ghanaian Internet Users Spend Five Hours Daily on Mobile Phones-CSA*. GNA. https://gna.org.gh/2022/09/ghanaian-internet-users-

Margonis, F. (2003). Paulo Freire and post-colonial dilemmas. *Studies in Philosophy and Education, 22*(2), 145–156. doi:10.1023/A:1022280930241

Markhaichuk, M., & Panshin, I. (2022). The Impact of Digital Literacy on Labor Productivity in the Context of the Educational Environment Transformation. *Eurasian Journal of Educational Research (EJER),* (97).

Marowa, I. (2015). Archives as extended memory of communities: The case of Dandawa Chiefdom in Hurungwe District, Zimbabwe. *ESARBICA Journal, 34*, 104–116.

Masoga, M. A., & Rugwiji, T. (2018). A Reflection on Ritual Murder in the Biblical text from an African Perspective. Scripture.Vol 117.Stellenbosch.

Masoga, M. A., & Rugwiji, T. (2018). A Reflection on Ritual Murder in the Biblical text from an African Perspective. Stellenbosch.

Mathison, S. (2005). *Encyclopedia of evaluation*. Sage Publications, Inc. doi:10.4135/9781412950558

McConnel, C. (2002). *Community Learning and Development: The making of an Empowering Profession. Edinburgh Community Learning Scotland Merriam and Brocket (1997). The Profession and Practice of Adult Education*. Jossey-Bass Publishers.

McCormack, R. (2020) 'Freire's literacy: Reading and writing our worlds', *Fine Print*, 43(August), 31–499. https://search.informit.org/doi/pdf/10.3316/informit.308301161064629

McDonough, C. C. (2016). The effect of ageism on the digital divide among older adults. *HSOA Journal of Gerontology & Geriatric Medicine, 2*(008), 1–7. doi:10.24966/GGM-8662/100008

McKay, V. (2007). Adult Basic Education and Training in South Africa. In: *Review of Adult Learning and Literacy, 7*. NSCALL. http://www.ncsall.net/fileadmin/resources/ann_rev/rall_v7_ch9.pdf

McLaren, P. (1992). Critical Literacy and Postcolonial Praxis: A Freirian Perspective. *College Literature, 19/20*(3/1), 7–27. https://www.jstor.org/stable/25111986%5Cnhttp://www.jstor.org/stable/pdfplus/25111986.pdf

McMillan, J., & Schumacher, S. (2014). *Research in Education: Evidence-Based Inquiry* (7th ed.). Pearson.

Merriam, S. B., & Baumgartner, L. M. (2020). *Learning in adulthood: A comprehensive guide*. John Wiley & Sons.

Merriam, S. B., Caffarella, R. S., & Baumgartner, L. M. (2007). *Learning in Adulthood: A Comprehensive Guide* (3rd ed.). Jossey-Bass.

Mezirow, J. (1997). Transformative learning: Theory to practice. *New Directions for Adult and Continuing Education, 1997*(74), 5–12. doi:10.1002/ace.7401

Mhlanga, D., & Moloi, T. (2020). COVID-19 and the digital transformation of education: What are we learning on 4IR in South Africa? *Education Sciences, 10*(7), 180. doi:10.3390/educsci10070180

Miller, C. (2008). The role of Adult Education in Community Development. Exploring the links. *International Journal of Lifelong Education*, *30*(4), 489–505.

Ministry of Communication. (2012). *National Broadband Policy and Implementation Strategy*. Government of Ghana.

Ministry of Education. (2019b). Education strategic plan (2018-2030). Ghana. MoE.

Mishra, P., & Koehler, M. J. (2008, March). Introducing technological pedagogical content knowledge. In *annual meeting of the American Educational Research Association* (*Vol. 1*, p. 16). AERA.

Mishra, P. (2019). Considering contextual knowledge: The TPACK diagram gets an upgrade. *Journal of Digital Learning in Teacher Education*, *35*(2), 76–78. doi:10.1080/21532974.2019.1588611

Modipa, M. E. 2014. "African values respect environment." Retrieved from https://www.iol.co.za/business-report/features/african-values-respect-environment-1668339 (accessed 30 October 2018).

Mohammed, A. K., & Kuyini, A. B. (2021). An evaluation of the free senior high school policy in Ghana. *Cambridge Journal of Education*, *51*(2), 143–172. doi:10.1080/0305764X.2020.1789066

Mokotso I.R (2015). A Sustainable educational response to the recent increased witch killing and ritual murder 'Liretlo' in Lesotho: Introducing Bosotho Traditional Religion in Lesotho School. *African Educational Research Journal, 3* (4), 209-220.

Mokotso I.R (2015). A Sustainable educational response to the recent increased witch killing and ritual murder 'Liretlo' in Lesotho: Introducing Bosotho Traditional Religion in Lesotho School. *African Educational Research Journal, 3*(4), 209-220.

Moloto (2006). Ritual Killings Conference. South African Government.

Moloto. (2006). *Ritual Killings Conference*. South African Government.

Moore, M. G. (1991). Distance education theory. *American Journal of Distance Education*, *5*(3), 1–6. doi:10.1080/08923649109526758

Moore, M. G. (1993). Theory of transactional distance. In M. Keegan (Ed.), *Theoretical principles of distance education* (pp. 22–38). Routledge.

Moore, M. G., & Kearsley, G. (2012). *Distance education: A systems view* (3rd ed.). Wadsworth.

Moroe, M. S. (2019). Strategies to motivate adult learners to complete the NQF 1 [Unpublished master's thesis, Academic. University of South Africa, Pretoria, South Africa].

Msila, V. (2007). From Apartheid Education to Revised National Curriculum Statement. *Nordic Journal of African Studies*, *16*(2), 146–160.

Mungai, W. M., Dorvlo, S. S., Nuwagirya, A., & Holmner, M. (2020). Influence of copyright exceptions and limitations on access to information in Kenya, Ghana, and Uganda libraries. *Library Management*, *41*(6/7), 565–577. doi:10.1108/LM-03-2020-0052

Murphy, E., & Rodriguez-Manzanares, M. A. (2008). Revisiting transactional theory in a context of web-based high school distance education. *Journal of Distance Education*, *22*(2), 1–14.

Murphy, M. P. (2020). COVID-19 and emergency eLearning: Consequences of the securitization of higher education for post-pandemic pedagogy. *Contemporary Security Policy*, *41*(3), 492–505. doi:10.1080/13523260.2020.1761749

Nafukho, F., Amutabi, M., & Otunga, R. (2005). *Foundations of Adult Education in Africa* [ebook]. UNESCO Institute for Education. https://unesdoc.unesco.org/images/0014/001413/141340E.pdf

Nakagomi, A., Shiba, K., Kawachi, I., Ide, K., Nagamine, Y., Kondo, N., Hanazato, M., & Kondo, K. (2022). Internet use and subsequent health and well-being in older adults: An outcome-wide analysis. *Computers in Human Behavior*, *130*, 107156. doi:10.1016/j.chb.2021.107156

Nathan, D. J. (2012). From preserving language Resources to Serving Language Speakers: New Prospects for Endangered Language Archives. *Language Documentation and Description*, *12*, 187–208.

NCVER (National Centre for Vocational Education Research). (2007). *VET regional partnerships at a glance*. NCVER.

Netanda, R. S., Mamabolo, J., & Themane, M. (2017). Do or die: Student support interventions for the survival of distance education institutions in a competitive higher education system. *Studies in Higher Education*. Advance online publication. doi:10.1080/03075079.2017.1378632

Netshakhuma, N. S. (2021). Incorporation of indigenous archives into Limpopo archives repository: a case of Venda indigenous archives. Global Knowledge, Memory, and Communication. doi:10.1108/GKMC-05-2020-0064

Netshakhuma, N. S. (2021a). Accessibility of Land Claims Records at Kruger National Park of South Africa. T. Robin (ed) Indigenous Research of Land, Self and Spirit. IGI Global. doi:10.4018/978-1-7998-3729-9.ch010

Neves, B. B., Waycott, J., & Malta, S. (2018). Old and afraid of new communication technologies? Reconceptualising and contesting the 'age-based digital divide'. *Journal of Sociology (Melbourne, Vic.)*, *54*(2), 236–248. doi:10.1177/1440783318766119

Ngoepe, M., & Katuu, S. (2017). Provision of Records Created in Networking Environments in the Curricula of Institutions of Higher Learning in Africa. *New Review of Information Networking*, *22*(1), 1–12. doi:10.1080/13614576.2017.1297731

Ngoepe, M., & Nkwe, M. (2018). Separating the wheat from the chaff with the winnowings fork: The eeny meeny mo appraisal approach of digital records in South Africa. *Records Management Journal*, *28*(2), 130–142. doi:10.1108/RMJ-09-2017-0027

Ngulube, P. (2015). Qualitative data analysis and interpretation: systematic search for meaning. *Addressing research challenges: making headway for developing researchers, 131*, 156. https://www.researchgate.net/publication/278961843

Nguyen, D. T., & Kieuthi, T. C. (2020). New trends in technology application in education and capacities of universities lecturers during the Covid-19 pandemic. [IJMPERD]. *International Journal of Mechanical and Production Engineering Research and Development, 10*(3), 1709–1714. https://www.researchgate.net/publication/343126027

Ng, W. (2012). Can we teach digital natives' digital literacy? *Computers & Education, 59*(3), 1065–1078. doi:10.1016/j.compedu.2012.04.016

Nicholls, S., Booker, L., Thorpe, K., Jackson, M., Girault, C., Briggs, R., & Jones, C. (2016). From Principles to Practice: Community consultation regarding access to indigenous language material in archival records at the State Library of New South Wales. *Archives and Manuscripts, 44*(3), 110–123. doi:10.1080/01576895.2016.1239116

Nimrod, G. (2018). Technophobia among older Internet users. *Educational Gerontology, 44*(2-3), 148–162. doi:10.1080/03601277.2018.1428145

O'Neal, L. J., Gibson, P., & Cotten, S. R. (2017). Elementary school teachers' beliefs about the role of technology in 21st-century teaching and learning. *Computers in the Schools, 34*(3), 192–206. doi:10.1080/07380569.2017.1347443

OECD. (2019). *Community Education and Training in South Africa*. (OECD Publishing)

OECD. (2019). *Community Education and Training in South Africa: Getting Skills Right*. OECD Publisher.

Ofosu-Adarkwa, K. (2012). National Broadband Policy and Implementation Strategy. *Ministry of Communications, Republic of Ghana.*

Ohemeng, F. L. K., & Ofosu-Adarkwa, K. (2014). Overcoming the digital divide in developing countries: An examination of Ghana's strategies to promote universal access to information communication technologies (ICTs). *Journal of Developing Societies, 30*(3), 297–322. doi:10.1177/0169796X14536970

Okello-Obura, C (2011) Records and Archives Legal and Policy Frameworks in Uganda. *Library Philosophy and Practice (e-journal),* 9.

Olatokun, M. W. (2008). A survey of Preservation and Conservation Practices and Techniques in Nigerian university libraries. *Libres Library and Information Science Research Electronic Journal, 18*(2), 1–18.

Ong, Y. K. (2018). Tackling Inequality Will Always Be Work in Progress and All Singaporeans Have a Part to Play. *TODAY.*

Ono, H., & Zavodny, M. (2007). Digital inequality: A five country comparison using microdata. *Social Science Research, 36*(3), 1135–1155. doi:10.1016/j.ssresearch.2006.09.001

Onyema, E. M., Eucheria, N. C., Obafemi, F. A., Sen, S., Atonye, F. G., Sharma, A., & Alsayed, A. O. (2020). Impact of Coronavirus pandemic on education. *Journal of Education and Practice*, *11*(13), 108–121. doi:10.7176/JEP/11-13-12

Ormond-Parker, L., & Sloggett, R. (2012). Local archives and community collecting in the digital age. *Archival Science*, *12*(2), 191–212. doi:10.100710502-011-9154-1

Owusu, A., Akpe-Doe, C. E., & Taana, I. H. (2022). Assessing the Effectiveness of E-Government Services in Ghana: A Case of the Registrar General's Department. [IJEGR]. *International Journal of Electronic Government Research*, *18*(1), 1–23. doi:10.4018/IJEGR.289827

Oyedotun, T. D. (2020). Sudden change of pedagogy in education driven by COVID-19: Perspectives and evaluation from a developing country. *Research in Globalization*, *2*, 100029. doi:10.1016/j.resglo.2020.100029

Pakistan Ministry of Education (MoE). (2018). National Education Policy 2018. services research, 42, 533-544. Islamabad: Government of Pakistan. doi:10.52223/JSSA20-010105-05

Palinkas, L. A., Horwitz, S. M., Green, C. A., Wisdom, J. P., Duan, N., & Hoagwood, K. (2015). Purposeful sampling for qualitative data collection and analysis in mixed method implementation research. *Administration and Policy in Mental Health*, *42*(5), 533–544. https://link.springer.com/article/10.1007/s10488-013-0528-y. doi:10.100710488-013-0528-y PMID:24193818

Patterson, W. (2008). Narratives of events: Labovian narrative analysis and its limitations. In M. Andrews, C. Squire, & M. Tamboukou (Eds.), *Doing narrative research* (pp. 22–40). Sage. doi:10.4135/9780857024992.d3

Pedraza, J. M. (2014). *What is organizational effectiveness How an organization could achieve it?* RSA.

Pereira, R. (2018). Assessing the implementation of the National Archives and Records Services Act at Eduardo Mondlane University in Mozambique. *ESARBICA Journal*, *37*, 222–239.

Petty, T., & Thomas, C. C. (2014). Approaches to a successful adult education programme. *College Student Journal*, 473–480.

Pinnick, J. (2017). Exploring digital preservation requirements: A case study from the National Geoscience Data Centre (NGDC). *Records Management Journal*, *27*(2), 175–191. doi:10.1108/RMJ-04-2017-0009

Pitsoe, V., & Baloyi, G. (2015). Conceptions of success in open distance learning. In M. Letseka (Ed.), *open distance learning in South Africa* (pp. 91–104). Nova.

Polat, R. K. (2012). Digital exclusion in Turkey: A policy perspective. *Government Information Quarterly*, *29*(4), 589–596. doi:10.1016/j.giq.2012.03.002

Poole, A. H. (2020). The information work of community archives: A systematic literature review. *The Journal of Documentation*, *76*(3), 657–687. doi:10.1108/JD-07-2019-0140

Population Review. (2021). *Gini coefficient by country 2021.* UNESCO.

Pouwels, J. (2019). We are in need of each other. Paulo Freire and the role of conflicts in education. *International Journal of Social Pedagogy, 7*(1), 1–15. doi:10.14324/111.444.ijsp.2019.v7.1.009

Prinsloo, M. (1999). Literacy in South Africa, An international hand book. Science Direct.

QDA Training Ltd. (2012). *Defining the Constant Comparison Method.* QDA Training. https://qdatraining.com/defining-the-constant-comparison-method/

Quan-Baffour, K.P. (2011). *Education for development: Adult basic education as a tool for socio-economic transformation.* Unpublished Inaugural lecture.

Quan-Haase, A., Williams, C., Kicevski, M., Elueze, I., & Wellman, B. (2018). Dividing the grey divide: Deconstructing myths about older adults' online activities, skills, and attitudes. *The American Behavioral Scientist, 62*(9), 1207–1228. doi:10.1177/0002764218777572

Rakemane, D., & Mosweu, O. (2021). Challenges of managing and preserving audio-visual archives in archival institutions in Sub-Saharan Africa: A literature review. *Collection and Curation, 40*(2), 42–50. doi:10.1108/CC-04-2020-0011

Ramagoshi, R. M. 2013. "The role of *letsema* in community struggles: Past and present." In Landman, C. (Ed.), *Hidden voices, untold stories and veiled memories: Oral history, representation and knowledge.* Proceedings of the Fifth Oral History Conference 2008, East London (pp. 49–57). ISBN 978-1-86888-736-1.

Rannditsheni, A. E., Masoga, A., & Mavhandu-Mudzusi, A. H. (2016). Some Perspectives on the Impacts of Ritual Murders in Vhembe District of South Africa: An Interpretive Phenomenological Approach. *Journal of Social Sciences, 48*(3), 239–245. doi:10.1080/09718923.2016.11893586

Rcfrey. 2012. "Structural analysis of the narrative." In *Annotations: Genre theory.* Retrieved from https://genretheoryannotations.wordpress.com/2012/02/15/structural-analysis-of-the-narrative (accessed 13 September 2018).

Reder, S. (2020). A Lifelong and Life-Wide Framework for Adult Literacy Education. *Adult Literacy Education: the International Journal of Literacy, Language, and Numeracy, 2*(1), 48–53. doi:10.35847/SReder.2.1.48

Reid, H., & Howard, V. (2016). Connecting with Community: The Importance of Community Engagement in Rural Public Library Systems. *Public Library Quarterly, 35*(3), 188–202. doi:10.1080/01616846.2016.1210443

Republic of Ghana (2003b). *The Ghana ICT for accelerated development (ICT4D) policy.* Republic of Ghana.

Republic of Ghana. (1992). *1992 constitution of the Republic of Ghana.* Ghana Publishing Corporation.

Republic of Ghana. (2008). *Education Act (Act 778).* Accra, Ghana: Republic of Ghana.

Robichaux, R. R., & Guarino, A. J. (2012). The impact of implementing a portfolio assessment system on pre-service teachers' daily teaching: Reflections on improvement, performance and professionalism. *Creative Education*, *3*(3), 290–292. doi:10.4236/ce.2012.33045

Rochat, L., Wilkosc-Debczynska, M., Zajac-Lamparska, L., Rothen, S., Andryszak, P., Gaspoz, J., Colombo, L., Khazaal, Y., & Achab, S. (2021). Internet use and problematic use in seniors: A comparative study in Switzerland and Poland. *Frontiers in Psychiatry*, *12*, 609190. doi:10.3389/fpsyt.2021.609190 PMID:34177634

Rothes, A., Lemos, M. S., & Goncalves, T. (2014). Motives and beliefs of learners enrolled in adult education. *Procedia: Social and Behavioral Sciences*, *112*, 939–948. http://www.sciencedirect.com/science/article/pii/S1877042814012695?via%3Dihub. doi:10.1016/j.sbspro.2014.01.1252

Rule, P. (2006). " The time is burning ": The right of adults to basic education in South Africa. *Journal of Education*, *39*, 113–135.

Rule, P., & Land, S. (2017). Finding the plot in South African reading education. *Reading and Writing*, *8*(1), 1–8. doi:10.4102/rw.v8i1.121

Ruys, I., Van Keer, H., & Aelterman, A. (2012). Examining pre-service teacher competence in lesson planning pertaining to collaborative learning. *Journal of Curriculum Studies*, *44*(3), 349–379. doi:10.1080/00220272.2012.675355

Satgour, U. (2015). Celebrating libraries in 20 years of democracy: An overview of library and information services in South Africa. *IFLA Journal*, *41*(2), 97–111. doi:10.1177/0340035215585100

Schelenz, L., & Schopp, K. (2018). Digitalization in Africa: Interdisciplinary perspectives on technology, development, and justice. *International Journal of Digital Society*, *9*(4), 1412–1420. doi:10.20533/ijds.2040.2570.2018.0175

Schellnack-Kelly, I (2020), Decolonising the archives: languages as enablers and barriers to accessing public archives in South Africa. *Archives and Manuscript. 40* (3), 291 - 299.

Scholtz, H. J., Philips, V. M., & Knobel, G. T. (1997). Muti or Ritual murder. National Library of Medicine Solisbury and Roberts (2012). An explanatory study on perceptions of factors influencing ritual murder. *htt://*vital.seals.ac.za:8080/vital/access/services/download/vital:40715/SOURCE *1.*

Scholtz, H. J., Philips, V. M., & Knobel, G. T. (1997). *Muti or Ritual murder*. National Library of Medicine.

Schreurs, K., Quan-Haase, A., & Martin, K. (2017). Problematizing the Digital Literacy Paradox in the Context of Older Adults' ICT Use: Aging, Media Discourse, and Self-Determination. *Canadian Journal of Communication*, *42*(2), 359–377. doi:10.22230/cjc.2017v42n2a3130

Schrum, L. (2000). Online teaching and learning: Essential conditions for success! In L. Lau (Ed.), *Distance learning technologies: Issues, trends and opportunities* (pp. 91–106). Idea Group., doi:10.4018/978-1-878289-80-3.ch008

SEAMEO Regional Centre for Higher Education and Development. (2021, September 26). *The 8th Meeting of the Working Group on Student Mobility and Quality Assurance of Higher Education among ASEAN Plus Three Countries (APT WG)*. SEAMEO RIHED. https://rihed.seameo.org/the-8th-meeting-of-aptwg/

Seifart, F., Drude, S., Franchetto, B., & Gasche, J. (2008). Language Documentation and Archives in South America. *Language Documentation and Conservation*, *2*(1), 130–140.

Seifert, A. (2020). The digital exclusion of older adults during the COVID-19 pandemic. *Journal of Gerontological Social Work*, *63*(6-7), 674–676. doi:10.1080/01634372.2020.1764687 PMID:32401181

Senge, P. (2006). *The fifth discipline: The art and practice of the learning organisations*. Currency, Doubleday.

Setlhodi, I. I. (2018). Mentoring in a web class for adult learners. In C. Fitzgerald, S. Laurian-Fitzgerald, & C. Popa (Eds.), *Student-centered strategies to transform adult learning in online environments* (pp. 206–220). IGI Global., doi:10.4018/978-1-5225-5085-3.ch010

Setlhodi, I. I. (2019a). The value of pacing in promoting self-directed learning. In F. Giuseffi (Ed.), *Self-Directed Learning Strategies in Adult Educational Contexts* (pp. 1–22). IGI Global., doi:10.4018/978-1-5225-8018-8.ch001

Setlhodi, I. I. (2019b). Ubuntu Leadership: An African Panacea for Improving School Performance, *Africa. Education Review*, *16*(2), 126–142. doi:10.1080/18146627.2018.1464885

Setlhodi, I. I. (2022). Values Centred Leadership: Insights from schools that underperform. *Open Journal of Social Sciences*, *10*(7), 10, 470–486. doi:10.4236/jss.2022.107036

Shepard, A. M. (2016). The Value–Added Language Archive: Increasing Cultural Compatibility for Native American Communities. Series: Emergent Use and Conceptualization of Language Archive. *Language Documentation and Conservation*, *10*, 458–479.

Shipp, N. J. (2016). Do I really need specialist qualifications to work as a professional in a gallery, library, archive or museum? *The Australian Library Journal*, *65*(4), 280–287. doi:10.1080/00049670.2016.1233604

Siemens, J. (2005). Connectivism: A learning theory for the digital age. *International Journal of Instructional Technology and Distance Learning*, *2*(1). http://www.itdl.org/spend-five-hours-daily-on-mobile-phones-csa/

Siko, J. P., & Barbour, M. K. (2022). Is it Any Wonder, I Reject You First: Pre-Pandemic Perceptions of K-12 Online Learning. *TechTrends*, *66*(2), 301–309. doi:10.100711528-022-00709-w PMID:35229084

Sipilä, K. (2014). Educational use of information and communications technology: Teachers' perspective. *Technology, Pedagogy and Education*, *23*(2), 225–241. doi:10.1080/1475939X.2013.813407

Sogunro, O. (2015). Motivating Factors for Adult Learners in Higher Education. *International Journal of Higher Education, 4*(1), 22–37. https://www.sciedu.ca/journal/index.php/ijhe/article/view/5874

Soudien, C., Reddy, V., & Harvey, J. (2021). *The impact of COVID-19 on a fragile education system: The case of South Africa.* Springer. . doi:10.1007/978-3-030-81500-4

South African Centre For Digital Language Resources. (n.d.). *Index.* SADILAR. https://sadilar.org/index.php/en/about

South African Qualifications Authority (SAQA). (n.d). *General Education and Training Certificate: Adult Basic Education and Training.* SAQA. https://regqs.saqa.org.za/viewQualification.php?id=71751.

Stey, (2005). *Multi- murders form South Africa: a case report.* National Library of Medicine. National Centre for Biotechnology Information.

Stey. (2005). *Multi- murders form South Africa: a case report. National Library of Medicine.* National Centre for Biotechnology Information.

Strom, M. (2012). The Congressional Archive: A breed apart. *Journal of Library Administration, 52*(3-4), 332–340. doi:10.1080/01930826.2012.684531

Su, N. (2018). Positivist qualitative methods. The Sage handbook of qualitative business and management research methods, 17-32.

Sum, S., Mathews, R. M., Hughes, I., & Campbell, A. (2008). Internet use and loneliness in older adults. *Cyberpsychology & Behavior, 11*(2), 208–211. doi:10.1089/cpb.2007.0010 PMID:18422415

Suoranta, J. (2021). Reinventing Paulo Freire's pedagogy in Finnish non-formal education: The case of life skills for all model. *Educational Philosophy and Theory, 0*(0), 1–15. doi:10.1080/00131857.2021.1974839

Sztompka, P. (1999). *Trust: A Sociological Theory.* Cambridge University Press.

Tadesse, S., & Muluye, W. (2020). The impact of COVID-19 pandemic on education system in developing countries: A review. *Open Journal of Social Sciences, 8*(10), 159–170. doi:10.4236/jss.2020.810011

Tafazoli, D. (2021). CALL teachers' professional development amid the COVID-19 outbreak: A qualitative study. *Call-Ej, 22*(2), 4-13. https://www.researchgate.net/publication/350604667_

Tagoe, M. A., & Abakah, E. (2023). Analysis of Ghana's adult learning and education policy environment and governance framework: Towards meeting the goal of lifelong learning for all. In M. Milana, Palle Rasmussen, & M. Bussi (Eds.), Research Handbook on Adult Education Policy. Edward (In Press)

Tait, A. (2017). European figures in distance and e-learning. *Journal of Learning for Development*, *4*(1), 5–11. doi:10.56059/jl4d.v4i1.197

Tan, S., Wijaya, T. T., Zou, L., & Hermita, N. (2020, October). Proving the formula for the area of a circle using Hawgent dynamic mathematics software. In Journal of Physics: Conference Series, 1655(1), 012052. IOP Publishing. doi:10.1088/1742-6596/1655/1/012052

Tennant, M. (2006). *Psychology and Adult Learning* (3rd ed.). Routledge.

Thobejane, T. D. (2013). History of Apartheid Education and the Problems of Reconstruction in South Africa. *Sociolinguistic Studies*, *3*(1), 1–12.

Thompson, J. (2001). *Emancipatory learning. NIACE Briefing Sheet*. NIACE.

Thompson, K. M., & Copeland, C. (2020). Inclusive considerations for optimal online learning in times of disasters and crises. *Information and Learning Sciences*, *121*(7/8), 481–486. doi:10.1108/ILS-04-2020-0083

Thorpe, K., & Galassi, M. (2014). Rediscovering Indigenous Languages: The Role and Impact of Libraries and Archives in Cultural Revitalisation. *Australian Academic and Research Libraries*, *45*(2), 81–100. doi:10.1080/00048623.2014.910858

Timms, K. (2009). New Partnerships for Old Sibling Rivals: The Development of Integrated Access Systems for the Holdings of Archives, Libraries and Museums. *Archivaria*, *68*, 67–95.

Todnem, R. (2005). Organisational change management: A critical review. *Journal of Change Management*, *5*(4), 369–380. doi:10.1080/14697010500359250

Tondeur, J., Scherer, R., Siddiq, F., & Baran, E. (2020). Enhancing pre-service teachers' technological pedagogical content knowledge (TPACK): A mixed-method study. *Educational Technology Research and Development*, *68*(1), 319–343. doi:10.100711423-019-09692-1

Trikoilis, D., & Papanastasiou, E. C. (2020). The potential of research for professional development in isolated settings during the COVID-19 crisis and beyond. *Journal of Technology and Teacher Education*, *28*(2), 295–300. https://www.learntechlib.org/primary/p/216071/

Trilsbeek, P., & König, A. (2014). Increasing the future usage of endangered language archives. In D. Nathan & P. K. Austin (Eds.), *Language Documentation and Description* (Vol. 12). Special Issue on Language Documentation and Archiving.

Tsugawa, S. (2022). Bridging the Digital Divide: Distance music learning among older adult musicians. *International Journal of Music Education*, 02557614221091888.

Tun, P. A., & Lachman, M. E. (2010). The association between computer use and cognition across adulthood: Use it so you won't lose it? *Psychology and Aging*, *25*(3), 560–568. doi:10.1037/a0019543 PMID:20677884

Tygel, A. F., & Kirsch, R. (2016). Contributions of Paulo Freire for a Critical Data Literacy: A Popular Education Approach. *The Journal of Community Informatics*, *12*(3), 108–121. doi:10.15353/joci.v12i3.3279

UN. (2020). *Education during COVID-19 and beyond.* UN. https://www.un.org/development/desa/dspd/wp-content/uploads/sites/22/ 2020/08/ sg_policy_brief_covid-19_and_education_august_2020.pdf

UNESCO Institute for Lifelong Learning (UIL). (2010). *Belém framework for action.* UNESCO.

UNESCO. (2010). *Reaching the marginalized. EFA Global Monitoring Report.* UNESCO.

UNESCO. (2015). *Recommendation on Adult Learning and Education.* UNESCO and UIL Publication.

UNHCR. (2023). Older Persons. *UNHCR Emergency Handbook.* UNHCR. https:/ /emergency.unhcr.org/entry/43935/older-persons#:~:text=An%20older%20person%20is%20defined,or%20age%2Drelated%20health%20conditions

United National Educational, Scientific and Cultural Organisation. (2017). *Literacy and numeracy from a lifelong learning perspective.* UNESCO. https://unesdoc.unesco.org/images/0024/002470/247094E.pdf

United Nations E-Government Survey (2018) *Gearing E-Government To Support Transformation Towards Sustainable And Resilient Societies.* United Nations Department of Economic and Social Affairs (UNDESA).

United Nations. (2018). *Sustainable Development Goals Knowledge Platform.* UN. https://sustainabledevelopment.un.org/?menu=1300

Upward, F; McKemmish, S and Reed B (2011). Counterpoint Archivists and Changing Information Spaces: A Continuum Approach to Recordkeeping and Archiving in Online Cultures. *The Journal of the Association of Canadian Archivists (Archivaria) 72.*

Vally Salim, M. E. (2022). The Making of Post-Apartheid State Policies for Workers, Adult and Community Education and Training : Abandoned Possibilities. *Education as Change*, *26*, 23. doi:10.25159/1947/11366

Van der Merwe, R. (2015). Collections create connections: Stitching the lives of marginalized women on the national memory canvas. *Museum Management and Curatorship*, *30*(4), 268–282. doi:10.1080/09647775.2015.1043022

Van Deursen, A. J., & Helsper, E. J. (2015). The third-level digital divide: Who benefits most from being online? In *Communication and information technologies annual* (Vol. 10, pp. 29–52). Emerald Group Publishing Limited. doi:10.1108/S2050-206020150000010002

Van Laar, E., Van Deursen, A. J., Van Dijk, J. A., & De Haan, J. (2017). The relation between 21st-century skills and digital skills: A systematic literature review. *Computers in Human Behavior*, *72*, 577–588. doi:10.1016/j.chb.2017.03.010

Van Wyk, M. (2017). An e-portfolio as empowering tool to enhance students' self-directed learning in a teacher education course: A case of a South African university. *South African Journal of Higher Education*, *31*(3), 274–291. doi:10.20853/31-3-834

Vaportzis, E., Giatsi Clausen, M., & Gow, A. J. (2017). Older adults' perceptions of technology and barriers to interacting with tablet computers: A focus group study. *Frontiers in Psychology*, *8*, 1687. doi:10.3389/fpsyg.2017.01687 PMID:29071004

Venson, L. S., Ngoepe, M., & Ngulube, P. (2014). The role of public archives in national development in selected countries in the East and Southern Africa Regional Branch of the International Council on Archives region. *Innovation*, *48*, 44–64.

Vittoria, P. (2018). Critical education in paulo freire: Educational action for social transformation. *Encyclopaideia*, *22*(51), 37–44. doi:10.6092/issn.1825-8670/8459

Wahlgren, B. & Mariager-Anderson, K. (2017). Improving Completion Rates in Adult Education through Social Responsibility. *Adult Learning*, *28*(1), 20-26. . doi:10.1177/1045159516634078

Wals, A. (2006). Action Research and Community-problem solving: Environmental education in an inner-city. *Journal Homepage.*, *17*, PP163–PP182.

Wasson, C., Holton, G., & Roth, S. H. (2016). Bringing user-centered Design to the Field of Archives. *Language Documentation and Conservation*, *10*, 641–681.

Watermeyer, R., Chen, Z., & Ang, B. J. (2022). 'Education without limits': The digital resettlement of post-secondary education and training in Singapore in the COVID-19 era. *Journal of Education Policy*, *37*(6), 861–882. doi:10.1080/02680939.2021.1933198

Webb, S., Holford, J., Hodge, S., Milana, M., & Waller, R. (2017). Lifelong learning for quality education: Exploring the neglected aspect of sustainable development goal 4. *International Journal of Lifelong Education*, *36*(5), 509–511. doi:10.1080/02601370.2017.1398489

Wells, K. (2011). *Narrative inquiry*. Oxford University Press. doi:10.1093/acprof:oso/9780195385793.001.0001

Wijaya, T. T. (2020). How chinese students learn mathematics during the coronavirus pandemic. . doi:10.46661/ijeri.4950

Wikipedia. (2013). *Talk*. Community Education.

Wildemeersch, D., & Jütte, W. (2017). Digital the new normal-multiple challenges for the education and learning of adults. *European journal for Research on the Education and Learning of Adults, 8*(1), 7-20.

WIPO. (2019). *WIPO and the sustainable development goals: innovation driving human progress*. WIPO. Https://www.wipo.int/edocs/pubdocs/en/wipo_pub_1061.pdf

Withers, D. (2017). Ephemeral Feminist Histories and the Politics of Transmission within Digital Culture. *Women's History Review*, *26*(5), 678–691. doi:10.1080/09612025.2016.1166887

World Bank. (2020). *Rapid response briefing note: Remote learning and COVID-19 outbreak*. The World Bank.

World Bank. (2021). *Egypt Economic Monitor, December 2021: The Far-Reaching Impact of Government Digitalization*. World Bank.

World Health Organisation. (2018). *Ethics and Health*. WHO. https://www.who.int/ethics/ research/en

Worldbank. (2022). *World Bank Provides $200 Million to Accelerate Ghana's Digital Transformation Agenda for Better Jobs*. World Bank. https://www.worldbank.org/en/ news/ press-release/2022/04/28/afw-world-bank-provides-200-million-to-accelerate-ghana-digital-transformation-agenda-for-better-jobs

Xavier, A. J., d'Orsi, E., de Oliveira, C. M., Orrell, M., Demakakos, P., Biddulph, J. P., & Marmot, M. G. (2014). English Longitudinal Study of Aging: Can Internet/E-mail use reduce cognitive decline? J*ournals of Gerontology Series A. The Journals of Gerontology. Series A, Biological Sciences and Medical Sciences*, *69*(9), 1117–1121. doi:10.1093/gerona/glu105 PMID:25116923

Xu, Z., Yuan, H., & Liu, Q. (2020). Student performance prediction based on blended learning. *IEEE Transactions on Education*, *64*(1), 66–73. doi:10.1109/TE.2020.3008751

Yeoh, E. K. K., & Chu, K. M. (2012). Literacy, education and economic development in contemporary China. *SSRN*, *2*(1&2), 11–30. doi:10.2139srn.2207559

Yılmaz, Z., Gülbağcı Dede, H., Sears, R., & Yıldız Nielsen, S. (2021). Are we all in this together? Mathematics teachers' perspectives on equity in remote instruction during pandemic. *Educational Studies in Mathematics*, *108*(1–2), 307–331. doi:10.100710649-021-10060-1 PMID:34934233

Yu, K., Wu, S., & Chi, I. (2021). Internet use and loneliness of older adults over time: The mediating effect of social contact. *The Journals of Gerontology. Series B, Psychological Sciences and Social Sciences*, *76*(3), 541–550. doi:10.1093/geronb/gbaa004 PMID:31942629

Yukl, G. (2013). *Leadership in organisations*. Pearson.

Zelinski, E. M., & Reyes, R. (2009). Cognitive benefits of computer games for older adults. *Gerontechnology: international journal on the fundamental aspects of technology to serve the ageing society*, *8*(4), 220.

Zhang, A. 2003. *Transactional distance in web-based college learning environments: Toward measurement and theory construction*. PhD. diss., Virginia Commonwealth University, Richmond, VA. Retrieved from https://wwwlib.umi.com/dissertations/fullcit/3082019 (accessed 28 September 2018).

Zhang, C., & Wang, Y. (2022). A study on internet use and well-being among Chinese older adults: based on CGSS (2012-2018) five-wave mixed interface survey data. *Europe PMC*.

Related References

To continue our tradition of advancing academic research, we have compiled a list of recommended IGI Global readings. These references will provide additional information and guidance to further enrich your knowledge and assist you with your own research and future publications.

Aburezeq, I. M., & Dweikat, F. F. (2017). Cloud Applications in Language Teaching: Examining Pre-Service Teachers' Expertise, Perceptions and Integration. *International Journal of Distance Education Technologies, 15*(4), 39–60. doi:10.4018/IJDET.2017100103

Acharjya, B., & Das, S. (2022). Adoption of E-Learning During the COVID-19 Pandemic: The Moderating Role of Age and Gender. *International Journal of Web-Based Learning and Teaching Technologies, 17*(2), 1–14. https://doi.org/10.4018/IJWLTT.20220301.oa4

Adams, J. L., & Thomas, S. K. (2022). Non-Linear Curriculum Experiences for Student Learning and Work Design: What Is the Maximum Potential of a Chat Bot? In S. Ramlall, T. Cross, & M. Love (Eds.), *Handbook of Research on Future of Work and Education: Implications for Curriculum Delivery and Work Design* (pp. 299–306). IGI Global. https://doi.org/10.4018/978-1-7998-8275-6.ch018

Adera, B. (2017). Supporting Language and Literacy Development for English Language Learners. In J. Keengwe (Ed.), *Handbook of Research on Promoting Cross-Cultural Competence and Social Justice in Teacher Education* (pp. 339–354). Hershey, PA: IGI Global. doi:10.4018/978-1-5225-0897-7.ch018

Ahamer, G. (2017). Quality Assurance for a Developmental "Global Studies" (GS) Curriculum. In I. Management Association (Ed.), Educational Leadership and Administration: Concepts, Methodologies, Tools, and Applications (pp. 438-477). Hershey, PA: IGI Global. https://doi.org/ doi:10.4018/978-1-5225-1624-8.ch023

Akayoğlu, S., & Seferoğlu, G. (2019). An Analysis of Negotiation of Meaning Functions of Advanced EFL Learners in Second Life: Negotiation of Meaning in Second Life. In M. Kruk (Ed.), *Assessing the Effectiveness of Virtual Technologies in Foreign and Second Language Instruction* (pp. 61–85). IGI Global. https://doi.org/10.4018/978-1-5225-7286-2.ch003

Akella, N. R. (2022). Unravelling the Web of Qualitative Dissertation Writing!: A Student Reflects. In A. Zimmerman (Ed.), *Methodological Innovations in Research and Academic Writing* (pp. 260–282). IGI Global. https://doi.org/10.4018/978-1-7998-8283-1.ch014

Alegre de la Rosa, O. M., & Angulo, L. M. (2017). Social Inclusion and Intercultural Values in a School of Education. In S. Mukerji & P. Tripathi (Eds.), *Handbook of Research on Administration, Policy, and Leadership in Higher Education* (pp. 518–531). Hershey, PA: IGI Global. doi:10.4018/978-1-5225-0672-0.ch020

Alexander, C. (2019). Using Gamification Strategies to Cultivate and Measure Professional Educator Dispositions. *International Journal of Game-Based Learning*, *9*(1), 15–29. https://doi.org/10.4018/IJGBL.2019010102

Anderson, K. M. (2017). Preparing Teachers in the Age of Equity and Inclusion. In I. Management Association (Ed.), Medical Education and Ethics: Concepts, Methodologies, Tools, and Applications (pp. 1532-1554). Hershey, PA: IGI Global. doi:10.4018/978-1-5225-0978-3.ch069

Awdziej, M. (2017). Case Study as a Teaching Method in Marketing. In D. Latusek (Ed.), *Case Studies as a Teaching Tool in Management Education* (pp. 244–263). Hershey, PA: IGI Global. doi:10.4018/978-1-5225-0770-3.ch013

Bakos, J. (2019). Sociolinguistic Factors Influencing English Language Learning. In N. Erdogan & M. Wei (Eds.), *Applied Linguistics for Teachers of Culturally and Linguistically Diverse Learners* (pp. 403–424). IGI Global. https://doi.org/10.4018/978-1-5225-8467-4.ch017

Banas, J. R., & York, C. S. (2017). Pre-Service Teachers' Motivation to Use Technology and the Impact of Authentic Learning Exercises. In L. Tomei (Ed.), *Exploring the New Era of Technology-Infused Education* (pp. 121–140). Hershey, PA: IGI Global. doi:10.4018/978-1-5225-1709-2.ch008

Barton, T. P. (2021). Empowering Educator Allyship by Exploring Racial Trauma and the Disengagement of Black Students. In C. Reneau & M. Villarreal (Eds.), *Handbook of Research on Leading Higher Education Transformation With Social Justice, Equity, and Inclusion* (pp. 186–197). IGI Global. https://doi.org/10.4018/978-1-7998-7152-1.ch013

Benhima, M. (2021). Moroccan English Department Student Attitudes Towards the Use of Distance Education During COVID-19: Moulay Ismail University as a Case Study. *International Journal of Information and Communication Technology Education, 17*(3), 105–122. https://doi.org/10.4018/IJICTE.20210701.oa7

Beycioglu, K., & Wildy, H. (2017). Principal Preparation: The Case of Novice Principals in Turkey. In I. Management Association (Ed.), Educational Leadership and Administration: Concepts, Methodologies, Tools, and Applications (pp. 1152-1169). Hershey, PA: IGI Global. https://doi.org/ doi:10.4018/978-1-5225-1624-8.ch054

Bharwani, S., & Musunuri, D. (2018). Reflection as a Process From Theory to Practice. In M. Khosrow-Pour, D.B.A. (Ed.), Encyclopedia of Information Science and Technology, Fourth Edition (pp. 1529-1539). Hershey, PA: IGI Global. doi:10.4018/978-1-5225-2255-3.ch132

Bhushan, A., Garza, K. B., Perumal, O., Das, S. K., Feola, D. J., Farrell, D., & Birnbaum, A. (2022). Lessons Learned From the COVID-19 Pandemic and the Implications for Pharmaceutical Graduate Education and Research. In C. Ford & K. Garza (Eds.), *Handbook of Research on Updating and Innovating Health Professions Education: Post-Pandemic Perspectives* (pp. 324–345). IGI Global. https://doi.org/10.4018/978-1-7998-7623-6.ch014

Bintz, W., Ciecierski, L. M., & Royan, E. (2021). Using Picture Books With Instructional Strategies to Address New Challenges and Teach Literacy Skills in a Digital World. In L. Haas & J. Tussey (Eds.), *Connecting Disciplinary Literacy and Digital Storytelling in K-12 Education* (pp. 38–58). IGI Global. https://doi.org/10.4018/978-1-7998-5770-9.ch003

Bohjanen, S. L., Cameron-Standerford, A., & Meidl, T. D. (2018). Capacity Building Pedagogy for Diverse Learners. In J. Keengwe (Ed.), *Handbook of Research on Pedagogical Models for Next-Generation Teaching and Learning* (pp. 195–212). Hershey, PA: IGI Global. doi:10.4018/978-1-5225-3873-8.ch011

Brewer, J. C. (2018). Measuring Text Readability Using Reading Level. In M. Khosrow-Pour, D.B.A. (Ed.), Encyclopedia of Information Science and Technology, Fourth Edition (pp. 1499-1507). Hershey, PA: IGI Global. doi:10.4018/978-1-5225-2255-3.ch129

Brookbanks, B. C. (2022). Student Perspectives on Business Education in the USA: Current Attitudes and Necessary Changes in an Age of Disruption. In A. Zhuplev & R. Koepp (Eds.), *Global Trends, Dynamics, and Imperatives for Strategic Development in Business Education in an Age of Disruption* (pp. 214–231). IGI Global. doi:10.4018/978-1-7998-7548-2.ch011

Brown, L. V., Dari, T., & Spencer, N. (2019). Addressing the Impact of Trauma in High Poverty Elementary Schools: An Ecological Model for School Counseling. In K. Daniels & K. Billingsley (Eds.), *Creating Caring and Supportive Educational Environments for Meaningful Learning* (pp. 135–153). IGI Global. https://doi.org/10.4018/978-1-5225-5748-7.ch008

Brown, S. L. (2017). A Case Study of Strategic Leadership and Research in Practice: Principal Preparation Programs that Work – An Educational Administration Perspective of Best Practices for Master's Degree Programs for Principal Preparation. In V. Wang (Ed.), *Encyclopedia of Strategic Leadership and Management* (pp. 1226–1244). Hershey, PA: IGI Global. doi:10.4018/978-1-5225-1049-9.ch086

Brzozowski, M., & Ferster, I. (2017). Educational Management Leadership: High School Principal's Management Style and Parental Involvement in School Management in Israel. In V. Potocan, M. Ünğan, & Z. Nedelko (Eds.), *Handbook of Research on Managerial Solutions in Non-Profit Organizations* (pp. 55–74). Hershey, PA: IGI Global. doi:10.4018/978-1-5225-0731-4.ch003

Cahapay, M. B. (2020). Delphi Technique in the Development of Emerging Contents in High School Science Curriculum. *International Journal of Curriculum Development and Learning Measurement, 1*(2), 1–9. https://doi.org/10.4018/IJCDLM.2020070101

Camacho, L. F., & Leon Guerrero, A. E. (2022). Indigenous Student Experience in Higher Education: Implementation of Culturally Sensitive Support. In P. Pangelinan & T. McVey (Eds.), *Learning and Reconciliation Through Indigenous Education in Oceania* (pp. 254–266). IGI Global. https://doi.org/10.4018/978-1-7998-7736-3.ch016

Cannaday, J. (2017). The Masking Effect: Hidden Gifts and Disabilities of 2e Students. In P. Dickenson, P. Keough, & J. Courduff (Eds.), *Preparing Pre-Service Teachers for the Inclusive Classroom* (pp. 220–231). Hershey, PA: IGI Global. doi:10.4018/978-1-5225-1753-5.ch011

Cederquist, S., Fishman, B., & Teasley, S. D. (2022). What's Missing From the College Transcript?: How Employers Make Sense of Student Skills. In Y. Huang (Ed.), *Handbook of Research on Credential Innovations for Inclusive Pathways to Professions* (pp. 234–253). IGI Global. https://doi.org/10.4018/978-1-7998-3820-3.ch012

Cockrell, P., & Gibson, T. (2019). The Untold Stories of Black and Brown Student Experiences in Historically White Fraternities and Sororities. In P. Hoffman-Miller, M. James, & D. Hermond (Eds.), *African American Suburbanization and the Consequential Loss of Identity* (pp. 153–171). IGI Global. https://doi.org/10.4018/978-1-5225-7835-2.ch009

Cohen, M. (2022). Leveraging Content Creation to Boost Student Engagement. In T. Driscoll III, (Ed.), *Designing Effective Distance and Blended Learning Environments in K-12* (pp. 223–239). IGI Global. https://doi.org/10.4018/978-1-7998-6829-3.ch013

Contreras, E. C., & Contreras, I. I. (2018). Development of Communication Skills through Auditory Training Software in Special Education. In M. Khosrow-Pour, D.B.A. (Ed.), Encyclopedia of Information Science and Technology, Fourth Edition (pp. 2431-2441). Hershey, PA: IGI Global. doi:10.4018/978-1-5225-2255-3.ch212

Cooke, L., Schugar, J., Schugar, H., Penny, C., & Bruning, H. (2020). Can Everyone Code?: Preparing Teachers to Teach Computer Languages as a Literacy. In J. Mitchell & E. Vaughn (Eds.), *Participatory Literacy Practices for P-12 Classrooms in the Digital Age* (pp. 163–183). IGI Global. https://doi.org/10.4018/978-1-7998-0000-2.ch009

Cooley, D., & Whitten, E. (2017). Special Education Leadership and the Implementation of Response to Intervention. In F. Topor (Ed.), *Handbook of Research on Individualism and Identity in the Globalized Digital Age* (pp. 265–286). Hershey, PA: IGI Global. doi:10.4018/978-1-5225-0522-8.ch012

Cosner, S., Tozer, S., & Zavitkovsky, P. (2017). Enacting a Cycle of Inquiry Capstone Research Project in Doctoral-Level Leadership Preparation. In I. Management Association (Ed.), Educational Leadership and Administration: Concepts, Methodologies, Tools, and Applications (pp. 1460-1481). Hershey, PA: IGI Global. doi:10.4018/978-1-5225-1624-8.ch067

Crawford, C. M. (2018). Instructional Real World Community Engagement. In M. Khosrow-Pour, D.B.A. (Ed.), Encyclopedia of Information Science and Technology, Fourth Edition (pp. 1474-1486). Hershey, PA: IGI Global. doi:10.4018/978-1-5225-2255-3.ch127

Crosby-Cooper, T., & Pacis, D. (2017). Implementing Effective Student Support Teams. In P. Dickenson, P. Keough, & J. Courduff (Eds.), *Preparing Pre-Service Teachers for the Inclusive Classroom* (pp. 248–262). Hershey, PA: IGI Global. doi:10.4018/978-1-5225-1753-5.ch013

Curran, C. M., & Hawbaker, B. W. (2017). Cultivating Communities of Inclusive Practice: Professional Development for Educators – Research and Practice. In C. Curran & A. Petersen (Eds.), *Handbook of Research on Classroom Diversity and Inclusive Education Practice* (pp. 120–153). Hershey, PA: IGI Global. doi:10.4018/978-1-5225-2520-2.ch006

Dass, S., & Dabbagh, N. (2018). Faculty Adoption of 3D Avatar-Based Virtual World Learning Environments: An Exploratory Case Study. In I. Management Association (Ed.), Technology Adoption and Social Issues: Concepts, Methodologies, Tools, and Applications (pp. 1000-1033). Hershey, PA: IGI Global. https://doi.org/ doi:10.4018/978-1-5225-5201-7.ch045

Davison, A. M., & Scholl, K. G. (2017). Inclusive Recreation as Part of the IEP Process. In C. Curran & A. Petersen (Eds.), *Handbook of Research on Classroom Diversity and Inclusive Education Practice* (pp. 311–330). Hershey, PA: IGI Global. doi:10.4018/978-1-5225-2520-2.ch013

DeCoito, I. (2018). Addressing Digital Competencies, Curriculum Development, and Instructional Design in Science Teacher Education. In M. Khosrow-Pour, D.B.A. (Ed.), Encyclopedia of Information Science and Technology, Fourth Edition (pp. 1420-1431). Hershey, PA: IGI Global. https://doi.org/ doi:10.4018/978-1-5225-2255-3.ch122

DeCoito, I., & Richardson, T. (2017). Beyond Angry Birds™: Using Web-Based Tools to Engage Learners and Promote Inquiry in STEM Learning. In I. Levin & D. Tsybulsky (Eds.), *Digital Tools and Solutions for Inquiry-Based STEM Learning* (pp. 166–196). Hershey, PA: IGI Global. doi:10.4018/978-1-5225-2525-7.ch007

Delmas, P. M. (2017). Research-Based Leadership for Next-Generation Leaders. In R. Styron Jr & J. Styron (Eds.), *Comprehensive Problem-Solving and Skill Development for Next-Generation Leaders* (pp. 1–39). Hershey, PA: IGI Global. doi:10.4018/978-1-5225-1968-3.ch001

Demiray, U., & Ekren, G. (2018). Administrative-Related Evaluation for Distance Education Institutions in Turkey. In K. Buyuk, S. Kocdar, & A. Bozkurt (Eds.), *Administrative Leadership in Open and Distance Learning Programs* (pp. 263–288). Hershey, PA: IGI Global. doi:10.4018/978-1-5225-2645-2.ch011

Dickenson, P. (2017). What do we Know and Where Can We Grow?: Teachers Preparation for the Inclusive Classroom. In P. Dickenson, P. Keough, & J. Courduff (Eds.), *Preparing Pre-Service Teachers for the Inclusive Classroom* (pp. 1–22). Hershey, PA: IGI Global. doi:10.4018/978-1-5225-1753-5.ch001

Ding, Q., & Zhu, H. (2021). Flipping the Classroom in STEM Education. In J. Keengwe (Ed.), *Handbook of Research on Innovations in Non-Traditional Educational Practices* (pp. 155–173). IGI Global. https://doi.org/10.4018/978-1-7998-4360-3.ch008

Dixon, T., & Christison, M. (2021). Teaching English Grammar in a Hybrid Academic ESL Course: A Mixed Methods Study. In K. Kelch, P. Byun, S. Safavi, & S. Cervantes (Eds.), *CALL Theory Applications for Online TESOL Education* (pp. 229–251). IGI Global. https://doi.org/10.4018/978-1-7998-6609-1.ch010

Donne, V., & Hansen, M. (2017). Teachers' Use of Assistive Technologies in Education. In L. Tomei (Ed.), *Exploring the New Era of Technology-Infused Education* (pp. 86–101). Hershey, PA: IGI Global. doi:10.4018/978-1-5225-1709-2.ch006

Donne, V., & Hansen, M. A. (2018). Business and Technology Educators: Practices for Inclusion. In I. Management Association (Ed.), Business Education and Ethics: Concepts, Methodologies, Tools, and Applications (pp. 471-484). Hershey, PA: IGI Global. https://doi.org/ doi:10.4018/978-1-5225-3153-1.ch026

Dos Santos, L. M. (2022). Completing Student-Teaching Internships Online: Instructional Changes During the COVID-19 Pandemic. In M. Alaali (Ed.), *Assessing University Governance and Policies in Relation to the COVID-19 Pandemic* (pp. 106–127). IGI Global. https://doi.org/10.4018/978-1-7998-8279-4.ch007

Dreon, O., Shettel, J., & Bower, K. M. (2017). Preparing Next Generation Elementary Teachers for the Tools of Tomorrow. In M. Grassetti & S. Brookby (Eds.), *Advancing Next-Generation Teacher Education through Digital Tools and Applications* (pp. 143–159). Hershey, PA: IGI Global. doi:10.4018/978-1-5225-0965-3.ch008

Durak, H. Y., & Güyer, T. (2018). Design and Development of an Instructional Program for Teaching Programming Processes to Gifted Students Using Scratch. In J. Cannaday (Ed.), *Curriculum Development for Gifted Education Programs* (pp. 61–99). Hershey, PA: IGI Global. doi:10.4018/978-1-5225-3041-1.ch004

Egorkina, E., Ivanov, M., & Valyavskiy, A. Y. (2018). Students' Research Competence Formation of the Quality of Open and Distance Learning. In V. Mkrttchian & L. Belyanina (Eds.), *Handbook of Research on Students' Research Competence in Modern Educational Contexts* (pp. 364–384). Hershey, PA: IGI Global. doi:10.4018/978-1-5225-3485-3.ch019

Ekren, G., Karataş, S., & Demiray, U. (2017). Understanding of Leadership in Distance Education Management. In I. Management Association (Ed.), Educational Leadership and Administration: Concepts, Methodologies, Tools, and Applications (pp. 34-50). Hershey, PA: IGI Global. https://doi.org/ doi:10.4018/978-1-5225-1624-8.ch003

Elmore, W. M., Young, J. K., Harris, S., & Mason, D. (2017). The Relationship between Individual Student Attributes and Online Course Completion. In K. Shelton & K. Pedersen (Eds.), *Handbook of Research on Building, Growing, and Sustaining Quality E-Learning Programs* (pp. 151–173). Hershey, PA: IGI Global. doi:10.4018/978-1-5225-0877-9.ch008

Ercegovac, I. R., Alfirević, N., & Koludrović, M. (2017). School Principals' Communication and Co-Operation Assessment: The Croatian Experience. In I. Management Association (Ed.), Educational Leadership and Administration: Concepts, Methodologies, Tools, and Applications (pp. 1568-1589). Hershey, PA: IGI Global. https://doi.org/ doi:10.4018/978-1-5225-1624-8.ch072

Everhart, D., & Seymour, D. M. (2017). Challenges and Opportunities in the Currency of Higher Education. In K. Rasmussen, P. Northrup, & R. Colson (Eds.), *Handbook of Research on Competency-Based Education in University Settings* (pp. 41–65). Hershey, PA: IGI Global. doi:10.4018/978-1-5225-0932-5.ch003

Farmer, L. S. (2017). Managing Portable Technologies for Special Education. In V. Wang (Ed.), *Encyclopedia of Strategic Leadership and Management* (pp. 977–987). Hershey, PA: IGI Global. doi:10.4018/978-1-5225-1049-9.ch068

Farmer, L. S. (2018). Optimizing OERs for Optimal ICT Literacy in Higher Education. In J. Keengwe (Ed.), *Handbook of Research on Mobile Technology, Constructivism, and Meaningful Learning* (pp. 366–390). Hershey, PA: IGI Global. doi:10.4018/978-1-5225-3949-0.ch020

Ferguson, B. T. (2019). Supporting Affective Development of Children With Disabilities Through Moral Dilemmas. In S. Ikuta (Ed.), *Handmade Teaching Materials for Students With Disabilities* (pp. 253–275). IGI Global. doi:10.4018/978-1-5225-6240-5.ch011

Fındık, L. Y. (2017). Self-Assessment of Principals Based on Leadership in Complexity. In I. Management Association (Ed.), Educational Leadership and Administration: Concepts, Methodologies, Tools, and Applications (pp. 978-991). Hershey, PA: IGI Global. https://doi.org/ doi:10.4018/978-1-5225-1624-8.ch047

Flor, A. G., & Gonzalez-Flor, B. (2018). Dysfunctional Digital Demeanors: Tales From (and Policy Implications of) eLearning's Dark Side. In I. Management Association (Ed.), The Dark Web: Breakthroughs in Research and Practice (pp. 37-50). Hershey, PA: IGI Global. https://doi.org/ doi:10.4018/978-1-5225-3163-0.ch003

Floyd, K. K., & Shambaugh, N. (2017). Instructional Design for Simulations in Special Education Virtual Learning Spaces. In T. Kidd & L. Morris Jr., (Eds.), *Handbook of Research on Instructional Systems and Educational Technology* (pp. 202–215). Hershey, PA: IGI Global. doi:10.4018/978-1-5225-2399-4.ch018

Freeland, S. F. (2020). Community Schools: Improving Academic Achievement Through Meaningful Engagement. In R. Kronick (Ed.), *Emerging Perspectives on Community Schools and the Engaged University* (pp. 132–144). IGI Global. https://doi.org/10.4018/978-1-7998-0280-8.ch008

Ghanbarzadeh, R., & Ghapanchi, A. H. (2019). Applied Areas of Three Dimensional Virtual Worlds in Learning and Teaching: A Review of Higher Education. In I. Management Association (Ed.), *Virtual Reality in Education: Breakthroughs in Research and Practice* (pp. 172-192). IGI Global. https://doi.org/10.4018/978-1-5225-8179-6.ch008

Giovannini, J. M. (2017). Technology Integration in Preservice Teacher Education Programs: Research-based Recommendations. In M. Grassetti & S. Brookby (Eds.), *Advancing Next-Generation Teacher Education through Digital Tools and Applications* (pp. 82–102). Hershey, PA: IGI Global. doi:10.4018/978-1-5225-0965-3.ch005

Good, S., & Clarke, V. B. (2017). An Integral Analysis of One Urban School System's Efforts to Support Student-Centered Teaching. In J. Keengwe & G. Onchwari (Eds.), *Handbook of Research on Learner-Centered Pedagogy in Teacher Education and Professional Development* (pp. 45–68). Hershey, PA: IGI Global. doi:10.4018/978-1-5225-0892-2.ch003

Guetzoian, E. (2022). Gamification Strategies for Higher Education Student Worker Training. In C. Lane (Ed.), *Handbook of Research on Acquiring 21st Century Literacy Skills Through Game-Based Learning* (pp. 164–179). IGI Global. https://doi.org/10.4018/978-1-7998-7271-9.ch009

Hamidi, F., Owuor, P. M., Hynie, M., Baljko, M., & McGrath, S. (2017). Potentials of Digital Assistive Technology and Special Education in Kenya. In C. Ayo & V. Mbarika (Eds.), *Sustainable ICT Adoption and Integration for Socio-Economic Development* (pp. 125–151). Hershey, PA: IGI Global. doi:10.4018/978-1-5225-2565-3.ch006

Hamim, T., Benabbou, F., & Sael, N. (2022). Student Profile Modeling Using Boosting Algorithms. *International Journal of Web-Based Learning and Teaching Technologies*, *17*(5), 1–13. https://doi.org/10.4018/IJWLTT.20220901.oa4

Henderson, L. K. (2017). Meltdown at Fukushima: Global Catastrophic Events, Visual Literacy, and Art Education. In R. Shin (Ed.), *Convergence of Contemporary Art, Visual Culture, and Global Civic Engagement* (pp. 80–99). Hershey, PA: IGI Global. doi:10.4018/978-1-5225-1665-1.ch005

Hudgins, T., & Holland, J. L. (2018). Digital Badges: Tracking Knowledge Acquisition Within an Innovation Framework. In I. Management Association (Ed.), Wearable Technologies: Concepts, Methodologies, Tools, and Applications (pp. 1118-1132). Hershey, PA: IGI Global. https://doi.org/ doi:10.4018/978-1-5225-5484-4.ch051

Hwang, R., Lin, H., Sun, J. C., & Wu, J. (2019). Improving Learning Achievement in Science Education for Elementary School Students via Blended Learning. *International Journal of Online Pedagogy and Course Design*, *9*(2), 44–62. https://doi.org/10.4018/IJOPCD.2019040104

Jančec, L., & Vodopivec, J. L. (2019). The Implicit Pedagogy and the Hidden Curriculum in Postmodern Education. In J. Vodopivec, L. Jančec, & T. Štemberger (Eds.), *Implicit Pedagogy for Optimized Learning in Contemporary Education* (pp. 41–59). IGI Global. https://doi.org/10.4018/978-1-5225-5799-9.ch003

Janus, M., & Siddiqua, A. (2018). Challenges for Children With Special Health Needs at the Time of Transition to School. In I. Management Association (Ed.), Autism Spectrum Disorders: Breakthroughs in Research and Practice (pp. 339-371). Hershey, PA: IGI Global. doi:10.4018/978-1-5225-3827-1.ch018

Jesus, R. A. (2018). Screencasts and Learning Styles. In M. Khosrow-Pour, D.B.A. (Ed.), Encyclopedia of Information Science and Technology, Fourth Edition (pp. 1548-1558). Hershey, PA: IGI Global. doi:10.4018/978-1-5225-2255-3.ch134

John, G., Francis, N., & Santhakumar, A. B. (2022). Student Engagement: Past, Present, and Future. In S. Ramlall, T. Cross, & M. Love (Eds.), *Handbook of Research on Future of Work and Education: Implications for Curriculum Delivery and Work Design* (pp. 329–341). IGI Global. https://doi.org/10.4018/978-1-7998-8275-6.ch020

Karpinski, A. C., D'Agostino, J. V., Williams, A. K., Highland, S. A., & Mellott, J. A. (2018). The Relationship Between Online Formative Assessment and State Test Scores Using Multilevel Modeling. In M. Khosrow-Pour, D.B.A. (Ed.), Encyclopedia of Information Science and Technology, Fourth Edition (pp. 5183-5192). Hershey, PA: IGI Global. doi:10.4018/978-1-5225-2255-3.ch450

Kats, Y. (2017). Educational Leadership and Integrated Support for Students with Autism Spectrum Disorders. In I. Management Association (Ed.), Educational Leadership and Administration: Concepts, Methodologies, Tools, and Applications (pp. 101-114). Hershey, PA: IGI Global. https://doi.org/ doi:10.4018/978-1-5225-1624-8.ch007

Kaya, G., & Altun, A. (2018). Educational Ontology Development. In M. Khosrow-Pour, D.B.A. (Ed.), Encyclopedia of Information Science and Technology, Fourth Edition (pp. 1441-1450). Hershey, PA: IGI Global. doi:10.4018/978-1-5225-2255-3.ch124

Keough, P. D., & Pacis, D. (2017). Best Practices Implementing Special Education Curriculum and Common Core State Standards using UDL. In P. Dickenson, P. Keough, & J. Courduff (Eds.), *Preparing Pre-Service Teachers for the Inclusive Classroom* (pp. 107–123). Hershey, PA: IGI Global. doi:10.4018/978-1-5225-1753-5.ch006

Kilburn, M., Henckell, M., & Starrett, D. (2018). Factors Contributing to the Effectiveness of Online Students and Instructors. In M. Khosrow-Pour, D.B.A. (Ed.), Encyclopedia of Information Science and Technology, Fourth Edition (pp. 1451-1462). Hershey, PA: IGI Global. doi:10.4018/978-1-5225-2255-3.ch125

Koban Koç, D. (2021). Gender and Language: A Sociolinguistic Analysis of Second Language Writing. In E. Hancı-Azizoglu & N. Kavaklı (Eds.), *Futuristic and Linguistic Perspectives on Teaching Writing to Second Language Students* (pp. 161–177). IGI Global. https://doi.org/10.4018/978-1-7998-6508-7.ch010

Konecny, L. T. (2017). Hybrid, Online, and Flipped Classrooms in Health Science: Enhanced Learning Environments. In I. Management Association (Ed.), Flipped Instruction: Breakthroughs in Research and Practice (pp. 355-370). Hershey, PA: IGI Global. https://doi.org/ doi:10.4018/978-1-5225-1803-7.ch020

Kupietz, K. D. (2021). Gaming and Simulation in Public Education: Teaching Others to Help Themselves and Their Neighbors. In N. Drumhiller, T. Wilkin, & K. Srba (Eds.), *Simulation and Game-Based Learning in Emergency and Disaster Management* (pp. 41–62). IGI Global. https://doi.org/10.4018/978-1-7998-4087-9.ch003

Kwee, C. T. (2022). Assessing the International Student Enrolment Strategies in Australian Universities: A Case Study During the COVID-19 Pandemic. In M. Alaali (Ed.), *Assessing University Governance and Policies in Relation to the COVID-19 Pandemic* (pp. 162–188). IGI Global. https://doi.org/10.4018/978-1-7998-8279-4.ch010

Lauricella, S., & McArthur, F. A. (2022). Taking a Student-Centred Approach to Alternative Digital Credentials: Multiple Pathways Toward the Acquisition of Microcredentials. In D. Piedra (Ed.), *Innovations in the Design and Application of Alternative Digital Credentials* (pp. 57–69). IGI Global. https://doi.org/10.4018/978-1-7998-7697-7.ch003

Llamas, M. F. (2019). Intercultural Awareness in Teaching English for Early Childhood: A Film-Based Approach. In E. Domínguez Romero, J. Bobkina, & S. Stefanova (Eds.), *Teaching Literature and Language Through Multimodal Texts* (pp. 54–68). IGI Global. https://doi.org/10.4018/978-1-5225-5796-8.ch004

Lokhtina, I., & Kkese, E. T. (2022). Reflecting and Adapting to an Academic Workplace Before and After the Lockdown in Greek-Speaking Cyprus: Opportunities and Challenges. In A. Zhuplev & R. Koepp (Eds.), *Global Trends, Dynamics, and Imperatives for Strategic Development in Business Education in an Age of Disruption* (pp. 126–148). IGI Global. https://doi.org/10.4018/978-1-7998-7548-2.ch007

Lovell, K. L. (2017). Development and Evaluation of Neuroscience Computer-Based Modules for Medical Students: Instructional Design Principles and Effectiveness. In J. Stefaniak (Ed.), *Advancing Medical Education Through Strategic Instructional Design* (pp. 262–276). Hershey, PA: IGI Global. doi:10.4018/978-1-5225-2098-6.ch013

Maher, D. (2019). The Use of Course Management Systems in Pre-Service Teacher Education. In J. Keengwe (Ed.), *Handbook of Research on Blended Learning Pedagogies and Professional Development in Higher Education* (pp. 196–213). IGI Global. https://doi.org/10.4018/978-1-5225-5557-5.ch011

Makewa, L. N. (2019). Teacher Technology Competence Base. In L. Makewa, B. Ngussa, & J. Kuboja (Eds.), *Technology-Supported Teaching and Research Methods for Educators* (pp. 247–267). IGI Global. https://doi.org/10.4018/978-1-5225-5915-3.ch014

Mallett, C. A. (2022). School Resource (Police) Officers in Schools: Impact on Campus Safety, Student Discipline, and Learning. In G. Crews (Ed.), *Impact of School Shootings on Classroom Culture, Curriculum, and Learning* (pp. 53–70). IGI Global. https://doi.org/10.4018/978-1-7998-5200-1.ch004

Marinho, J. E., Freitas, I. R., Leão, I. B., Pacheco, L. O., Gonçalves, M. P., Castro, M. J., Silva, P. D., & Moreira, R. J. (2022). Project-Based Learning Application in Higher Education: Student Experiences and Perspectives. In A. Alves & N. van Hattum-Janssen (Eds.), *Training Engineering Students for Modern Technological Advancement* (pp. 146–164). IGI Global. https://doi.org/10.4018/978-1-7998-8816-1.ch007

McCleskey, J. A., & Melton, R. M. (2022). Rolling With the Flow: Online Faculty and Student Presence in a Post-COVID-19 World. In S. Ramlall, T. Cross, & M. Love (Eds.), *Handbook of Research on Future of Work and Education: Implications for Curriculum Delivery and Work Design* (pp. 307–328). IGI Global. https://doi.org/10.4018/978-1-7998-8275-6.ch019

McCormack, V. F., Stauffer, M., Fishley, K., Hohenbrink, J., Mascazine, J. R., & Zigler, T. (2018). Designing a Dual Licensure Path for Middle Childhood and Special Education Teacher Candidates. In D. Polly, M. Putman, T. Petty, & A. Good (Eds.), *Innovative Practices in Teacher Preparation and Graduate-Level Teacher Education Programs* (pp. 21–36). Hershey, PA: IGI Global. doi:10.4018/978-1-5225-3068-8.ch002

McDaniel, R. (2017). Strategic Leadership in Instructional Design: Applying the Principles of Instructional Design through the Lens of Strategic Leadership to Distance Education. In V. Wang (Ed.), *Encyclopedia of Strategic Leadership and Management* (pp. 1570–1584). Hershey, PA: IGI Global. doi:10.4018/978-1-5225-1049-9.ch109

McKinney, R. E., Halli-Tierney, A. D., Gold, A. E., Allen, R. S., & Carroll, D. G. (2022). Interprofessional Education: Using Standardized Cases in Face-to-Face and Remote Learning Settings. In C. Ford & K. Garza (Eds.), *Handbook of Research on Updating and Innovating Health Professions Education: Post-Pandemic Perspectives* (pp. 24–42). IGI Global. https://doi.org/10.4018/978-1-7998-7623-6.ch002

Meintjes, H. H. (2021). Learner Views of a Facebook Page as a Supportive Digital Pedagogical Tool at a Public South African School in a Grade 12 Business Studies Class. *International Journal of Smart Education and Urban Society, 12*(2), 32–45. https://doi.org/10.4018/IJSEUS.2021040104

Melero-García, F. (2022). Training Bilingual Interpreters in Healthcare Settings: Student Perceptions of Online Learning. In J. LeLoup & P. Swanson (Eds.), *Handbook of Research on Effective Online Language Teaching in a Disruptive Environment* (pp. 288–310). IGI Global. https://doi.org/10.4018/978-1-7998-7720-2.ch015

Meletiadou, E. (2022). The Use of Peer Assessment as an Inclusive Learning Strategy in Higher Education Institutions: Enhancing Student Writing Skills and Motivation. In E. Meletiadou (Ed.), *Handbook of Research on Policies and Practices for Assessing Inclusive Teaching and Learning* (pp. 1–26). IGI Global. https://doi.org/10.4018/978-1-7998-8579-5.ch001

Memon, R. N., Ahmad, R., & Salim, S. S. (2018). Critical Issues in Requirements Engineering Education. In I. Management Association (Ed.), Computer Systems and Software Engineering: Concepts, Methodologies, Tools, and Applications (pp. 1953-1976). Hershey, PA: IGI Global. doi:10.4018/978-1-5225-3923-0.ch081

Mendenhall, R. (2017). Western Governors University: CBE Innovator and National Model. In K. Rasmussen, P. Northrup, & R. Colson (Eds.), *Handbook of Research on Competency-Based Education in University Settings* (pp. 379–400). Hershey, PA: IGI Global. doi:10.4018/978-1-5225-0932-5.ch019

Mense, E. G., Griggs, D. M., & Shanks, J. N. (2018). School Leaders in a Time of Accountability and Data Use: Preparing Our Future School Leaders in Leadership Preparation Programs. In E. Mense & M. Crain-Dorough (Eds.), *Data Leadership for K-12 Schools in a Time of Accountability* (pp. 235–259). Hershey, PA: IGI Global. doi:10.4018/978-1-5225-3188-3.ch012

Mense, E. G., Griggs, D. M., & Shanks, J. N. (2018). School Leaders in a Time of Accountability and Data Use: Preparing Our Future School Leaders in Leadership Preparation Programs. In E. Mense & M. Crain-Dorough (Eds.), *Data Leadership for K-12 Schools in a Time of Accountability* (pp. 235–259). Hershey, PA: IGI Global. doi:10.4018/978-1-5225-3188-3.ch012

Mestry, R., & Naicker, S. R. (2017). Exploring Distributive Leadership in South African Public Primary Schools in the Soweto Region. In I. Management Association (Ed.), Educational Leadership and Administration: Concepts, Methodologies, Tools, and Applications (pp. 1041-1064). Hershey, PA: IGI Global. doi:10.4018/978-1-5225-1624-8.ch050

Monaghan, C. H., & Boboc, M. (2017). (Re) Defining Leadership in Higher Education in the U.S. In V. Wang (Ed.), *Encyclopedia of Strategic Leadership and Management* (pp. 567–579). Hershey, PA: IGI Global. doi:10.4018/978-1-5225-1049-9.ch040

Morall, M. B. (2021). Reimagining Mobile Phones: Multiple Literacies and Digital Media Compositions. In C. Moran (Eds.), *Affordances and Constraints of Mobile Phone Use in English Language Arts Classrooms* (pp. 41-53). IGI Global. https://doi.org/10.4018/978-1-7998-5805-8.ch003

Mthethwa, V. (2022). Student Governance and the Academic Minefield During COVID-19 Lockdown in South Africa. In M. Alaali (Ed.), *Assessing University Governance and Policies in Relation to the COVID-19 Pandemic* (pp. 255–276). IGI Global. https://doi.org/10.4018/978-1-7998-8279-4.ch015

Muthee, J. M., & Murungi, C. G. (2018). Relationship Among Intelligence, Achievement Motivation, Type of School, and Academic Performance of Kenyan Urban Primary School Pupils. In M. Khosrow-Pour, D.B.A. (Ed.), Encyclopedia of Information Science and Technology, Fourth Edition (pp. 1540-1547). Hershey, PA: IGI Global. https://doi.org/ doi:10.4018/978-1-5225-2255-3.ch133

Naranjo, J. (2018). Meeting the Need for Inclusive Educators Online: Teacher Education in Inclusive Special Education and Dual-Certification. In D. Polly, M. Putman, T. Petty, & A. Good (Eds.), *Innovative Practices in Teacher Preparation and Graduate-Level Teacher Education Programs* (pp. 106–122). Hershey, PA: IGI Global. doi:10.4018/978-1-5225-3068-8.ch007

Nkabinde, Z. P. (2017). Multiculturalism in Special Education: Perspectives of Minority Children in Urban Schools. In J. Keengwe (Ed.), *Handbook of Research on Promoting Cross-Cultural Competence and Social Justice in Teacher Education* (pp. 382–397). Hershey, PA: IGI Global. doi:10.4018/978-1-5225-0897-7.ch020

Nkabinde, Z. P. (2018). Online Instruction: Is the Quality the Same as Face-to-Face Instruction? In J. Keengwe (Ed.), *Handbook of Research on Digital Content, Mobile Learning, and Technology Integration Models in Teacher Education* (pp. 300–314). Hershey, PA: IGI Global. doi:10.4018/978-1-5225-2953-8.ch016

Nugroho, A., & Albusaidi, S. S. (2022). Internationalization of Higher Education: The Methodological Critiques on the Research Related to Study Overseas and International Experience. In H. Magd & S. Kunjumuhammed (Eds.), *Global Perspectives on Quality Assurance and Accreditation in Higher Education Institutions* (pp. 75–89). IGI Global. https://doi.org/10.4018/978-1-7998-8085-1.ch005

Nulty, Z., & West, S. G. (2022). Student Engagement and Supporting Students With Accommodations. In P. Bull & G. Patterson (Eds.), *Redefining Teacher Education and Teacher Preparation Programs in the Post-COVID-19 Era* (pp. 99–116). IGI Global. https://doi.org/10.4018/978-1-7998-8298-5.ch006

O'Connor, J. R. Jr, & Jackson, K. N. (2017). The Use of iPad® Devices and "Apps" for ASD Students in Special Education and Speech Therapy. In Y. Kats (Ed.), *Supporting the Education of Children with Autism Spectrum Disorders* (pp. 267–283). Hershey, PA: IGI Global. doi:10.4018/978-1-5225-0816-8.ch014

Okolie, U. C., & Yasin, A. M. (2017). TVET in Developing Nations and Human Development. In U. Okolie & A. Yasin (Eds.), *Technical Education and Vocational Training in Developing Nations* (pp. 1–25). Hershey, PA: IGI Global. doi:10.4018/978-1-5225-1811-2.ch001

Pack, A., & Barrett, A. (2021). A Review of Virtual Reality and English for Academic Purposes: Understanding Where to Start. *International Journal of Computer-Assisted Language Learning and Teaching*, *11*(1), 72–80. https://doi.org/10.4018/IJCALLT.2021010105

Pashollari, E. (2019). Building Sustainability Through Environmental Education: Education for Sustainable Development. In L. Wilson, & C. Stevenson (Eds.), *Building Sustainability Through Environmental Education* (pp. 72-88). IGI Global. https://doi.org/10.4018/978-1-5225-7727-0.ch004

Paulson, E. N. (2017). Adapting and Advocating for an Online EdD Program in Changing Times and "Sacred" Cultures. In I. Management Association (Ed.), Educational Leadership and Administration: Concepts, Methodologies, Tools, and Applications (pp. 1849-1876). Hershey, PA: IGI Global. https://doi.org/doi:10.4018/978-1-5225-1624-8.ch085

Petersen, A. J., Elser, C. F., Al Nassir, M. N., Stakey, J., & Everson, K. (2017). The Year of Teaching Inclusively: Building an Elementary Classroom for All Students. In C. Curran & A. Petersen (Eds.), *Handbook of Research on Classroom Diversity and Inclusive Education Practice* (pp. 332–348). Hershey, PA: IGI Global. doi:10.4018/978-1-5225-2520-2.ch014

Pfannenstiel, K. H., & Sanders, J. (2017). Characteristics and Instructional Strategies for Students With Mathematical Difficulties: In the Inclusive Classroom. In C. Curran & A. Petersen (Eds.), *Handbook of Research on Classroom Diversity and Inclusive Education Practice* (pp. 250–281). Hershey, PA: IGI Global. doi:10.4018/978-1-5225-2520-2.ch011

Phan, A. N. (2022). Quality Assurance of Higher Education From the Glonacal Agency Heuristic: An Example From Vietnam. In H. Magd & S. Kunjumuhammed (Eds.), *Global Perspectives on Quality Assurance and Accreditation in Higher Education Institutions* (pp. 136–155). IGI Global. https://doi.org/10.4018/978-1-7998-8085-1.ch008

Preast, J. L., Bowman, N., & Rose, C. A. (2017). Creating Inclusive Classroom Communities Through Social and Emotional Learning to Reduce Social Marginalization Among Students. In C. Curran & A. Petersen (Eds.), *Handbook of Research on Classroom Diversity and Inclusive Education Practice* (pp. 183–200). Hershey, PA: IGI Global. doi:10.4018/978-1-5225-2520-2.ch008

Randolph, K. M., & Brady, M. P. (2018). Evolution of Covert Coaching as an Evidence-Based Practice in Professional Development and Preparation of Teachers. In V. Bryan, A. Musgrove, & J. Powers (Eds.), *Handbook of Research on Human Development in the Digital Age* (pp. 281–299). Hershey, PA: IGI Global. doi:10.4018/978-1-5225-2838-8.ch013

Rell, A. B., Puig, R. A., Roll, F., Valles, V., Espinoza, M., & Duque, A. L. (2017). Addressing Cultural Diversity and Global Competence: The Dual Language Framework. In L. Leavitt, S. Wisdom, & K. Leavitt (Eds.), *Cultural Awareness and Competency Development in Higher Education* (pp. 111–131). Hershey, PA: IGI Global. doi:10.4018/978-1-5225-2145-7.ch007

Richards, M., & Guzman, I. R. (2020). Academic Assessment of Critical Thinking in Distance Education Information Technology Programs. In I. Management Association (Ed.), *Learning and Performance Assessment: Concepts, Methodologies, Tools, and Applications* (pp. 1-19). IGI Global. https://doi.org/10.4018/978-1-7998-0420-8.ch001

Riel, J., Lawless, K. A., & Brown, S. W. (2017). Defining and Designing Responsive Online Professional Development (ROPD): A Framework to Support Curriculum Implementation. In T. Kidd & L. Morris Jr., (Eds.), *Handbook of Research on Instructional Systems and Educational Technology* (pp. 104–115). Hershey, PA: IGI Global. doi:10.4018/978-1-5225-2399-4.ch010

Roberts, C. (2017). Advancing Women Leaders in Academe: Creating a Culture of Inclusion. In S. Mukerji & P. Tripathi (Eds.), *Handbook of Research on Administration, Policy, and Leadership in Higher Education* (pp. 256–273). Hershey, PA: IGI Global. doi:10.4018/978-1-5225-0672-0.ch012

Rodgers, W. J., Kennedy, M. J., Alves, K. D., & Romig, J. E. (2017). A Multimedia Tool for Teacher Education and Professional Development. In C. Martin & D. Polly (Eds.), *Handbook of Research on Teacher Education and Professional Development* (pp. 285–296). Hershey, PA: IGI Global. doi:10.4018/978-1-5225-1067-3.ch015

Romanowski, M. H. (2017). Qatar's Educational Reform: Critical Issues Facing Principals. In I. Management Association (Ed.), Educational Leadership and Administration: Concepts, Methodologies, Tools, and Applications (pp. 1758-1773). Hershey, PA: IGI Global. https://doi.org/ doi:10.4018/978-1-5225-1624-8.ch080

Ruffin, T. R., Hawkins, D. P., & Lee, D. I. (2018). Increasing Student Engagement and Participation Through Course Methodology. In M. Khosrow-Pour, D.B.A. (Ed.), Encyclopedia of Information Science and Technology, Fourth Edition (pp. 1463-1473). Hershey, PA: IGI Global. doi:10.4018/978-1-5225-2255-3.ch126

Sabina, L. L., Curry, K. A., Harris, E. L., Krumm, B. L., & Vencill, V. (2017). Assessing the Performance of a Cohort-Based Model Using Domestic and International Practices. In I. Management Association (Ed.), Educational Leadership and Administration: Concepts, Methodologies, Tools, and Applications(pp. 913-929). Hershey, PA: IGI Global. https://doi.org/ doi:10.4018/978-1-5225-1624-8.ch044

Samkian, A., Pascarella, J., & Slayton, J. (2022). Towards an Anti-Racist, Culturally Responsive, and LGBTQ+ Inclusive Education: Developing Critically-Conscious Educational Leaders. In E. Cain-Sanschagrin, R. Filback, & J. Crawford (Eds.), *Cases on Academic Program Redesign for Greater Racial and Social Justice* (pp. 150–175). IGI Global. https://doi.org/10.4018/978-1-7998-8463-7.ch007

Santamaría, A. P., Webber, M., & Santamaría, L. J. (2017). Effective School Leadership for Māori Achievement: Building Capacity through Indigenous, National, and International Cross-Cultural Collaboration. In I. Management Association (Ed.), Educational Leadership and Administration: Concepts, Methodologies, Tools, and Applications (pp. 1547-1567). Hershey, PA: IGI Global. https://doi.org/ doi:10.4018/978-1-5225-1624-8.ch071

Santamaría, L. J. (2017). Culturally Responsive Educational Leadership in Cross-Cultural International Contexts. In I. Management Association (Ed.), Educational Leadership and Administration: Concepts, Methodologies, Tools, and Applications (pp. 1380-1400). Hershey, PA: IGI Global. https://doi.org/ doi:10.4018/978-1-5225-1624-8.ch064

Segredo, M. R., Cistone, P. J., & Reio, T. G. (2017). Relationships Between Emotional Intelligence, Leadership Style, and School Culture. *International Journal of Adult Vocational Education and Technology*, *8*(3), 25–43. doi:10.4018/IJAVET.2017070103

Shalev, N. (2017). Empathy and Leadership From the Organizational Perspective. In Z. Nedelko & M. Brzozowski (Eds.), *Exploring the Influence of Personal Values and Cultures in the Workplace* (pp. 348–363). Hershey, PA: IGI Global. doi:10.4018/978-1-5225-2480-9.ch018

Siamak, M., Fathi, S., & Isfandyari-Moghaddam, A. (2018). Assessment and Measurement of Education Programs of Information Literacy. In R. Bhardwaj (Ed.), *Digitizing the Modern Library and the Transition From Print to Electronic* (pp. 164–192). Hershey, PA: IGI Global. doi:10.4018/978-1-5225-2119-8.ch007

Siu, K. W., & García, G. J. (2017). Disruptive Technologies and Education: Is There Any Disruption After All? In I. Management Association (Ed.), Educational Leadership and Administration: Concepts, Methodologies, Tools, and Applications (pp. 757-778). Hershey, PA: IGI Global. https://doi.org/ doi:10.4018/978-1-5225-1624-8.ch037

Slagter van Tryon, P. J. (2017). The Nurse Educator's Role in Designing Instruction and Instructional Strategies for Academic and Clinical Settings. In J. Stefaniak (Ed.), *Advancing Medical Education Through Strategic Instructional Design* (pp. 133–149). Hershey, PA: IGI Global. doi:10.4018/978-1-5225-2098-6.ch006

Slattery, C. A. (2018). Literacy Intervention and the Differentiated Plan of Instruction. In *Developing Effective Literacy Intervention Strategies: Emerging Research and Opportunities* (pp. 41–62). Hershey, PA: IGI Global. doi:10.4018/978-1-5225-5007-5.ch003

Smith, A. R. (2017). Ensuring Quality: The Faculty Role in Online Higher Education. In K. Shelton & K. Pedersen (Eds.), *Handbook of Research on Building, Growing, and Sustaining Quality E-Learning Programs* (pp. 210–231). Hershey, PA: IGI Global. doi:10.4018/978-1-5225-0877-9.ch011

Souders, T. M. (2017). Understanding Your Learner: Conducting a Learner Analysis. In J. Stefaniak (Ed.), *Advancing Medical Education Through Strategic Instructional Design* (pp. 1–29). Hershey, PA: IGI Global. doi:10.4018/978-1-5225-2098-6.ch001

Spring, K. J., Graham, C. R., & Ikahihifo, T. B. (2018). Learner Engagement in Blended Learning. In M. Khosrow-Pour, D.B.A. (Ed.), Encyclopedia of Information Science and Technology, Fourth Edition (pp. 1487-1498). Hershey, PA: IGI Global. doi:10.4018/978-1-5225-2255-3.ch128

Storey, V. A., Anthony, A. K., & Wahid, P. (2017). Gender-Based Leadership Barriers: Advancement of Female Faculty to Leadership Positions in Higher Education. In V. Wang (Ed.), *Encyclopedia of Strategic Leadership and Management* (pp. 244–258). Hershey, PA: IGI Global. doi:10.4018/978-1-5225-1049-9.ch018

Stottlemyer, D. (2018). Develop a Teaching Model Plan for a Differentiated Learning Approach. In *Differentiated Instructional Design for Multicultural Environments: Emerging Research and Opportunities* (pp. 106–130). Hershey, PA: IGI Global. doi:10.4018/978-1-5225-5106-5.ch005

Stottlemyer, D. (2018). Developing a Multicultural Environment. In *Differentiated Instructional Design for Multicultural Environments: Emerging Research and Opportunities* (pp. 1–27). Hershey, PA: IGI Global. doi:10.4018/978-1-5225-5106-5.ch001

Swagerty, T. (2022). Digital Access to Culturally Relevant Curricula: The Impact on the Native and Indigenous Student. In E. Reeves & C. McIntyre (Eds.), *Multidisciplinary Perspectives on Diversity and Equity in a Virtual World* (pp. 99–113). IGI Global. https://doi.org/10.4018/978-1-7998-8028-8.ch006

Swami, B. N., Gobona, T., & Tsimako, J. J. (2017). Academic Leadership: A Case Study of the University of Botswana. In N. Baporikar (Ed.), *Innovation and Shifting Perspectives in Management Education* (pp. 1–32). Hershey, PA: IGI Global. doi:10.4018/978-1-5225-1019-2.ch001

Swanson, K. W., & Collins, G. (2018). Designing Engaging Instruction for the Adult Learners. In M. Khosrow-Pour, D.B.A. (Ed.), Encyclopedia of Information Science and Technology, Fourth Edition (pp. 1432-1440). Hershey, PA: IGI Global. doi:10.4018/978-1-5225-2255-3.ch123

Swartz, B. A., Lynch, J. M., & Lynch, S. D. (2018). Embedding Elementary Teacher Education Coursework in Local Classrooms: Examples in Mathematics and Special Education. In D. Polly, M. Putman, T. Petty, & A. Good (Eds.), *Innovative Practices in Teacher Preparation and Graduate-Level Teacher Education Programs* (pp. 262–292). Hershey, PA: IGI Global. doi:10.4018/978-1-5225-3068-8.ch015

Taliadorou, N., & Pashiardis, P. (2017). Emotional Intelligence and Political Skill Really Matter in Educational Leadership. In I. Management Association (Ed.), Educational Leadership and Administration: Concepts, Methodologies, Tools, and Applications (pp. 1274-1303). Hershey, PA: IGI Global. https://doi.org/doi:10.4018/978-1-5225-1624-8.ch060

Tandoh, K. A., & Ebe-Arthur, J. E. (2018). Effective Educational Leadership in the Digital Age: An Examination of Professional Qualities and Best Practices. In J. Keengwe (Ed.), *Handbook of Research on Digital Content, Mobile Learning, and Technology Integration Models in Teacher Education* (pp. 244–265). Hershey, PA: IGI Global. doi:10.4018/978-1-5225-2953-8.ch013

Tobin, M. T. (2018). Multimodal Literacy. In M. Khosrow-Pour, D.B.A. (Ed.), Encyclopedia of Information Science and Technology, Fourth Edition (pp. 1508-1516). Hershey, PA: IGI Global. doi:10.4018/978-1-5225-2255-3.ch130

Torres, K. M., Arrastia-Chisholm, M. C., & Tackett, S. (2019). A Phenomenological Study of Pre-Service Teachers' Perceptions of Completing ESOL Field Placements. *International Journal of Teacher Education and Professional Development*, *2*(2), 85–101. https://doi.org/10.4018/IJTEPD.2019070106

Torres, M. C., Salamanca, Y. N., Cely, J. P., & Aguilar, J. L. (2020). All We Need is a Boost! Using Multimodal Tools and the Translanguaging Strategy: Strengthening Speaking in the EFL Classroom. *International Journal of Computer-Assisted Language Learning and Teaching*, *10*(3), 28–47. doi:10.4018/IJCALLT.2020070103

Torres, M. L., & Ramos, V. J. (2018). Music Therapy: A Pedagogical Alternative for ASD and ID Students in Regular Classrooms. In P. Epler (Ed.), *Instructional Strategies in General Education and Putting the Individuals With Disabilities Act (IDEA) Into Practice* (pp. 222–244). Hershey, PA: IGI Global. doi:10.4018/978-1-5225-3111-1.ch008

Toulassi, B. (2017). Educational Administration and Leadership in Francophone Africa: 5 Dynamics to Change Education. In S. Mukerji & P. Tripathi (Eds.), *Handbook of Research on Administration, Policy, and Leadership in Higher Education* (pp. 20–45). Hershey, PA: IGI Global. doi:10.4018/978-1-5225-0672-0.ch002

Umair, S., & Sharif, M. M. (2018). Predicting Students Grades Using Artificial Neural Networks and Support Vector Machine. In M. Khosrow-Pour, D.B.A. (Ed.), Encyclopedia of Information Science and Technology, Fourth Edition (pp. 5169-5182). Hershey, PA: IGI Global. doi:10.4018/978-1-5225-2255-3.ch449

Vettraino, L., Castello, V., Guspini, M., & Guglielman, E. (2018). Self-Awareness and Motivation Contrasting ESL and NEET Using the SAVE System. In M. Khosrow-Pour, D.B.A. (Ed.), Encyclopedia of Information Science and Technology, Fourth Edition (pp. 1559-1568). Hershey, PA: IGI Global. doi:10.4018/978-1-5225-2255-3.ch135

Wiemelt, J. (2017). Critical Bilingual Leadership for Emergent Bilingual Students. In I. Management Association (Ed.), Educational Leadership and Administration: Concepts, Methodologies, Tools, and Applications (pp. 1606-1631). Hershey, PA: IGI Global. doi:10.4018/978-1-5225-1624-8.ch074

Wolf, F., Seyfarth, F. C., & Pflaum, E. (2018). Scalable Capacity-Building for Geographically Dispersed Learners: Designing the MOOC "Sustainable Energy in Small Island Developing States (SIDS)". In U. Pandey & V. Indrakanti (Eds.), *Open and Distance Learning Initiatives for Sustainable Development* (pp. 58–83). Hershey, PA: IGI Global. doi:10.4018/978-1-5225-2621-6.ch003

Woodley, X. M., Mucundanyi, G., & Lockard, M. (2017). Designing Counter-Narratives: Constructing Culturally Responsive Curriculum Online. *International Journal of Online Pedagogy and Course Design*, *7*(1), 43–56. doi:10.4018/IJOPCD.2017010104

Yell, M. L., & Christle, C. A. (2017). The Foundation of Inclusion in Federal Legislation and Litigation. In C. Curran & A. Petersen (Eds.), *Handbook of Research on Classroom Diversity and Inclusive Education Practice* (pp. 27–52). Hershey, PA: IGI Global. doi:10.4018/978-1-5225-2520-2.ch002

Zinner, L. (2019). Fostering Academic Citizenship With a Shared Leadership Approach. In C. Zhu & M. Zayim-Kurtay (Eds.), *University Governance and Academic Leadership in the EU and China* (pp. 99–117). IGI Global. https://doi.org/10.4018/978-1-5225-7441-5.ch007

About the Contributors

Sampson Tawiah holds a PhD in Education from the University of South Africa. He is an Associate Lecturer at the Durban University of Technology. His research interests are in General Education, Educational Foundations and Adult Education for workplace inclusion and employment. His main intellectual interest is in youths, adults and community development. His research focuses on women in South Africa and Africa in general and the links between race and vocational education for livelihood, social inclusion, inequality, and poverty reduction. His work epitomizes scientific data and theoretical foundations of education including work and skills development.

Itumeleng I. Setlhodi is an associate professor in the school of Educational Studies, college of Education, at the University of South Africa. She is currently acting Director in the Academic Quality Assurance and Enhancement Unit, within the Vice principal Teaching and Learning office. She supervises Masters and Doctoral students within educational studies field. She holds a Doctor of Education qualification. Research interests are in educational leadership, adult education, quality assurance, mentorship and coaching, higher education, and gender.

***

Ellen Abakah (Ph.D.) is a trained adult educator with experience in higher education teaching. She is currently an early career researcher with the Department of Adult Education and Human Resource Studies, University of Ghana. Her research interests include adult learning and education, teacher learning and continuing professional learning development and gender and political participation.

Kofi Konadu Berko is an MPhil in Adult Education student at the Department of Adult Education and Human Resource Studies, University of Ghana. His current research interests are Adult literacy, lifelong learning, indigenous education and education for sustainable development.

Motlagoiloe Senzenina Moroe is a Provincial Manager for the Wholesale & Retail Sector Education and Training Authority. She is currently pursuing her PhD in Sector Education Management and Advancement. Research interests are in Adult Education, Education and Training, and Community Colleges Leadership and Management.

Nkholedzeni Sidney Netshakhuma is currently the Postdoctoral Research Fellowship with the University of Cape Town, Centre for African Studies effective from January 2023. His research interest includes Records Management, Archives management and Heritage management, and Political and liberation movements archives. He has published more than 60 articles and book chapters. He currently served as a Deputy Chairperson of the South Africa Higher Education Records and Archives Management Forum. He reviewed more than 60 research articles and book chapters. He obtained Ph.D. Information Science, Masters of Information Science, Post Diploma in Archival Studies, BTECH (Archival Studies at the University of South Africa (UNISA), BPHIL (Information Science at the University of Stellenbosch), BA (History and Political Studies at the University of Venda.

Index

G

H

I

L

M

O

P

R

S

T

U

www.ingramcontent.com/pod-product-compliance
Lightning Source LLC
LaVergne TN
LVHW081327300926
849161LV00008B/1899
* 9 7 8 1 6 6 8 4 6 6 2 5 4 *